PRIZE ESSAYS

OF THE

AMERICAN HISTORICAL ASSOCIATION

1914

ANGLO-AMERICAN ISTHMIAN DIPLOMACY

1815-1915

ANGLO-AMERICAN ISTHMIAN DIPLOMACY
1815-1915

BY

MARY WILHELMINE WILLIAMS, Ph. D.

NEW YORK

RUSSELL & RUSSELL · INC

1965

FIRST PUBLISHED IN 1916
REISSUED, 1965, BY RUSSELL & RUSSELL, INC.
L. C. CATALOG CARD NO: 65—13935

PRINTED IN THE UNITED STATES OF AMERICA

TO MY FATHER AND MY MOTHER
CHARLES WILLIAMS
AND
CAROLINE K. WILLIAMS

PREFACE.

Though the diplomatic relations of England and the United States over the Central American isthmus have received frequent consideration of a general character by writers on American diplomacy, no exhaustive study of the subject appears to have been before attempted. It is the aim of the following essay to present the result of a detailed investigation into Anglo-American isthmian diplomacy, from the first emergence of Central America as a subject of diplomatic interest between the two countries down to the immediate present.

The work here presented is to a large extent based upon new material. Part of this is in the form of printed sources, drawn upon to some degree by previous writers but by no means exhausted. The most important writings of this class are the British *Parliamentary Papers* and the *United States Documents*. But a much larger and more valuable contribution was made by the manuscript archives for the period 1815 to 1861, found in the Public Record Office in London and in the Department of State at Washington. Only a comparatively small portion of the archives bearing upon the subject of this study have been printed, and the unprinted material has hitherto been entirely untouched by research students.

Chapter I, which is merely introductory, makes no pretense at being an original contribution. The authorities upon which it is founded, however, have largely the character of sources, and these have been used critically with a view to ascertaining the facts behind the conflicting statements of various contemporary writers. Chapters II to VIII, inclusive, which are based to a considerable but varying degree upon previously unused material, are the most original part of the essay. Access to manuscript archives made possible not only a presentation of many hitherto unknown facts, but also led to a new, and, it is believed, more accurate, interpretation of numerous phases of the subject considered by previous writers. Chapter IX, which covers a period subsequent to that for which the archives are open, presents some fresh viewpoints resulting from the new light thrown upon preceding events. The period covered by chapter X is too recent for a satisfactory treatment; hence, this chapter aims primarily to present in broad outline the latest phases of the general subject, in their proper relations. The concluding chapter, XI, summarizes the result of the whole study.

Certain irregularities appearing in connection with the bibliographical citations may need an explanation. In some instances more than one authority has been cited for a given statement. This has been done with two purposes in view: (1) to strengthen by a multiplication of witnesses statements based upon non-documentary writings—generally in the nature of travel sketches, largely made up of personal observations and reports from hearsay evidence; (2) to aid the reader who may wish to make a further study of the point in question. The authority believed to be the most reliable has been placed first on the list. Throughout the study, writings of a generally untrustworthy character have been used only in a supplementary manner. References to manuscript sources are in every case as definite as possible. Wherever despatch or page numbers exist they have been given. Letters in the archives from important diplomatic or consular agents are as a rule numbered, but those from less important agents—particularly those written from Central America—are frequently unnumbered. Drafts of correspondence are generally unnumbered, as are also private letters from officials, while letters from private individuals are always without numbers.

This study was originally written as a thesis under the direction of Professor Ephraim D. Adams, in connection with my candidacy for the degree of Doctor of Philosophy at Leland Stanford Junior University. For his painstaking supervision of my work and for his stimulating interest in it, I am especially indebted to Professor Adams. My gratitude is also due to Professor Henry L. Cannon of Stanford University for many suggestions which were of value in the later revision of the manuscript. Through the friendly interest of Mr. Hubert Hall, Assistant Keeper of the Public Records, in London, I secured access to the British manuscript archives, the most valuable part of my source material. My sister, Miss Edle Carolyn Williams, gave much assistance in the preparation of the accompanying map.

Mary Wilhelmine Williams.

Wellesley, Massachusetts,
May 20, 1915.

CONTENTS.

(xi)

CHAPTER VII.

CHAPTER VIII.

CHAPTER IX.

CHAPTER X.

CHAPTER XI.

MAP.

CHAPTER I.

THE BRITISH IN CENTRAL AMERICA BEFORE 1815.

For more than a century before the government of the United States came into existence, the subjects of Great Britain had been actively interested in that part of the North American continent which, geographically, is included under the term " Central America ".[1] By various and fluctuating degrees of political control their government protected them, and, in consequence, there gradually developed a close relationship between Great Britain and certain parts of Central America. It was the existence of this British connection with the isthmus and the fact that the connection was time-honored when the attention of the United States was first seriously attracted to the region that rendered subsequent British-American isthmian relations so complicated and difficult of adjustment. Shortly after the United States had become a rival of the British in Central America, so delicate had the situation grown that the American government, despairing of any other peaceful settlement, for the first and only time in its history compromised with the Monroe doctrine and made an agreement with Great Britain which later came to be known as the Clayton-Bulwer treaty. This instrument, instead of removing the difficulty, as had

---

[1] This account assumes a general knowledge of Central American history on the part of the reader. Bancroft's three-volume work is the best and most comprehensive history of Central America; Fortier and Ficklen's *Central America and Mexico* gives a good brief account.

I

been hoped, only magnified it to an alarming degree and brought into being the long-lived and vexatious " Central American question ".

These early British interests were divided between three different portions of Central America: Belize Settlement, the Bay Islands, and the Mosquito Shore. For the purpose of making clear the subsequent chapters, a brief account of the early English connections with the places named is here given.

Belize Settlement.

The British settlement of Belize was a direct outgrowth of the buccaneering era in the Western World. At an early date the exclusive commercial policy of Spain tempted the subjects of other nations to acquire a share in her prosperity by irregular and violent methods. During the long and frequent wars they operated as privateers; in times of peace they were undisguised freebooters, or buccaneers. As time passed, the West Indies became the chief centre of operations for these " brethren of the coast "; and from here they made daring and profitable attacks upon Spanish vessels homeward bound from the colonies.[2] With the conquest of Jamaica by Cromwell, in 1655, the strength of the English buccaneers increased; for the early governors of the island as a rule not only connived at the marauding expeditions, but at times even shared in the plunder.[3] Indeed, Captain Morgan, notorious for sacking and burning many cities on the

[2] For a detailed account of the buccaneers see Haring, *Buccaneers in the West Indies*; Burney, *Buccaneers of America*; Johnson, *General History of the Pyrates*; Esquemeling, *Buccaneers of America*.

[3] Johnson, *Pyrates*, I, 25; Long, *History of Jamaica*, I, 300; Squier, *Notes on Central America*, 369.

coasts of Spanish America, as well as for preying upon Spanish vessels, was knighted by the British government and made lieutenant-governor of Jamaica.[4]

At first, when attacking Spanish ships, the freebooters aimed primarily to rob them of the wealth carried from the mines; this accomplished, the vessels, which frequently carried mahogany or logwood, were set afire and abandoned. Almost by accident a shipload of logwood was spared and taken to London, where the ready market which it commanded quickly revealed its value to the buccaneers. After this, logwood-laden vessels were eagerly captured for the sake of their cargoes.[5]

When Spanish prizes became scarcer the freebooters gradually took to cutting their own logwood on the thinly-settled portions of the Spanish coast.[6] This change began a few years after the English took possession of Jamaica.[7] The new enterprise was favored by Modyford, the governor of the island, as plundering Spanish bottoms had come to be frowned upon by the home government.[8] Spain was now too weak to do more than partially police her coasts and to seize the vessels containing plunder from her forests; consequently, for a time the British Council for the Plantations approved of the connivance of Modyford's successor.[9]

[4] *Cal. St. P., Col., Am. and W. I., 1675-1676*, 343; Long, *Jamaica*, I, 301; Haring, *Buccaneers*, 205.

[5] Dampier, *Voyages*, II, pt. 2, p. 47; Gibbs, *British Honduras*, 24.

[6] Dampier, *Voyages*, II, pt. 2, pp. 47-48; *Cal. St. P., Col., Am. and W. I., 1669-1674*, 121, 311, 426, 427, 428; Gibbs, *British Honduras*, 24.

[7] Haring, *Buccaneers*, 208-209; *Parl. Papers*, 1847, *Coms.*, LXIV, "Spanish-American Republics", 3.

[8] Haring, *Buccaneers*, 209.

[9] *Ibid.*, 210; *Cal. St. P., Col., Am. and W. I., 1677-1680*, 343, 406; *1681-1685*, 284.

Naturally, log-cutting settlements grew up with the development of this new British industry. One of the earliest establishments of this sort was made in Yucatan, on the Belize River, in 1662.[10] As logwood was plentiful on this part of the coast, the settlement prospered and was soon on a firm basis.

The reprisals of the Spanish upon the English logwood cargoes continued, however, in spite of precautions;[11] therefore in 1670 the British government attempted to secure by treaty a sanction or defense of the actions of its subjects. The seventh article of an agreement made with Spain in this year reads:

It is agreed that the most serene King of Great Britain, his heirs and successors, shall have, hold, keep and enjoy forever with plenary right of sovereignty, dominion, possession and propriety, all those lands, regions, islands, colonies, and places, whatsoever, being or situated in the West Indies, or any part of America, which the said King of Great Britain or his subjects do at present hold or possess.[12]

Though the clause appears to have been inserted in the treaty ostensibly and primarily for the purpose of settling a dispute over the possession of Jamaica,[13] the British negotiators evidently aimed to secure a wording which might include the British log-cutting settlements on the Belize and on other parts of the Spanish

---

[10] L. L., " Balize ", in *Nouvelles Annales*, C, 52; *Parl. Papers*, 1847, *Coms.*, LXIV, " Spanish-American Republics ", 13; Gibbs, *British Honduras*, 26. This was probably not the first British settlement in the region, for it seems that as early as 1638 a number of shipwrecked British sailors established themselves there. *Ibid.*, 26; Lucas, *Historical Geography of the British Colonies*, II, 297; Trendell, *Her Majesty's Colonies*, 347.

[11] Haring, *Buccaneers*, 211.

[12] Hertslet, *Treaties between Great Britain and Foreign Powers*, II, 196-197.

[13] *U. S. Docs.*, ser. no. 660, doc. 27, p. 80.

coast.[14] This interpretation was attempted by the governors of Jamaica and by the Board of Trade,[15] but the Spaniards had no intention of acknowledging that such concessions had been made; therefore they continued to capture the logwood vessels of the British, and repeatedly destroyed their log-cutting settlements;[16] Belize suffered like the rest, and in about the year 1732 the settlers were driven away and their homes demolished. They promptly returned, however, and defeated all further expeditions sent against them.[17]

Belize was occupied by the British under the equivocal title of 1670 until the formation of the peace of 1763, which concluded the Seven Years' War. Whether or not the negotiators of this treaty were ignorant of the terms of that made in 1670 and of its possible application to Belize is not apparent.[18] In any case, by the later treaty England agreed to demolish all fortifications erected by British subjects in the Bay of Honduras; but the Spanish government permitted the log-cutters to remain, and guaranteed them protection, though, obviously, Spain still held full sovereignty over the settlement.[19]

Again, in 1779, when Spain had allied herself with the revolting English colonies, the Spaniards returned to Belize. This time the settlement was pillaged and many of its inhabitants taken as prisoners to Havana.

[14] Long, *Jamaica*, I, 341; *Parl. Papers*, 1847, *Coms.*, LXIV, " Spanish-American Republics ", 13; Gibbs, *British Honduras*, 27.

[15] *Parl. Papers*, 1847, *Coms.*, LXIV, " Spanish-American Republics ", 14; Burney, *Buccaneers*, 99-100.

[16] Wafer, *New Voyage to America*, 34; Long, *Jamaica*, I, 341; *Parl. Papers*, 1847, *Coms.*, LXIV, " Spanish-American Republics ", 13-14.

[17] Bancroft, *Central America*, II, 625-628.

[18] Long, *Jamaica*, I, 342.

[19] MacDonald, *Select Charters*, 265.

But in the following year Omoa, in Honduras, was captured by British officers, who, by convention with the Spanish authorities, arranged for the redemption of the " Baymen ", as the settlers were called.[20]

By the treaty of 1783, which concluded the American Revolution, Belize still remained under Spanish sovereignty, and by this treaty definite boundaries were for the first time agreed upon for the settlement.   The boundary line was given in great detail, but, generally speaking, the northern limit of settlement was to be Rio Hondo, and the southern, Belize River.[21]

Notwithstanding the stipulations of 1783, the British continued to spread; therefore a treaty made three years later extended the southern boundary as far as the Sibun River.   Besides this extension of territory, the new agreement gave the settlers additional privileges within the district.   Not only were they permitted to cut and carry away logwood, but they were also allowed to take mahogany and all other woods, as well as to gather and sell all other uncultivated products; but it was definitely agreed that no plantations were to be made or factories of any sort to be established, since the undisputed possession of the territory by Spain precluded the right of the English to form settlements of that kind.[22]   A Spanish commissioner, in company with one representing the English government, was to be admitted to the settlement twice a year to examine into the condition of affairs.[23]

[20] Ann. Reg., 1780, " History ", 212-214; Parl. Papers, 1847, Coms., LXIV, " Spanish-American Republics ", 15; Henderson, British Settlement of Honduras, 5-7.

[21] Ann. Reg., 1783, "State Papers ", 334-335.

[22] Ibid., 1786, pp. 262-264.

[23] Parl. Papers, 1847, Coms., LXIV, " Spanish-American Republics ", 17-18.

For many years the Spanish government held the settlers rigidly to the terms specified. Commissioners made regular visits for this purpose, and saw that the boundary limits were not exceeded, as well as that the other agreements were complied with. Repeatedly they uprooted and destroyed young plantations started by the residents.[24]

The jealous vigilance of the Spanish authorities was shared by the rival Spanish wood-cutters. This jealousy, and the fact that the British settlers tried constantly to exceed the terms of the treaty, led to repeated threats of hostilities on the part of the Spaniards. The Baymen, who were not permitted to erect fortifications, were alarmed at these demonstrations, and appealed to their government for protection. In response, Colonel Barrow was sent to the place with both military and civil commissions, and took charge of affairs as superintendent, January 1, 1797.[25]

In 1798, when England and Spain were again at war, a determined attempt was made to drive out the settlers. A combined expedition was sent from Campeachy and Bacalar, under Governor O'Niel of Yucatan. The Baymen, however, prepared for a desperate resistance. They burned the houses on Saint George's Cay, to prevent them from falling into the hands of the enemy, and met the invaders at sea.[26] With the aid of a small naval force under Captain Moss in the *Merlin*,

[24] Crowe, *Gospel in Central America*, 196; Gibbs, *British Honduras*, 50.
[25] Trendell, *Her Majesty's Colonies*, 348.
[26] Henderson, *British Settlement of Honduras*, 8; Crowe, *Gospel in Central America*, 196; Lucas, *Historical Geography*, II, 307. The population at this time, white and colored, was probably not more than six or seven hundred. Henderson, *British Settlement of Honduras*, 85.

they drove off the Spaniards after two days' fighting.[27] This appears to have been the last attempt of the Spanish actively to interfere with the Belize settlement.

During the remainder of the period previous to 1815 the same relations prevailed between the British government and Belize as formerly.[28] By at least three treaties in this period England virtually acknowledged that the settlement was upon the basis established in 1786. The third article of the peace of Amiens of 1802 reads:

His Britannic majesty restores to the French republic and its allies, viz. his Catholic majesty and the Batavian republic, all the possessions and colonies which respectively belonged to them, and which have been either occupied or conquered by the British forces during the course of the present war.[29]

The only exceptions mentioned are the island of Trinidad and the Dutch possessions in Ceylon.[30] Again, in 1809, Great Britain and Spain formed an alliance in which the two powers agreed upon "an entire and lasting oblivion of all acts of hostility done on their side in the course of the late wars" in which they had been engaged against each other.[31] The last and most important of these treaties was that of 1814; it confirmed the first article of the treaty of 1786.[32]

In view of what has just been said, there seems to be absolutely no basis for the statement made by more

[27] Bird, "Sketch of the East Coast of Central America", in *Jr. Roy. Geog. Soc.*, XI, 81; Bancroft, *Central America*, II, 635; Henderson, *British Settlement of Honduras*, 8; Crowe, *Gospel in Central America*, 196-197.

[28] L. L., "Balize", in *Nouvelles Annales*, C, 54.

[29] *Ann. Reg.*, 1802, p. 609.

[30] *Ibid.*

[31] *Ibid.*, 1809, p. 737.

[32] Hertslet, *Treaties*, II, 245, 271.

recent writers, that the victory won by the Baymen in
1789 was a conquest of the Belize territory, and the
event which led directly to the extension of full British
sovereignty over the region.[33] The victory seems really
to have attracted but little attention from the home
government, and it was not until after a lapse of more
than fifty years that enlarged claims were made in consequence of it. In 1815, and for many years subsequent
to that date, as will be shown later, the British government merely regarded Belize as a settlement of British
subjects upon soil the sovereignty of which rested in
Spain.

The Bay Islands.

In the Bay of Honduras, close to the shores of the
Honduran republic, lie the Bay Islands, a group of
some half dozen islands, of which Ruatan[34] is by far
the largest and most important. This island is about
thirty miles long and eight or nine broad, and is possessed of excellent harbors, easily defended.[35]

While on his fourth voyage, in 1502, Columbus discovered and took possession of Ruatan and another
island of the group, now generally known as Bonacca,
in the names of the Spanish sovereigns.[36] The ownership of Spain was not disputed until towards the
middle of the seventeenth century, when the buccaneers swarmed in the western seas.[37] The advantages

[33] See Gibbs, *British Honduras*; Egerton, *British Colonial Policy*;
Keane, *Central and South America*; Woodward, *Expansion of the British
Empire*.

[34] Also written Roatan or Rattan.

[35] Long, *Jamaica*, I, 333; Roberts, *Central America*, 276; Alcedo, *Dictionary of America and the West Indies*, IV, 334.

[36] Roberts, *Central America*, 275; Squier, *Notes on Central America*,
369. The name of Bonacca is sometimes rendered " Guanacca ".

[37] Squier, *Notes on Central America*, 369; Travis, *Clayton-Bulwer
Treaty*, 3; Edgington, *Monroe Doctrine*, 65.

offered by the islands as a rendezvous early appealed
to the freebooters, who landed on them in 1642.[38] The
Indians, who were apparently the only inhabitants at
the time, made no resistance and the intruders established themselves on the islands. From this retreat,
and particularly from the sheltered harbors of Ruatan,
attacks were made upon the Spanish.[39]

The bishop of Comayagua, however, soon became
much concerned over the injurious effect of the hereti-
cal British upon the religion of the natives, and helped
incite the Spanish authorities to action against the
usurpers. A strong force was organized under the
leadership of various colonial officials, and in August,
1650, the buccaneers were dislodged.[40] But no attempt
was made to guard Ruatan or the other islands against
future seizure by the British. The few natives, whom
the pirates had spared and enslaved, were too frightened to remain, and were therefore removed to the
adjoining coast and allotted lands by the government.[41]

From this time until 1742, when war existed between
Spain and England, the Bay Islands appear to have had
no permanent inhabitants.[42] During this struggle, however, the English planned to gain control of the whole
Atlantic coast of Guatemala. They captured and fortified several important places on the mainland, and later

---

[38] Strangeways, *Mosquito Shore,* 42; Juarros, *Guatemala,* 318; Crowe,
Gospel in Central America, 184.

[39] Juarros, *Guatemala,* 319; Crowe, *Gospel in Central America,* 184;
Squier, *Notes on Central America,* 370.

[40] Juarros, *Guatemala,* 319-321; Crowe, *Gospel in Central America,*
184-185; Gibbs, *British Honduras,* 25.

[41] Squier, *Notes on Central America,* 370; *De Bow's Review,* XXVII,
555-556.

[42] Long, *Jamaica,* I, 335; Juarros, *Guatemala,* 321; Squier, *Notes on
Central America,* 370.

took possession of Ruatan.[43] Following this, they made a strong effort to colonize the island, but after the treaty of Aix-la-Chapelle the settlements were broken up and the inhabitants removed.[44] Spain then tried to encourage colonization, but her efforts failed; and for some time the islands, though recognized as Spanish territory, seem to have been practically deserted.[45]

Later, however, a few British appear to have settled upon the islands, but when war again broke out, in 1780, they were driven away by the Guatemalans,[46] and the treaty of 1783 definitely stipulated that all English settlers should, without exception, retire from the Spanish continent and its dependent islands.[47] These terms appear to have been evaded, but a supplementary convention, formed three years later, containing more definite stipulations to the same effect,[48] resulted in British evacuation of the coveted territory.[49]

Yet when war again existed in 1796, they once more returned. British officers transported Caribs from

[43] Juarros, *Guatemala*, 321; Squier, *Notes on Central America*, 370-371.
[44] Long, *Jamaica*, I, 335.
[45] *Ibid.*, 335-336. Long, in his history, published in 1774, repeatedly urged (I, 334, and *passim*), the acquisition and settlement of Ruatan by England. He stated (p. 333), that two Jamaica traders had patents for grazing mules on the island.

Squier, *Notes on Central America*, 371, and Trendell, *Her Majesty's Colonies*, 348, give the impression that during this whole period the islands were definitely held by the British; the latter states (p. 348), that the government of Ruatan and Bonacca was connected with that of Belize, and that the administrative officers had their residence on Ruatan. With regard to this point, however, Long seems to be the best authority.

[46] Long, *Jamaica*, I, 333; Squier, *Notes on Central America*, 371.
[47] *Ann. Reg.*, 1783, " State Papers ", 334-335.
[48] *Ibid.*, 1786, p. 263.
[49] Squier seems uncertain upon this point, *Notes on Central America*, 371; but Juarros gives a clear impression that the English abandoned the islands, *Guatemala*, 321.

Saint Vincent and the Leeward Islands to Ruatan and made that place a penal settlement. A guard of 2,000 negroes was stationed there for the defense of the islands. As soon, however, as these encroachments became known to the Spanish colonial officials, steps were taken towards the reconquest of the place; and in May, 1797, the Indians and negroes surrendered to a Spanish naval commander, after which the Spanish flag was hoisted and the territory formally declared a possession of Spain.[50]

After this, as long as Spain retained her dominion over Guatemalan territory, she remained in undisputed possession of the Bay Islands. About the year 1804 Captain Henderson, the superintendent of Belize, landed upon Ruatan, and, in writing of the incident, stated definitely that the island belonged to Spain.[51] Moreover, as has already been stated,[52] a treaty made between Spain and England in 1814 confirmed the first article of the treaty of 1786, which referred to British settlers on Central American territory. Therefore, if at any time previous Spanish control of the islands had lapsed, it was revived at this time and distinctly recognized by the British government.

The Mosquito Shore.

During the period considered in this chapter the term " Mosquito Shore " was applied in a vague way to the east coast of the captain-generalcy of Guate-

[50] Juarros, *Guatemala*, 321; Squier, *Notes on Central America*, 371; Gibbs, *British Honduras*, 52; Galindo, " Notice of the Caribs in Central America ", in *Jr. Roy. Geog. Soc.*, III, 290.

[51] Henderson, *British Settlement of Honduras*, 168; Squier, *Notes on Central America*, 372.

[52] See above, p. 8.

mala, but particularly to that part lying between Cape Honduras and the mouth of the San Juan River.[53]

The name was derived from the Moscos, or Mosquitos, the semi-nomadic population which inhabited the district.[54] These people were a mixture of at least three races. Those to whom the term Mosquito was originally applied were American aborigines, partly composed of Caribs who invaded the coast from the West Indies.[55] To these was added, probably in the early part of the seventeenth century, an Ethiopian element through the wreck of an African slaver somewhere upon the coast.[56] Because of this infusion of negro blood, the name " Sambos " was at times applied to the population of the region, or at least to the more negroid portion of it.[57] As time passed, traders and buccaneers who frequented the shore contributed a Caucasian strain to the earlier mixture;[58] and more African blood was occasionally added by fugitive slaves from the adjoining settlements.[59]

The aboriginal inhabitants of the shore were never completely subjugated by the conquerors of Guatemala;[60] but the cruel treatment which they suffered

[53] Long, *Jamaica*, I, 314; *Parl. Papers*, 1847, *Coms.*, LXIV, " Spanish-American Republics ", 27; *Kemble Papers*, II, 419, in N. Y. Hist. Soc., *Colls.*, 1884.

[54] Squier, *Notes on Central America*, 48; Keane, *Central and South America*, II, 237; Churchill, *Voyages*, VI, 287; *Kemble Papers*, II, 419.

[55] Keane, *Central and South America*, II, 235.

[56] Churchill, *Voyages*, VI, 293; Henderson, *British Settlement of Honduras*, 216; Strangeways, *Mosquito Shore*, 328; Bonnycastle, *Spanish-America*, I, 172.

[57] *Kemble Papers*, II, 419; Roberts, *Central America*, 152-153; Strangeways, *Mosquito Shore*, 239; Bonnycastle, *Central America*, I, 172.

[58] Bard, *Waikna*, 337-338.

[59] Scherzer, *Travels in Central America*, II, 30-31; Squier, *Notes on Central America*, 208; Keane, *Central and South America*, II, 236.

[60] *Cal. St. P., Col., Am. and W. I.*, 1669-1674, 303; Alcedo, *Dictionary*, III, 347; Long, *Jamaica*, I, 315, 317; Roberts, *Central America*, 54.

from the would-be conquerors bred in them a deep hatred for the Spanish people and their government.[61] This feeling was shared by the English buccaneers who infested the coast and worked harm to the Spaniards;[62] and they found it to their interest to foster it in the natives. But while encouraging opposition to the Spaniards, the freebooters themselves cultivated friendly relations with the Indians. They taught them the use of firearms and won their favor in various ways; and the Mosquitos in return helped the English in their attacks on the Spanish settlements.[63] Other adventurers came to the shore, especially from Jamaica, and traded with the Mosquitos for the natural products of the region.[64] With the aid of the Mosquitos as middlemen, they also exchanged British goods for the gold of the Spaniards, within the Spanish settlements.[65] The Mosquito coast was thus made a sort of " underground railroad " connecting the Spanish colonies, commercially, with the outside world.

As time passed, the freebooters and other British subjects made permanent settlements on the shore at Cape Gracias á Dios, Bluefields, and other points;[66] and thus the British influence grew. Shortly after the

[61] Dampier, *Voyages*, I, 8; Hist. MSS. Comm., *Report on MSS. of Mrs. Stopford-Sackville*, II, 289; Henderson, *British Settlement of Honduras*, 212, 225; Roberts, *Central America*, 153.

[62] Churchill, *Voyages*, VI, 286, 289, 291; Bard, *Waikna*, 337; Keane, *Central and South America*, II, 237.

[63] Long, *Jamaica*, I, 315, 317; Churchill, *Voyages*, VI, 287; Dampier, *Voyages*, I, 8, 10.

[64] Churchill, *Voyages*, VI, 286; Long, *Jamaica*, I, 319-320; *Parl. Papers*, 1847, Coms., LXIV, " Spanish-American Republics ", 29.

[65] Long, *Jamaica*, I, 317; *Kemble Papers*, II, 428; *Parl. Papers*, 1847, Coms., LXIV, " Spanish-American Republics ", 29.

[66] *Parl. Papers*, 1847, " Coms.", LXIV, " Spanish-American Republics ", 36; Bonnycastle, *Spanish-America*, I, 172; Bard, *Waikna*, 337.

English conquest of Jamaica this influence was much increased, for Oldman, the chief of the Mosquitos, was taken to England, where he formed some sort of alliance with the English government,[67] in consequence of which the Mosquitos regarded themselves as subjects of the King of England.[68] After some years, however, the alliance seems to have been forgotten by the English government, for when Jeremy, the heir of Oldman, came into power he was sent to Jamaica, evidently at the instigation of British residents of the shore, to ask for British protection for his people.[69] Whether the request was granted at this time is not certain;[70] but at some subsequent date the governors of Jamaica adopted the plan of appointing justices of the peace for the shore, who in addition to their regular duties were empowered to decide commercial questions of contracts and debts.[71]

This policy was continued until the war of 1739-1748 with Spain. During this struggle the British government came quickly to realize the importance of the Mosquitos as military allies and as agents for carrying on illicit trade with the Spanish colonies.[72] Gov-

[67] Oldman received from the English king a " crown " and a " commission ", which were but a " lacd hat " and a " ridiculous piece of writing " purporting that he should kindly use and relieve such straggling Englishmen as came to the shore. Churchill, *Voyages*, VI, 288.

[68] Dampier, *Voyages*, I, pt. 2, p. 11; Edwards, *British West Indies*, V, 203.

[69] Sloane, *History of Jamaica*, I, 76; *Cal. St. P., Col., Am. and W. I., 1669-1674*, 493; Long, *Jamaica*, I, 316.

[70] Sloane says that Albemarle, the governor of Jamaica, did nothing in the matter, as he feared that it was a trick to set up a government of buccaneers. *History of Jamaica*, I, 76; *cf.* Keasbey, *Nicaragua Canal*, 82-84.

[71] *Parl. Papers*, 1847, *Coms.*, LXIV, " Spanish-American Republics ", 29.

[72] *Ibid.*, 1856, *Coms.*, LX, " Correspondence with the United States respecting Central America ", 202.

ernor Trelawney of Jamaica, in 1740, wrote to the home government describing a plan for producing revolt in the Spanish colonies by aid from the Mosquitos.[73] For the purpose of executing the scheme, Captain Robert Hodgson was promptly sent to the shore to take possession of it in the name of the British government.[74] Hodgson called a meeting of the leading Mosquitos and made known his purpose to them. Then, probably through a liberal use of promises and rum, he secured their assent to a series of articles which he drew up.[75] These articles formally transferred the sovereignty of the shore to the British government, and made a Sambo chief, to whom the others were required to swear allegiance, the local ruler.[76]

Hodgson's attempt to produce a revolt of the back-country Indians failed, as did also Anson's and Vernon's expeditions, so there were no British conquests in Central America in consequence of Trelawney's scheme.[77] The British government, however, was now determined to secure a firm hold upon the Mosquito Shore. Therefore Hodgson was appointed superintendent of the region, and in 1749 he erected a fort at Black River, hoisted a British flag, and established a garrison of 100 men sent from Jamaica.[78] His action

---

[73] *U. S. Docs.*, ser. no. 660, doc. 27, p. 83.

[74] *Parl. Papers*, 1847, *Coms.*, LXIV, " Spanish-American Republics ", 29; Bard, *Waikna*, 340.

[75] *U. S. Docs.*, ser. no. 660, doc. 27, pp. 85-86; Bard, *Waikna*, 340-343.

[76] *Parl. Papers*, 1847, *Coms.*, LXIV, " Spanish-American Republics ", 29; *U. S. Docs.*, ser. no. 660, doc. 27, p. 84; Bard, *Waikna*, 340-342; Scherzer, *Travels in Central America*, II, 31.

[77] *U. S. Docs.*, ser. no. 660, doc. 27, p. 86; Travis, *Clayton-Bulwer Treaty*, 24; Bancroft, *Central America*, II, 601.

[78] *Parl. Papers*, 1847, *Coms.*, LXIV, " Spanish-American Republics ", 29; Bard, *Waikna*, 343; Lucas, *Historical Geography*, II, 299.

really amounted to a formal assumption of possession on the part of the British government. His function was to look after British interests generally, and particularly those of a commercial nature. This latter duty included the cultivation and preservation of friendship with the Mosquitos.[79]

In the autumn of 1739, before the arrival of Hodgson, the Spanish ambassador to England had complained that the English of Jamaica incited the Mosquitos to attacks on the adjacent Spanish settlements.[80] After the arrival of the superintendent and the formal occupation of the region, protests were uttered again and again. In 1750 the Spanish threatened to expel the intruders by force.[81] By way of reply to this, Hodgson, at Trelawney's instructions, represented that the object in stationing a superintendent on the shore was to prevent British hostilities against the Spanish.[82] For a time the Spaniards were, or pretended to be, deceived, and complimented Hodgson with the title of colonel for his professed services.[83] But the aggressions of the British continued, and the Spanish finally prepared for hostile action.[84]

The British settlers, who numbered about a thousand at the time,[85] were alarmed at this, as was also Governor Knowles, Trelawney's successor.[86] Knowles lacked

---

[79] *Parl. Papers,* 1847, *Coms.,* LXIV, " Spanish-American Republics ", 29.

[80] Bard, *Waikna,* 343.

[81] *Ibid.*; Bancroft, *Central America,* II, 601-602; Keane, *Central and South America,* II, 237.

[82] Bard, *Waikna,* 343; Bancroft, *Central America,* II, 602.

[83] Bard, *Waikna,* 343-344; Bancroft, *Central America,* II, 602.

[84] Bard, *Waikna,* 344; Bancroft, *Central America,* II, 602.

[85] *Parl. Papers,* 1847, *Coms.,* LXIV, " Spanish-American Republics ", 36.

[86] Bard, *Waikna,* 344.

the enthusiasm for British territorial expansion which had moved his predecessor; accordingly he wrote to the home government that the whole Mosquito affair was "a job", and that if Hodgson were not checked or recalled he would involve the nation in difficulties.[87] While waiting for a reply from home, Knowles wrote to the captain-general of Guatemala in an effort to preserve peace.[88] In consequence of these endeavors, a more pacific spirit was displayed by the Spaniards.[89] But with the accession of a new governor the old difficulties returned, and helped produce a conflict with Spain.[90]

By the treaty of 1763 which concluded this conflict, Great Britain agreed not only to demolish all fortifications erected by British subjects in the Bay of Honduras, but also in "other places of the territory of Spain in that part of the world".[91] In the following year, orders were given for the destruction of the fort at Black River, and the withdrawal of the garrison;[92] and the orders were executed.[93] But the settlers were reluctant to leave the shore, and the British government, probably influenced by Otway, the existing superintendent,[94] soon changed its policy.

In view of their bitter opposition to British interference in Mosquito territory, it is certain that the Spanish

[87] Bard, *Waikna*, 344; Travis, *Clayton-Bulwer Treaty*, 26.
[88] Bard, *Waikna*, 344.
[89] Travis, *Clayton-Bulwer Treaty*, 26.
[90] *Ibid.*; Bard, *Waikna*, 344; Bancroft, *Central America*, II, 602.
[91] *Ann. Reg.*, 1762, "State Papers", 239.
[92] *Parl. Papers*, 1847, *Coms.*, LXIV, "Spanish-American Republics", 30.
[93] Travis, *Clayton-Bulwer Treaty*, 26.
[94] *Parl. Papers*, 1847, *Coms.*, LXIV, "Spanish-American Republics", 30.

authorities intended the terms of the treaty to apply to this whole territory as well as to the settlements strictly upon the shores of the Bay of Honduras; but in the wording of the agreement the British saw a chance for evasion. Could the whole of the Mosquito Shore be regarded as lying in the Bay-of-Honduras "part of the world"? Black River might be so considered, but not the settlement at Cape Gracias á Dios, and surely not Bluefields, which was far to the south and near the mouth of the San Juan River.

Apparently certain of good ground for defense of their action, the British soon resumed occupation of the shore, under pretense that they had been imposed upon by the Spanish court when they gave orders for evacuation of the region.[95] The system of appointing superintendents was restored. Robert Hodgson, son of the first superintendent, held office from 1767 to 1775, when, as a new plan of government was decided upon, he was recalled.[96] This plan provided for a superintendent and an elective council of twelve members. With the approval of the Jamaican authorities these officers could make police regulations for the country.[97]

While the British were establishing themselves more firmly upon the Mosquito Shore, the Spanish were by no means passive. They protested emphatically, and at times resorted to retaliatory measures;[98] but the well-known weakness of Spain and the evident value of the

[95] *Ibid.*

[96] Travis, *Clayton-Bulwer Treaty*, 27.

[97] *Parl. Papers*, 1847, *Coms.*, LXIV, " Spanish-American Republics ", 32; Travis, *Clayton-Bulwer Treaty*, 27.

[98] *Parl. Papers*, 1847, *Coms.*, LXIV, " Spanish-American Republics ", 32-34; Bancroft, *Central America*, II, 602-604.

coast led the British to take a more bold and open attitude than formerly. In reply to Spanish protests, the British government declared that the Mosquito territory had never been conquered by the Spaniards; consequently, its king was an independent sovereign and quite capable of acting politically as such.[99]

The indignation of the Spanish government at these claims influenced it to aid the revolting American colonies in 1779.[100] England, in retaliation for this unfriendly act, formed a daring plan for indemnifying herself through conquests from Spain for the probable loss of her Atlantic colonies.[101] By means of aid from the Mosquitos, the Spanish colonial dominions were to be cut into two parts, along the line of the San Juan River and Lake Nicarauga, after which each section was to be conquered separately.[102] Governor Dalling of Jamaica, with whom the plan originated, was put in control of the bold undertaking.[103] The Mosquitos did not give so much aid as had been counted upon, however, and in some cases even went over to the enemy.[104] The rainy season set in, and with it came disease. Adequate food and clothing and medical supplies were lacking, and the whole enterprise ended

---

[99] *Parl. Papers*, 1847, *Coms.*, LXIV, " Spanish-American Republics ", 30; Travis, *Mosquito History*, 8; *De Bow's Review*, XXVII, 553.

[100] Travis, *Clayton-Bulwer Treaty*, 27.

[101] Fortier and Ficklen, *Central America and Mexico*, 115.

[102] *Ibid.* Cf. Edwards, *British West Indies*, V, 212, 214.

[103] *Kemble Papers*, II, " Preface," 7.

[104] *Kemble Papers*, II, 7, 406; Hist. MSS. Comm., *Report on MSS. of Mrs. Stopford-Sackville*, II, 287-288; Crowe, *Gospel in Central America*, 187.

in great disaster.[105] Of the more than 2,000 men sent out only 380 returned to Jamaica.[106]

At first the Spanish were also successful on the Mosquito coast itself, for the British garrison had been reduced.[107] The fort at Black River was captured in March, 1782, and the settlers were forced to take refuge at Cape Gracias á Dios.[108] But reinforcements were sent, and in five months the whole region was in control of the British, in whose hands it was when the war ended.[109]

When the treaty of 1783 was being negotiated, the question of British settlements in Central America gave considerable anxiety to the British cabinet. After the ambitious plans for conquest of Spanish soil had failed, the British government had no intention of relaxing the hold maintained on Mosquito territory previous to the war. The Spanish, however, were determined to drive the enemy from all of their territory except Belize; therefore the definitive treaty of peace stipulated by its sixth article that all English settlers except those at Belize should retire from the " Spanish continent ".[110] The British cabinet objected to the article on the ground that it gave greater concessions than were warranted by the preliminaries, and wished to defer for six months the agreement regard-

---

[105] *Kemble Papers*, II, 3-65, *passim*; Crowe, *Gospel in Central America*, 187; Fortier and Ficklen, *Central America and Mexico*, 117; Mahan, *Interest of America in Sea Power*, 80; Bancroft, *Central America*, II, 611.

[106] Crowe, *Gospel in Central America*, 187; Fortier and Ficklen, *Central America and Mexico*, 117.

[107] *Parl. Papers*, 1847, *Coms.*, LXIV, " Spanish-American Republics ", 34.

[108] *Ibid.*, 34-35.

[109] *Ibid.*, 35; Travis, *Clayton-Bulwer Treaty*, 28.

[110] *Ann. Reg.*, 1783, " State Papers ", 334-335.

ing the question covered by the article.[111] But as it seemed desirable to sign the treaties as soon as possible, Fox pointed out to the King that the British government could put its own interpretation upon the words " Spanish continent ", and could determine whether the Mosquito Shore came under that description or not.[112] The King gave his consent, and Fox instructed the Duke of Manchester to accede to the objectionable article unless he could prevail upon the other negotiators to defer the consideration of it.[113] Further delay seemed undesirable, and the treaty was signed with this article unchanged.

After the agreement was ratified the British made no move towards the evacuation of the Mosquito Shore, and, in reply to the protests of Spain, declared that the shore was not a part of the " Spanish continent ", but of the " American continent ".[114] Nevertheless the Spanish government was determined, and as England was crippled by a long and unsuccessful war, and by discontent at home, she was forced to yield. After a long and bitter discussion, the treaty of 1786, which left no loophole for British evasion, was signed.[115] This stipulated that " His Britannic Majesty's subjects, and the other colonists who have hitherto enjoyed the protection of England, shall evacuate the country of the Mosquitos, as well as the continent in general, and the islands adjacent, without exception, situated beyond the

---

[111] Fox, *Memoirs and Correspondence*, II, 122, 124.

[112] *Ibid.*, 122-123.

[113] *Ibid.*, 124.

[114] *Parl. Papers*, 1847, *Coms.*, LXIV, " Spanish-American Republics ", 35-36; Bard, *Waikna*, 344; Keane, *Central and South America*, II, 238.

[115] *Parl. Papers*, 1847, *Coms.*, LXIV, " Spanish-American Republics ", 36; Burney, *Buccaneers of America*, 102.

line hereinafter described ".[116] The line referred to was the new and more comprehensive boundary for Belize settlement.

The Indians were much opposed to the arrangement,[117] and in their opposition were probably supported by the settlers, some of whom remained in defiance of the treaty,[118] and by the traders.[119] Several attempts were made by the Spaniards to subjugate the Indians and to establish permanent settlements upon the coast, but all in vain. In 1796 the Mosquitos recaptured the last settlement—that on Black River— and drove out the Spaniards.[120] This seems to have been the last effort of Spain to secure control of the Mosquito Shore.

After the treaty of 1786 the British gave up all open political relations with the Mosquitos.[121] Yet the influence of the contraband traders, to whom the Indians were still invaluable, did much towards preserving a friendly feeling for Great Britain. This friendliness was also fostered by a continuance, by the Belize authorities, of an old custom of feasting the leading Mosquitos and of distributing presents among them.[122] Because of this attention the Mosquitos seem to have

---

[116] *Ann. Reg.*, 1786, " State Papers ", p. 263. This treaty was very unpopular and led to a vote of censure by the House of Lords against the government. After a long, sharp debate the motion was defeated. *Ann. Reg.*, 1787, " History ", 111-114.

[117] Stout, *Nicaragua*, 168.

[118] *Parl. Papers*, 1847, *Coms.*, LXIV, " Spanish-American Republics ", 36; Roberts, *Central America*, 283; Bancroft, *Central America*, II, 606.

[119] *Kemble Papers*, II, 428; Bonnycastle, *Spanish America*, I, 174.

[120] Bancroft, *Central America*, II, 607; Travis, *Clayton-Bulwer Treaty*, 30.

[121] Bard, *Waikna*, 345; Bancroft, *Central America*, II, 606-607.

[122] Henderson, *British Settlement of Honduras*, 165-182; Edwards, *British West Indies*, V, 206.

considered themselves as still under British protection, and the Spanish tacitly permitted them to do so.[123]

As long as Spain retained dominion over Central America, the British government refrained from all further attempts at interference with the Mosquitos, and showed no special interest in the shore. In 1814, by a treaty already described, she confirmed Spain in her sovereignty over it. Shortly after this a captain in the corps of royal British engineers, who had made a voyage in the region, wrote: " The Mosquito shore . . . has been claimed by the British. The English held this country for eighty years, and abandoned it in 1787 and 1788. The Spaniards call it a part of Honduras,[124] which it really is, and claim it as such." [125] This statement seems to reflect the view of the British government at the time. The British protectorate no longer existed, and British control on the shore was a thing of the past.

Such was the character of British influence in Central America, extending over a period of more than a century and a half. At one time Great Britain had some basis for asserting a legal claim to all of the territory towards which her interests were directed;[126] and at times she exercised full control, now over one portion and now over another, in disregard of Spanish sovereign rights, and frequently in defiance of treaty stipulations. After a long struggle, largely devoid of success, Spain was finally able to strike an effective blow by the treaty of 1786. By means of this she

---

[123] Stout, *Nicaragua,* 168.
[124] The northern, or Honduran, part of the shore had been described by the writer.
[125] Bonnycastle, *Spanish America,* I, 171.
[126] The treaty of 1670.

drove the British from the Bay Islands and from the
Mosquito Shore, but permitted the retention of the
Belize concession, while carefully keeping in the Spanish Crown the sovereignty over Belize territory. The
years which followed were largely occupied by the
French Revolution and the Napoleonic wars. During
this period, Great Britain, from lack of inclination or
lack of opportunity, failed to recover the hold which
she had lost. Therefore, at the date with which the
next chapter opens her Central American relations
were on the same basis as immediately after the treaty
of 1786.

CHAPTER II.

BRITISH AGGRESSIONS; AMERICAN I
AWAKENED, 1815-1850.

With the year 1815 there opened a new
United States. Though in the War of 181
ary Republican party had utterly failed in
for conquest, yet the nation had fought its
and, while frequently defeated and disco
finally won an inspiring victory at New C
conflict roused the American people as a whole to
national consciousness and filled them with a confidence in their own possibilities, hitherto lacking. With
the close of the struggle the country assumed a more
secure and dignified position among the nations.

After this second war for independence, the attitude
of England, especially, was altered towards the United
States. She not only showed a sincere desire to refrain
from any unseemly meddling with American affairs,
but even displayed a real anxiety to avoid all chances
for future trouble. Actual concessions were as a rule
reluctantly granted, but the discussion of subjects out
of which serious differences might arise was avoided
if possible, or postponed. It was this determination on
the part of the British to maintain a pacific policy that
prevented embarrassing complications as a result of
Jackson's violent proceedings in Florida;[1] and it was
undoubtedly also influential in effecting the temporary

[1] Reddaway, *Monroe Doctrine*, 14, 33. *Cf.* Rush, *Residence at the Court of London*, 399-413.

arrangements regarding Oregon, made by the convention of 1818.[2]

Up to 1823 nothing had arisen seriously to disturb the good feeling between the two governments. When, therefore, the " Monroe doctrine " was first given expression in December of that year, popular enthusiasm was roused in America for the British government because of the well-known position of Canning towards the designs of the Holy Alliance. Few outside of the American cabinet suspected that the attitude displayed by the President's message was not welcome to England, and might prove an embarrassing obstruction in the execution of plans which she herself cherished for the extension of power in the western world.[3]

Nevertheless, Canning was decidedly taken aback by this independent stand of the American government. However, without revealing his own views, and carefully refraining from all open acts which might rouse antagonism, he proceeded to adopt and carry out a policy calculated to render ineffective the Monroe doctrine in so far as it conflicted with British designs.[4] Canning's general policy was to prevent Latin America from looking towards the United States for help and from seeking alliances with her.[5] For this purpose the

[2] Beaumarchais, *La doctrine de Monroë,* 2, 6-7.

[3] Reddaway, *Monroe Doctrine,* 88.

[4] J. Q. Adams early discerned the unfriendly character of Canning's attitude (Adams, *Memoirs,* III, 437), and upon learning of Canning's death in 1827, wrote in his diary: " May this event, in the order of Providence, avert all the evils which he would, if permitted, have drawn down upon us, and all evil counsels formed against our peace and prosperity be baffled and defeated! " *Ibid.,* VII, 328.

[5] Chatfield to Palmerston, Oct. 28, 1835, F. O., Cen. Am., vol. 16, no. 26; Temperley, " Later American Policy of George Canning ", in *Am. Hist. Rev.,* XI, 783, 787-788. For instance, on February 8, 1826, Canning wrote to Vaughan: " The avowed pretension of the United States to put

British government was to secure a preponderating influence, politically and economically, in the new states.[6]

Great Britain was especially interested in Central America because of early relations there, and, in consequence of Monroe's proclamation, suspected the American government of watching with particular attention British movements in that quarter. However, at this period the American government did not merit the suspicion directed towards it. As yet the United States as a nation had hardly secured her bearings; she was a second rate power with an uncertain future. Her population numbered but little more than ten million, and was confined to the eastern fourth of the present settled area. In proportion as her national strength was less than it is now, so also were her interests less comprehensive. The Monroe doctrine, though boldly uttered, was merely defensive in aim; and for many years it was applied only to territory actually contiguous to American borders. The great triangle of Mexican domain shut off the attention of the United States government from Central America.

Though Central America as well as the other Spanish-American republics received Monroe's declaration with enthusiasm and looked towards the north

---

themselves at the head of the confederacy of all the Americas, and to sway that confederacy against Europe, (Great Britain included), is *not* a pretension identified with our interests, or one that we can countenance as tolerable.

" It is however a pretension which there is no use in contesting in the abstract; but we must not say anything that seems to admit the principle." Mass. Hist. Soc., *Proc.*, XLVI, 234; *cf.* Rush, *The Court of London from 1819 to 1825*, pp. 431-433, 471.

[6] Turner, *Rise of the New West*, 222; Paxson, *Independence of the South American Republics*, 178-252, *passim*.

for protection from European enemies, there is nothing
in either the English or the American archives to show
that, for the first two decades following the proclamation, the United States government took any special
interest in British encroachments on the American
isthmus, or made any active attempts to check them.[7]

In 1825 the government was invited to send delegates
to a great pan-American congress at which was to be
discussed, among other questions, the manner in which
all colonization of European powers on the American
continent should be resisted.[8] It is true that on this
occasion much interest was shown by the United States,[9]
but in the instructions given the American representatives no special mention was made of Central America,
or of British aggressions in that region.[10] Moreover, it
should be borne in mind that Great Britain also was
invited to the congress. However, as is well known,
party opposition to President Adams prevented the
American delegates from reaching Panama in time,
and the congress itself came to nothing.

In fact, for a long period the United States government not only ignored Central America so far as the

---

[7] In 1824 the United States government decided to send an informal
agent, Mann, to Guatemala. J. Q. Adams, the secretary of state, instructed Mann that the first object of his mission would be to gather
information about the new republic. Guatemala, Adams wrote in his
diary, was important because of its location on the isthmus, and because
of the " commercial connections, and lodgments on the soil by the British,
with the neighboring bay of Honduras and Mosquito shore ". *Memoirs*,
VI, 325. No note of resentment towards British interests in Central
America is evident in the words just quoted. If such resentment had
been felt by the American government, it seems probable that Adams's
jealous patriotism would have caused him promptly to reflect it. See
above, note 4.

[8] *Brit. and For. State Papers*, XIII, 397.

[9] *Am. State Papers, For. Relats.*, V, 916-919; VI, 356-366.

[10] *Brit. and For. State Papers*, XV, 832-862.

principles of the Monroe doctrine were concerned, but also quite neglected that country itself. Only occasionally were agents of the United States sent there, and those who were sent appear to have lacked both interest and efficiency.[11] In their instructions, the American agents were often directed to emphasize to the restless states the importance of union to the maintenance of republican government,[12] but though the history of British encroachments in Central America must have been pretty well known to the Washington authorities, nothing appears in the instructions regarding the matter; furthermore, the despatches of the agents contain no allusion to it.

Meanwhile the British improved their opportunity. During the last years of Spanish control and in the period of the Central American confederation they advanced but slowly, largely content to keep off all intruders and to hold the ground previously gained.[13] At this time a desire to be on good terms with the United States, as well as the lack of special interest, prevented the British government itself from adopting a very strong policy in Central America, though its agents in the region displayed much aggressiveness. But almost simultaneously with the dissolution of the confederation in 1839, and the consequent loss of power of united resistance, appeared a greater jealousy of

[11] Dept. of State, Inst., Am. States, vol. 15, p. 15; Squier to Clayton, Aug. 20, 1849, Dept. of State, Des., Guat., vol. 2.

[12] Dept. of State, Inst., Am. States, vol. 14, p. 212, and *passim.*

[13] Schenley to Planta, May 21, 1826, F. O., Cen. Am., vol. 5; Memorandum from the British Premier, 1829, C. O., Hond., vol. 40; Palmerston to Granville, Oct. 4, 1831, *ibid.*, vol. 42; Granville to Palmerston, Oct. 24, 1831, *ibid.*

American designs, which overcame the earlier hesitation, and the policy of the government became as aggressive as its agents could desire. With the approval of their superiors, the British representatives intrigued to prevent further union,[14] and set one weak state or warring faction against the other to the advantage of their country, and at the same time extended their hold upon Central American territory. The British interference to prevent a closer union of states will be shown later, but attention is now directed to the British plan of acquiring more territory.

In the early part of the period under consideration the center of British influence was Belize. During the last years of Spanish sovereignty, when commissioners no longer visited the region, the settlers gradually spread south of the Sibun River into Guatemalan territory, and at the time of Central American independence had reached the Sarstoon.[15] After the overthrow of Spanish power, the British government was anxious to preserve to the settlers the rights granted by Spain. Consequently, suspicious over the wording of a treaty of alliance made between Guatemala and Colombia in 1825,[16] it required a distinct declaration from each state that neither designed to arrogate pretensions to a territorial authority which might possibly clash with British possessory rights in Belize.[17] In a treaty made with Mexico in 1826, Great Britain also secured the introduction of a clause guaranteeing to the British at Belize

[14] Froebel, *Seven Years in Central America*, 193-194; Scherzer, *Travels in Central America*, II, 31.
[15] Codd to Goderich, Nov. 24, 1827, C. O., Hond., vol. 38.
[16] *Brit. and For. State Papers*, XII, 802-811.
[17] Chatfield to Palmerston, Feb. 3, 1834, F. O., Cen. Am., vol. 14.

the same terms as were given by Spain forty years
before.[18]

Bad feeling arose between the Central American
confederation and the British settlers almost immediately.[19]   As a result of complaints from the latter the
British colonial secretary consulted the legal adviser
of the Crown regarding the status of Belize.   That
official, basing his judgment upon the treaties of 1802,
1809, and 1814, referred to in the preceding chapter,
gave the opinion that the treaties of 1783 and 1786
were still in force.[20]   This decision prevented the establishment of full British sovereignty over the territory,
for which the settlers had hoped;[21]   consequently the
inimical relations continued.   Soon complaints against
the Central Americans were again made to the home
government, accompanied by the statement that the
unfriendly Central American attitude was caused by
the presence of people from the United States.[22]   A
little later the superintendent announced that North
Americans were planning to settle in the region between the Sibun and the Sarstoon rivers.[23]   This report
seemed to rouse the British premier to consider the
situation seriously.   He admitted as undeniable the
right of Spain to the Belize territory, but felt it desirable to determine whether she would not relinquish her

---

[18] *Brit. and For. State Papers,* XIV, 625.   A little later an attempt to
secure the same agreement with Central America failed because the
Central American agent in London lacked the necessary powers.   Edgington, *Monroe Doctrine,* 64.

[19] Codd to Bathurst, Feb. 6, 1825, F. O., Cen. Am., vol. 4.

[20] Robinson to Bathurst, July 8, 1825, C. O., Hond., vol. 36.

[21] Codd to Goderich, Nov. 24, 1827, *ibid.,* vol. 38.

[22] Schenley to Planta, May 31, 1826, F. O., Cen. Am., vol. 5.

[23] Memorandum of British Premier, 1829, C. O., Hond., vol. 40.   The
report was evidently false, for nothing further was said regarding the
matter.

claims. Should she be unwilling to do this, he thought it might be well to regard the territory as a part of the state of Guatemala, and to offer the Central American government an earlier recognition in return for the cession of it.[24]

Nothing resulted from the suggestion at the time, however, but when the Liberals under lead of Morazan gained control of the Central American government they demanded that the British settlers retreat to the territory beyond the Sibun, the southern boundary established by the treaty of 1786.[25] This led the British agents to support the Serviles, who were more indifferent to British encroachments, and to work for the overthrow of Morazan.[26] The demand of the Liberals also caused Palmerston to oppose a suggestion[27] to settle the strife by means of a treaty with Guatemala,[28] and to instruct Chatfield, the British consul, to refrain from all discussion of the question of boundaries with the Central American government, warning him not to give them any reason to think that the British government considered the question one with which they had any concern.[29]

Insistent upon maintaining what it regarded as its rights, the Central American government confirmed a cession of tracts of territory between the Sibun and the Sarstoon, made by the state of Guatemala, to a land

---

[24] *Ibid.*

[25] Cockburn to Goderich, Jan. 26, 1833, F. O., Cen. Am., vol. 13, no. 52.

[26] Chatfield to Palmerston, Feb. 3, 1834, F. O., Am., vol. 14; Squier, *Nicaragua*, II, 412-414; Stephens, *Central America*, II, 47-49.

[27] Backhouse to Cockburn, Feb. 19, 1834, C. O., Hond., vol. 45.

[28] Cockburn to Goderich, Jan. 30, 1833, F. O., Cen. Am., vol. 13.

[29] Palmerston to Chatfield, Mar. 19, 1834, *ibid.*, vol. 14, no. 5; Palmerston to Chatfield, Sept. 22, 1834, *ibid.*, vol. 15.

company and to one Colonel Galindo,[30] an Irishman by birth, but a Central American by adoption.[31] This roused Cockburn, the Belize superintendent, to declare that the British government would resist to the utmost all encroachments upon this territory.[32] As Chatfield, true to his instructions, had refused to discuss the question of boundaries, the Guatemalan government decided to send Galindo to London to secure terms.[33] He was to go by way of Washington and endeavor to secure American aid against the British. But Chatfield, anticipating this move,[34] notified Vaughan, the English minister to the United States.[35] Vaughan took the hint and later wrote to Palmerston that he " had no difficulty in convincing Mr. Forsyth that the United States could not possibly listen to any such proposal from Colonel Galindo ".[36] Therefore, when Galindo made known his errand, he was informed that the United States government deemed it inexpedient to interfere in the matter. He then proceeded to London, but the British government refused to receive him as a diplomatic agent on the ground that he was a British subject, and his mission ended in failure.[37]

Meanwhile the quarrel between the British settlers and the Central American government had increased in bitterness, partly because of discriminatory duties

[30] Chatfield to Palmerston, Nov. 13, 1834, C. O., Hond., vol. 47, no. 23.

[31] *U. S. Docs.*, ser. no. 660, doc. 27, pp. 12-13.

[32] Chatfield to Palmerston, Nov. 13, 1834, C. O., Hond., vol. 47, no. 23; Palmerston to Chatfield, May 13, 1836, F. O., Cen. Am., vol. 18, no. 7.

[33] *U. S. Docs.*, ser. no. 660, doc. 27, p. 12.

[34] Chatfield to Palmerston, Dec. 29, 1834, F. O., Cen. Am., vol. 14, no. 29.

[35] Chatfield to Vaughan, Dec. 29, 1834, F. O., Cen. Am., vol. 14; Chatfield to Vaughan, Jan. 10, 1835, F. O., Cen. Am. vol. 16.

[36] Vaughan to Palmerston, July 4, 1835, C. O., Hond., vol. 47.

[37] *U. S. Docs.*, ser. no. 660, doc. 27, pp. 3-13.

charged by the latter upon all goods coming into the republic from Belize.[38] Consequently the residents took matters into their own hands; they held a convention, changed the name of the place to British Honduras, adopted a colonial form of government,[39] and, in November, 1834, sent a petition to London asking that the settlement be declared a regular British colony.[40]

As a result, the British government decided to settle the whole question. Its plan involved a definite recognition of sovereignty over the Belize territory as still existing in the Spanish Crown, for the purpose of securing the relinquishment of this sovereignty to Great Britain. Accordingly, in March, 1835, Villiers, the British representative at Madrid, was instructed to try to obtain from the Spanish government a concession to the whole tract of land occupied by the Belize settlers, as far south as the Sarstoon.[41] Villiers broached the matter to the Spanish foreign secretary,[42] hinting that if the cession was not made the settlement would be declared a British colony anyway.[43] He received an encouraging reply from the secretary,[44] but the question seems never to have been considered by the Spanish government, and the English ambassador thought it inexpedient to press the matter.[45] Palmer-

[38] Chatfield to Palmerston, Dec. 30, 1834, F. O., Cen. Am., vol. 14, no. 28.

[39] Keasbey, *Nicaragua Canal*, 171; Walker, *Ocean to Ocean*, 50.

[40] *U. S. Docs.*, ser. no. 660, doc. 27, p. 4; Crowe, *Gospel in Central America*, 206.

[41] Wellington to Villiers, Mar. 12, 1835, F. O., Spain, vol. 439, no. 19.

[42] Villiers to Wellington, April 8, 1835, *ibid.*, vol. 441, no. 61.

[43] Miller to Glenelg, May 18, 1835, C. O., Hond., vol. 47.

[44] *Ibid.*

[45] Palmerston to Glenelg, Sept. 15, 1838, F. O., Cen. Am., vol. 21.

ston thereupon determined that it was best to " let the Spaniards quietly forget it ",[46] and to permit whatever interests and claims the latter possessed to lapse.

The continued lack of interest in Belize on the part of the United States made this policy a safe one for the British government; and though the settlers were dissatisfied with the equivocal situation, their government consistently maintained its former stand, unwilling needlessly to attract the attention of the American or the Spanish governments to the region. In November, 1840, a new superintendent, Macdonald, proclaimed the law of England to be the law of the " settlement or colony of British Honduras ", and sent a new petition to the home government;[47] But as Aberdeen thought it unwise again to open the question, and feared that a declaration of British sovereignty over Belize would be offensive to Spanish dignity,[48] nothing was done. Again, in 1846, Belize was heard from. A petition presented to the British government in behalf of Belize merchants asked that goods from Belize be admitted at British ports free from the discriminating duty charged upon foreign goods.[49] But the Colonial Office replied that the sovereignty of Belize territory rested not in Great Britain, but in Spain, under the treaties of 1783 and 1786.[50] Therefore the petition could not be granted. This seems to have been the last attempt of the Belize settlers for a long period to put themselves on a complete colonial basis.

[46] Palmerston to Glenelg, Sept. 15, 1838, F. O., Cen. Am., vol. 21; Strangeways to Stephen, Mar. 20, 1839, C. O., Hond., vol. 56.

[47] Crowe, *Gospel in Central America,* 205-206; Gibbs, *British Honduras,* 50.

[48] Canning to Hope, Dec. 13, 1841, C. O., Hond., vol. 61.

[49] Hawes to Parker, Oct. 12, 1846, *ibid.,* vol. 71.

[50] *Ibid.*

For many years the British agents in Central America tried to rouse their government to the importance of securing the island of Ruatan,[51] and in 1830 the Belize superintendent, hoping to be sustained in his act, seized the island, on the excuse that the Central Americans had refused to return fugitive slaves.[52] But remonstrance being made by the Central American authorities, the seizure was disavowed by the British government, and the island abandoned.[53] The English authorities were nevertheless alive to the value of Ruatan, and, while from policy they could not countenance an occupation of it by their subjects, they kept close watch lest other nations seize it.[54] When Villiers was instructed regarding Belize, he was also directed to try to secure from the Spanish government the cession of Ruatan and Bonacca,[55] but his efforts in this regard were equally fruitless.

As the right of Great Britain to the islands was, in the opinion of the British government, " to say the least, exceedingly questionable ",[56] it was felt that the revival of a dominant claim might by objected to by other European powers, and by the United States;[57] therefore the same policy was pursued as with Belize.

[51] Schenley to Planta, May 31, 1826, F. O., Cen. Am., vol. 5; Cockburn to Goderich, Jan. 30, 1833, *ibid.,* vol. 13, no. 52; Cooke to Howickl, Aug. 13, 1831, *ibid.,* vol. 11; Prowett to Glenelg, April 15, 1837, C. O., Hond., vol. 51: Grey to Backhouse, Nov. 30, 1837, *ibid.*

[52] Squier, *Notes on Central America,* 372-373.

[53] *Ibid.*

[54] Palmerston to Granville, Oct. 4, 1831, C. O., Hond., vol. 42; Granville to Palmerston, Oct. 24, 1831, *ibid.;* Chatfield to Palmerston, Oct. 8, 1838, F. O., Cen. Am., vol. 20, no. 58; Palmerston to Chatfield, Sept. 21, 1839, *ibid.,* vol. 22, no. 7.

[55] Wellington to Villiers, Mar. 12, 1835, F. O., Spain, vol. 4, no. 21.

[56] Colonial Office Memorandum of Correspondence respecting Ruatan or Rattan, Dec. 31, 1838, F. O., Cen. Am., vol. 38.

[57] *Ibid.*

The British cabinet shrewdly kept open the question of ownership of the islands, and watched developments.[58]

When the Central American confederation had fallen to pieces, partly as a result of British influence,[59] the time seemed ripe for a bolder stand. In 1838 a party of liberated slaves from the Grand Cayman Islands came to Ruatan to settle. The Honduran commandant stationed on the island informed them that before they could establish themselves there they must obtain permission from the republic of Honduras. Some of the immigrants asked for permission, but others refused to do so and appealed to the Belize superintendent. Macdonald, noted for his aggressive policy, held the office at the time. He soon landed on Ruatan, hauled down the Central American flag, and hoisted that of Great Britain. Scarcely had he departed, however, before the commandant again ran up the Central American colors. Macdonald returned, seized the commandant and his soldiers and carried them to the mainland, threatening them with death if they attempted to return.[60] The government of Honduras protested and once more unfurled the flag of Central America on the island,[61] but it was hauled down by orders of the British government, and Chatfield was instructed to inform the Central Americans that the British government did not deem it necessary to discuss with them the right of British sovereignty over Rua-

---

[58] Chatfield to Palmerston, Jan. 30, 1836, F. O., Cen. Am., vol. 18, no. 2; Chatfield to Palmerston, Oct. 8, 1838, *ibid.*, vol. 20, no. 58.

[59] Squier to Clayton, Aug. 20, 1849, Dept. of State, Des., Guat., vol. 2.

[60] Squier, *Notes on Central America*, 373.

[61] Palmerston to Chatfield, Sept. 21, 1839, F. O., Cen. Am., vol. 22, no. 7; Squier, *Notes on Central America*, 374.

tan.[62] At this time Honduras was acting alone and was too weak to do more than protest; therefore the British remained in control.[63]

In 1841 the British government went a step further. It informed the governor of Jamaica that should any foreign power take possession of Ruatan he was to order the departure of the intruders, and he was authorized to use forcible measures for their ejectment, without further instructions, if the order was not obeyed.[64]

Meanwhile to the Cayman Island population had been added some English settlers,[65] and Macdonald, seeing his opportunity, offered to appoint magistrates for them if they so desired.[66] Some time later the offer was accepted, and subsequently magistrates were regularly appointed by the Belize superintendent.[67]

On the Mosquito Shore, as in Belize and the Bay Islands, the same slow but decided advance was made towards British control. In 1816 the heir of the Mosquitos was at his own request crowned at Belize,[68] and the custom was followed with his successors.[69] In spite of this, however, British interest in the Mosquitos seems temporarily to have declined, for the practice of giving them presents was discontinued, and was only

[62] Palmerston to Chatfield, Sept. 21, 1839, F. O., Cen. Am., vol. 22, no. 7; Chatfield to Palmerston, Jan. 25, 1840, *ibid.*, vol. 23, no. 2.

[63] Squier, *Notes on Central America*, 375.

[64] Palmerston to Bulwer, Mar. 14, 1850, F. O., Am., vol. 509, no. 25.

[65] Fancourt to Elgin, Jan. 15, 1845, C. O., Hond., vol. 69, no. 1.

[66] Squier, *Notes on Central America*, 375.

[67] Fancourt to Elgin, Jan. 15, 1845, C. O., Hond., vol. 69, no. 1.

[68] Bard, *Waikna*, 345-346; Stout, *Nicaragua*, 168.

[69] Codd to Manchester, April 3, 1824, C. O., Hond., vol. 35.

revived in 1830, after the Indians had protested against English neglect.[70]

In the early thirties, when the Central American government was trying to secure a settlement with England regarding the Belize boundaries, an attempt was also made to induce the British to relinquish all claims to the Mosquito Shore, but Chatfield diplomatically evaded a discussion of the subject.[71] However, the claims of the Central Americans to the shore succeeded in reviving the interest of the British government; and as the Central American confederation weakened the British interest increased. In 1837 the Colonial Office ordered that the custom of giving presents be continued and that the Indians be protected from Central American encroachments.[72] In the following year Palmerston directed that the old connection with the Mosquitos be maintained, and, if anything, be drawn closer, because circumstances might arise to make the dependence of the Mosquito country politically and commercially useful to England.[73]

[70] Arthur to Bathurst, Jan. 15, 1821, *ibid.*, vol. 30; Cockburn to the Colonial Secretary [n. d.], *ibid.*, vol. 41. In view of later events, it is of interest to note the opinion held at this time by the Belize superintendent with regard to the southern boundary of the Mosquito territory. In 1830 the Mosquito king granted a tract of land, apparently lying between Bluefields and the San Juan River, to one McLeLachein who evidently intended to make a British settlement there. In referring to this circumstance, Cockburn wrote that he was not aware of any recognized right by which the king could make such a grant. Moreover, the settlement contemplated would be regarded with increased jealousy by the Central Americans because of its proximity to the San Juan River, by means of which it was proposed to open up a canal. Cockburn to Twiss, Feb. 7, 1830, *ibid.*

[71] Chatfield to Palmerston, July 5, 1834, F. O., Cen. Am., vol. 14, no. 3.

[72] Stephen to Backhouse, June 15, 1837, *ibid.*, vol. 19.

[73] Strangeways to Stephen, Mar. 28, 1838, *ibid.*, vol. 21; Dept. of State, Inst., Am. States, vol. 15, p. 52.

But no very active measures were taken to increase British influence over that region until the appointment of the enterprising Macdonald to the superintendency of Belize. Macdonald quickly saw the use which might be made of the Mosquito protectorate, and in 1840 wrote to Russell urging the importance of keeping the Central Americans from possessing the mouth of the San Juan for transit purposes. To retain the river mouth for the Mosquito king, he declared, would promote British commercial prosperity, and strengthen national and political power.[74]

In August, 1841, Macdonald, accompanied by the Mosquito king, went in a British vessel to San Juan, the little town at the mouth of the river. Here he raised the Mosquito flag, laid claim to the port in the name of the Mosquito king, and announced the protectorate of England over the Indians.[75] The Central Americans were ordered to leave the place by the first of the following March.[76] The Nicaraguan commandant of the port[77] refused to recognize the sovereign of the Mosquitos, and was thereupon taken aboard the vessel and carried to Cape Gracias á Dios, where he was put ashore and left to get back as best he could.[78]

Macdonald's expedition was evidently made without instructions from his government, but, judging from Chatfield's reply to a protest from Nicaragua,[79] it was

---

[74] C. O., Hond., vol. 57, no. 45.

[75] *Niles' Register*, LXI, 98; Latané, *Diplomatic Relations*, 191.

[76] *Niles' Register*, LXI, 98.

[77] In 1832 the Nicaraguans had moved to the north bank of the San Juan River, *Parl. Papers*, 1847-1848, *Coms.*, LXV, " Correspondence respecting the Mosquito Territory ", 84.

[78] *U. S. Docs.*, ser. no. 579, doc. 75, p. 24.

[79] *Ibid.*, pp. 24-26.

entirely approved.[80]　In this letter Chatfield outlined
the history of the British protectorate over the Mosquitos, stated that the Mosquio territory extended to
the south bank of the port, and declared that as the
British government recognized the sovereignty of the
Mosquitos it would not regard with indifference the
usurpation of their territory.[81]　Chatfield's letter not
only had the full approval of the Foreign Office, but
was clearly written in compliance with instructions
from the foreign secretary.[82]　In reply, the secretary-
general of Nicaragua entered into further protests,
accompanied by a long argument to prove that the
Mosquitos had never been recognized as an independent nation by any sovereign power in Central America.[83]　This seems to have ended the quarrel for the
time, and, in spite of British plans and acts, the Nicaraguan authorities remained at the port of San Juan
unmolested for many years.

Before laying claim to San Juan in behalf of the
Mosquito king, Macdonald had attempted to establish
practical British sovereignty on the shore by placing
the government in charge of a commission to which he
intended to delegate his authority.　This body was to
be composed chiefly of British subjects and was to sit

[80] Soon after his appointment Macdonald found among the Belize
archives documents showing the close alliance which had formerly existed
between the Mosquitos and the British government.　Perceiving the use
to which these documents could be put, he sent them to his government.
The result was a distinct increase of interest in the Mosquitos on the
part of the British cabinet.　Murphy to the Secretary of State, Jan. 20,
1842, Dept. of State, Des., Cen. Am., vol. 2.

[81] *U. S. Docs.*, ser. no. 579, doc. 75, p. 24.

[82] Memorandum on Mosquito Shore, written Dec. 15, 1843, upon a
Colonial Office letter of November 27, 1840, F. O., Cen. Am., vol. 36.

[83] *U. S. Docs.*, ser. no. 579, doc. 75, pp. 30-34.

at Belize.[84] The superintendent evidently appointed the commissioners without instructions, after which he outlined his plans for the Mosquito government, expecting that they would meet with favor from the British cabinet. Palmerston was strongly inclined to the scheme and wished it executed, but Russell, who at that time was colonial secretary, opposed it on the ground that it would make the shore in fact a British colony.[85] As Russell stood firm, the superintendent was informed that there was no objection to a commission composed of Englishmen, provided that they were considered solely as Mosquito, and not as British, agents.[86] Nothing further appears to have been done towards changing the government before 1842, when the death of the Mosquito king created an unsettled state of affairs.[87] As a result of this disorganized condition, frequent complaints of lack of protection, and of the encroachments of the Central American states on Mosquito territory, were made by British subjects on the shore.[88]

Finding that his earlier plans were unacceptable, Macdonald wrote in 1842, apparently shortly after the Mosquito king's death, urging that a British resident be appointed for the shore.[89] In the following year the Foreign Office took the matter seriously into consideration. A memorandum written at that time states that the question now was how to show interest in the Mosquito coast with determination as to foreign powers, but without adopting measures which might

[84] Memorandum on Mosquito Shore, written Dec. 15, 1843, upon a Colonial Office letter of Nov. 27, 1840, F. O., Cen. Am., vol. 36.
[85] *Ibid.*   [86] *Ibid.*   [87] *Ibid.*   [88] *Ibid.*
[89] Macdonald to Metcalf, April 30, 1842, C. O., Hond., vol. 63.

lead to unnecessary quarrels with them.[90]   It was finally decided to adopt Macdonald's suggestion and station a British resident on the shore.[91]   The selection of the official seems to have been left to Macdonald, who, in 1844, appointed Patrick Walker, his private secretary,[92] to the position, and established him at Bluefields.[93]   The territory was renamed Mosquitia, and a new flag, closely modelled after the Union Jack, was given to the Indians.[94]

While the British were thus establishing themselves more securely in Central America, events in the United States had produced a renewal of the earlier British policy of blocking American advance to the southwest by supporting Mexico [95]—a policy which had not been vigorously pursued after Canning's death.   At an early date when citizens of the United States began moving into Texas, the migration was not overlooked by the British agent in Mexico.   He saw the danger and called Canning's attention to the probable outcome of the movement; but whether, in consequence, warning was offered to Mexico by the British government is not evident.[96]   When Texas declared her independence and

[90] Memorandum on Mosquito Shore, written Dec. 15, 1843, upon a Colonial Office letter of November 27, 1840, F. O., Cen. Am., vol. 36.

[91] *Ibid.*; Chatfield to Aberdeen, July 1, 1844, F. O., Cen. Am., vol. 37, no. 24.

[92] Keasbey, *Nicaragua Canal,* 169.

[93] Chatfield to Aberdeen, July 1, 1844, F. O., Cen. Am., vol. 37, no. 24.

[94] Crowe, *Gospel in Central America,* 213.

[95] Temperley, "Later American Policy of George Canning", in *Am. Hist. Rev.,* XI, 781; Adams, *British Interests and Activities in Texas,* 15, 239.

[96] After reporting the movement to his government, Ward, the British agent, remarked: "Not knowing in how far His Majesty's Government may conceive the possession of Texas by the Americans, to be likely to affect the interests of Great Britain, I have not thought it right to go beyond such general observations upon the subject, in my communication

expressed a desire to enter the American Union, the uneasiness and jealousy naturally increased, and Great Britain promptly took measures to preserve the independence of this new republic, and to maintain it as a strong buffer state against the extension of American power.[97] This reinforced jealousy of the British undoubtedly was influential in increasing their activities in Central America, as well as in determining their attitude on the Oregon question.

The United States appears, however, to have taken but little notice for some time of this revived policy of general aggressiveness against American interests,[98] and it was not until 1843 that the Washington authorities were really aroused regarding the situation in Texas. They then realized that British influence there was very strong, and believed that it aimed,

---

with this Government, as appeared to me calculated to make it perceive the danger, to which it is wilfully exposing itself." Paxson, " England and Mexico, 1824-1825 ", in *Colo. Univ. Studies*, III, 118.

[97] Adams, *British Interests and Activities in Texas, 1838-1846*; Smith, *Annexation of Texas, passim*.

[98] In 1841, Murphy, a special and confidential agent of the United States, was sent to Central America with directions to learn the cause for the failure of Galindo's mission, and also to determine the existing state of the Belize boundary controversy. To his instructions Webster added: " This information you will endeavor to supply by proper inquiries, which, however, should be cautiously made and so as not to let it be supposed that this government takes any more interest in the matter now than it did at the time of the visit of Colonel Galindo to Washington, or that it is inclined to deviate from the course which was pursued upon that occasion." Dept. of State, Inst., Am. States, vol. 15, pp. 48-49. These words suggest an intention to adopt a more vigorous Central American policy. However, though Murphy secured the desired information, gave details regarding other British encroachments in Central America, and urged that a commercial treaty be made with Nicaragua to prevent the British from gaining control of the San Juan, no further steps were taken by the American government at this time. Murphy to the Secretary of State, Jan. 20, and Feb. 4, 1842, Dept. of State, Des., Cen. Am., vol. 2. The failure to act may have been due to the transfer of American attention to British interests in Texas.

among other things, at the abolition of slavery.[99] Thereupon, the American government began immediately to prepare for Texan annexation.[100] Simultaneously with this movement came the proclamation of the expansionist policy of the Democrats.[101] The election of Polk followed, and in the next year the admission of Texas to the Union.

These events were clearly disconcerting to British plans; but the policy of hindering American advance towards the southwest was stubbornly maintained, and was even given greater impetus when war between the United States and Mexico became imminent, and with it the American acquisition of California. Aberdeen, then British foreign secretary, even thought of active interference to prevent the latter event. He gave up his idea of doing so only in consideration that the Oregon question was still capable of peaceful settlement. Should the Oregon boundary negotiations end in war, aid was to be given Mexico.[102] As the Oregon boundary dispute was settled peaceably, Mexico fought her battles alone—and lost California.

This triumph of American expansionist schemes was certain to have a profound effect upon British policy in Central America. For centuries the importance of Central America for a transisthmian route had been recognized, and recently the line via Nicaragua had been considered the most feasible.[103] The significance of such a route at that time becomes evident only when

---

[99] Garrison, *Westward Extension*, 110-114; Reeves, *American Diplomacy under Tyler and Polk*, 132-134.
[100] Garrison, *Westward Extension*, 114-115.
[101] Rives, " Mexican Diplomacy ", in *Am. Hist. Rev.*, XVIII, 275.
[102] *Ibid.*, 286-291.
[103] Travis, *Mosquito History*, 11; Snow, *American Diplomacy*, 330.

it is remembered that before the Civil War little faith was entertained that a railroad could be successfully built to the Pacific, or operated even if it should be built.[104] Therefore, upon gaining territory on the Pacific coast, the interest of the United States in Central America must increase tremendously.

As England clearly saw the outcome of the Mexican War before it began, she lost little time in preparing for it. Early in 1847 Palmerston, who had succeeded Aberdeen in the preceding July, wrote to Chatfield, and Walker, the Mosquito superintendent, and to O'Leary, the British representative at Bogotá,[105] asking, first, for the most authentic information procurable as to the boundary claimed by the king of the Mosquitos; and, secondly, for their opinions as to the boundary which the British government should insist upon as "absolutely essential for the security and well-being of the Mosquito state." [106] The replies varied to some extent regarding the limits claimed by the Mosquito king, though in general all indicated that he had pretended to dominion pretty well south to Chiriqui Lagoon, near the Isthmus of Panama; but all agreed that the boundary which the British should insist upon to the south was the San Juan River.[107]

A detailed report on the Mosquito Shore, which had been called for by the Committee of the Privy Council for Trade and Plantations, was made by John Mc-

---

[104] Travis, *Mosquito History*, 12-13.

[105] New Granada as well as Nicaragua claimed the Mosquito Shore.

[106] *Parl. Papers,* 1847-1848, *Coms.,* LXV, " Correspondence respecting the Mosquito Territory ", 1.

[107] *Ibid.,* 2-52. Had the Mosquitos been recognized as sovereign and independent, the claims, when compared with the evidence submitted by Chatfield and Walker, would have been quite reasonable.

Gregor on February 1.[108] The foreign secretary apparently availed himself of the information contained in this report, for on June 30, before receiving replies to his inquiries, he wrote to Chatfield stating that the encroachments committed by the states of Honduras and Nicaragua upon the territory of the Mosquitos had given rise to the question of boundaries. Therefore, after carefully examining various documents relative to the subject, the British government was of the opinion that the Mosquito king's right should be maintained as extending from Cape Honduras to the mouth of the San Juan River.[109] Chatfield was accordingly instructed to notify the Central American states concerned, and to inform them that the British government would not view with indifference any attempt to encroach upon the rights or territory of the Mosquito king, who was under the protection of the British Crown.[110]

The instruction was followed by Chatfield, who, in speaking of the southern boundary, took the precaution to add the words, " without prejudice to the right of the Mosquito king to any territory south of the River San Juan ".[111] The two weak Central American states, roused to a fear for their independence, protested vigorously that they did not recognize the Mosquito kingdom, and declared their intention to resist the attempts

[108] *Parl. Papers,* 1847, *Coms.,* LXIV, " Spanish-American Republics ", 26-61. The report of McGregor also gave detailed information regarding Belize, the Bay Islands, and Central America in general.

[109] These boundaries coincide with those given by McGregor as existing in 1777. *Parl. Papers,* 1847, *Coms.,* LXIV, " Spanish-American Republics ", 27.

[110] *Parl. Papers,* 1847-1848, *Coms.,* LXV, " Correspondence respecting the Mosquito Territory ", 1.

[111] *Ibid.,* 56.

of the British to commit aggressions upon Central American territory in the name of the Mosquitos.[112] But unfortunately they were too helpless and distracted to unite against the aggressor.

In October, notice came from the " Council of State " of the Mosquito king [113] to the government of Nicaragua, that the Nicaraguans would be given until January 1, 1848, to withdraw from the San Juan. After that time, forcible means would be employed to maintain the king's authority.[114] On the same date, Walker, in company with the king, went to San Juan, hauled down the Nicaraguan flag, hoisted that of the Mosquitos, and fired a royal salute to the latter.[115]

The Nicaraguan government was, obviously, too weak to do more than protest, which it did, emphatically denying the existence of the Mosquito kingdom, and declaring that the Mosquito Shore, by the treaties of 1783 and 1786, had been Spanish territory, and that with independence from Spain the shore had become a part of the Central American states.[116] Twice, also, was appeal made to Washington by the Nicaraguans for aid against the British,[117] but no reply was returned at the time by the United States government.[118]

Before the opening of the new year the small Nicaraguan garrison evacuated the mouth of the San Juan

[112] *Ibid.*, 66-69.
[113] This was apparently Walker's development of Macdonald's idea for government by commission, and was made possible by the increasingly aggressive policy of the British government, as well as by the fact that Grey, and not Russell, was now colonial secretary.
[114] *Parl. Papers*, 1847-1848, *Coms.*, LXV, " Correspondence respecting the Mosquito Territory ", 58.
[115] *Ibid.*, 57.
[116] *Ibid.*, 75-76, 93-94.
[117] *U. S. Docs.*, ser. no. 579, doc. 75, pp. 11-14, 79-80.
[118] Richardson, *Messages and Papers*, V, 34.

and retired up the river to Serapaqui. On January 1,
Walker, again accompanied by the Mosquito king, went
to San Juan and hauled down the Nicaraguan flag
which he found flying, and hoisted that of the Mosquitos, saluting it as before. He left a small party at
the place and gave the Nicaraguan officials a short time
in which to clear out the customs house. Again the
Nicaraguans issued their protest, and a few days later
the force at Serapaqui descended upon San Juan,
hoisted the flag of the republic, seized the British officials stationed at the port, and carried them as prisoners
to Serapaqui. On February 12 the fort at the latter
place was destroyed by two British war vessels, the
Alarm and the *Vixen,* sent to punish the defiant act of
the Nicaraguans.[119]

Following the battle at Serapaqui Captain Loch of
the *Alarm* made a treaty with the Nicaraguans. This
provided for the surrender of the British prisoners,
with apologies for all violent acts committed at San
Juan, and also contained an agreement by the Nicaraguans not to disturb the Mosquito authorities at that
place. But by the last article of the treaty the Nicaraguans tried to secure a loophole for escape. This
article stipulated that nothing in the treaty should prevent Nicaragua from soliciting, by means of a commissioner, a final settlement of the difficulties with
England.[120] Walker had been drowned at Serapaqui;[121] therefore Loch appointed an officer to fill his

[119] *Parl. Papers,* 1847-1848, *Coms.,* LXV, " Correspondence respecting
the Mosquito Territory ", 94-104; Squier, *Nicaragua,* I, 101; Crowe,
Gospel in Central America, 215.

[120] *Parl. Papers,* 1847-1848, *Coms.,* LXV, " Correspondence respecting
the Mosquito Teritory ", 121.

[121] *Ibid.,* 104.

place, and also named a collector of customs for San Juan,[122] which was shortly afterwards renamed Greytown, in honor of the governor of Jamaica.[123]

In February, 1848, Palmerston, basing his action upon the reports of Chatfield and Walker, extended the southern boundary of the Mosquito territory to the Colorado branch of the San Juan, which was many miles south of the port.[124] The purpose of this extension was obviously to shut Nicaragua from both banks of the river and thus leave her no share in any interoceanic canal arrangements. In the following month, upon learning of the retaliatory measures taken by the Nicaraguans against the British at San Juan, the foreign secretary showed his determination by directing that the Nicaraguan authorities be notified that a British war vessel would be ordered to visit San Juan from time to time to maintain the officials stationed there. Furthermore, if the Nicaraguans persisted in intruding themselves in San Juan, measures of an unfriendly character would be resorted to upon parts of their own coast.[125]

These acts of Palmerston gave Nicaragua little reason to expect favorable results from negotiation; but since protest and appeal as well as attempt at physical resistance had proved vain, negotiation seemed the only hope left. Accordingly, Francisco Castellon was appointed Nicaraguan chargé d'affaires at London in the

[122] *Ibid.*, 123.
[123] Bancroft to Buchanan, Jan. 26, 1849, Dept. of State, Des., Eng., vol. 59, no. 114; Addington to Hawes, Jan. 12, 1849, C. O., Hond., vol. 78.
[124] *Parl. Papers*, 1847-1848, *Coms.*, LXV, " Correspondence respecting the Mosquito Territory ", 94.
[125] *Ibid.*, 102.

autumn of 1848,[126] with instructions to try to secure terms from the British government. For many months Castellon remained in London, hoping to arrive at an agreement regarding Greytown, but Palmerston refused to do anything that would intimate that San Juan did not belong exclusively to the Mosquitos, and warned the Nicaraguan agent against counting on aid from the United States, as it was " a matter of total indifference to her Majesty's government " what the American government might say or do. Finally, in July, 1849, after all hopes of making a direct settlement with the British government had disappeared, Castellon returned to Central America.[127]

While the British were thus incited by American expansion to renew their encroachments in Central America, the people of the United States and their government were anything but indifferent to the situation. Once roused by the cry of British interference in Texas, American jealousy and suspicion of England long survived. Moreover, through the successful annexation of Texas and the settlement of the vexed boundary questions, the nation had become intoxicated with the " manifest destiny " idea.[128] The knowledge of European interference in an attempt to preserve a " balance of power " in the New World only served further to increase American aggressiveness, which was reflected in Polk's version of the Monroe doctrine set forth in the annual message of December, 1845.[129] In accordance with the policy then declared, the govern-

[126] Castellon went by way of Washington and made a third appeal for aid, but no reply appears to have been given to his communication during Polk's administration. *U. S. Docs.*, ser. no. 579, doc. 75, pp. 91, 92.

[127] *Ibid.*, pp. 172-180.

[128] *Dem. Rev.*, XVII, 5-10, 193-204.

[129] Richardson, *Messages and Papers*, IV, 398-399.

ment, as far as circumstances permitted, systematically worked to frustrate what was believed to be the design of the British.

An interoceanic canal was part of Polk's general expansionist policy.[130] The British had a grip on the isthmus of Nicaragua and were suspected of having designs on Panama also.[131] In order to insure a route for the United States, a prompt arrangement seemed necessary in 1846. Because of the war just opened with Mexico, it was probably deemed unwise to negotiate for the Nicaragua route, and thus risk entanglement with the question of Mosquito claims. Therefore, a treaty was negotiated with New Granada giving to the United States and its citizens the right of way across the Isthmus of Panama by any available method of transit. In return for the concession the United States guaranteed the complete neutrality of the isthmus and the right of sovereignty possessed by New Granada over it.[132]

For some years the American government had suspected Great Britain of designs upon California.[133] This territory had attracted the Americans also, and President Polk especially coveted San Francisco harbor.[134] Therefore American attention was attracted towards the region, and the Mexican War had scarcely begun before it was in control of the United States authorities.

[130] Garrison, *Westward Extension*, 287.
[131] Grahame, " The Canal Diplomacy ", in *N. Am. Rev.*, CXCVII, 33.
[132] *Brit. and For. State Papers*, XL, 968-969.
[133] Professor Adams, *British Interests and Activities in Texas*, 234-264, has shown that these designs were entirely limited to British agents who received no encouragement from their government. The British interest in California just before the Mexican War was due simply to a desire to save it from falling into American hands.
[134] Polk, *Diary*, I, 71.

This much accomplished, Polk's administration undoubtedly would have pursued a more vigorous policy towards the British encroachments in Central America, had it not been for the Mexican War. But while handicapped by the struggle with Mexico the government had no desire to venture into a more serious one with Great Britain.[135] However, before the war was over the United States government had determined to act. A hint of coming developments appeared in the presidential message of 1847, through Polk's assertion that no European power should, with the consent of the American government, secure any foothold upon the continent.[136] Early in the next year Elijah Hise was appointed chargé d'affaires in Guatemala. As the fate of the treaty of peace with Mexico had not yet been learned when Hise received his instructions, it was determined to proceed cautiously. The general plan was first to reunite the Central American states and thus aid them to resist British encroachments.[137] The purpose of the mission was to determine the extent of British aggressions, and to urge upon the states the necessity for union; and Hise was instructed accordingly.[138] When his report should be received the government meant to settle upon a more definite policy, calculated to put an end to British interference on the isthmus.[139]

[135] " Letters of Bancroft and Buchanan ", in *Am. Hist. Rev.,* V, 98, 99; Buchanan, *Works,* VIII, 379.

[136] Richardson, *Messages and Papers,* IV, 539-540.

[137] " Letters of Bancroft and Buchanan ", in *Am. Hist. Rev.,* V, 98-99; Buchanan, *Works,* VIII, 379, 380.

[138] *Ibid.,* 78-84.

[139] " Letters of Bancroft and Buchanan ", in *Am. Hist. Rev.,* V, 99. At this time, an American agent, Savage, was in Guatemala. He had announced the British seizure of San Juan, and in reporting the intentions of the British, had stated " all eyes are turned towards the United

The British government realized that as soon as the Mexican War was over the United States could be expected to interfere in Central American affairs. Therefore, Palmerston was on the alert. When, as a result of speeches of Senator Dix, delivered early in 1848, the American nation was being more actively roused against the British movements in Central America,[140] the foreign secretary furnished Crampton, the British representative at Washington, with a history of the Mosquito protectorate,[141] and instructed him to say in reply to inquiries that his government would be ready to vindicate its proceedings at San Juan whenever called upon to do so by any party having the right to question it.[142]

When the proposed mission became known to Palmerston, he wrote to Chatfield, stating that he understood that the principal object of Hise would be to urge a union of the Central American states in order better to resist any interference of the British government in the affairs of Mosquito. In consequence of this, Chatfield was instructed to take such steps as might be necessary or useful to defeat the policy of the United States so far as its object was hostile to the interests of Great Britain.[143] But Chatfield was in some way misled regarding the object of Hise's visit, and thought that he was merely to arrange a commercial treaty.[144] Therefore he was but little suspicious of the

---

States of America for the solution of this problem ", but he gave no details regarding the general situation. Savage to Buchanan, Jan. 14, 1848, and Dec. 25, 1847, Dept. of State, Des., Guat., vol. 1.

[140] Crampton to Palmerston, Feb. 9, 1848, F. O., Am., vol. 484, no. 19, and April 2, 1848, *ibid.*, vol. 485, no. 35.

[141] *Ibid.*, vol. 483, no. 13.

[142] *Ibid.*, no. 20; vol. 497, no. 38.

[143] F. O., Guat., vol. 50, no. 24.

[144] Chatfield to Palmerston, Jan. 12, 1849, *ibid.*, vol. 57, no. 6.

American chargé d'affaires. Nevertheless he reported to Palmerston his intention to anticipate any possible designs of the Americans by private correspondence calculated to show the Central American states the uselessness of looking to North America for real sympathy at any time.[145]

Unfortunately for the plans of the Polk government, Hise was delayed by sickness and other causes [146] and did not reach Central America until late in October, 1848.[147] At the time of his arrival the Central American states were in the utmost confusion and on the verge of anarchy, a condition partially produced by the intrigues of the British agents. Honduras and Nicaragua, because of the Mosquito claims, hated and feared England, as did also Salvador, and looked towards the United States for aid.[148] The Servile party, to which the British gave preference, was in power in Costa Rica and in Guatemala; consequently the British government was in favor with those states.[149] The existence of a boundary dispute between Nicaragua and Costa Rica [150] also inclined the latter to look to Great Britain for protection against her stronger neighbor; and the suspicion of American designs roused by the Mexican War naturally caused Guatemala to hold aloof from the United States.[151]

After two months spent in investigation, Hise wrote his government that he was convinced that the British

---

[145] Chatfield to Palmerston, Jan. 12, 1849, F. O., Guat., vol. 57, no. 6.
[146] Buchanan, *Works*, VIII, 380.
[147] Dept. of State, Des., Am. States, vol. 15, p. 52.
[148] Chatfield to Palmerston, Jan. 11, 1848, F. O., Guat., vol. 51, no. 2, and Dec. 15, 1848, *ibid.*, vol. 53, no. 115.
[149] Travis, *Clayton-Bulwer Treaty*, 55.
[150] *U. S. Docs.*, ser. no. 579, doc. 75, p. 136.
[151] Savage to Buchanan, Dec. 25, 1847, Dept. of State, Des., Guat., vol. 1; Savage to Webster, April 21, 1851, *ibid.*, vol. 3, no. 6.

designed to make themselves owners and occupants of the points on the coasts of Nicaragua which would become the termini of any interoceanic canal communication by way of the San Juan and Lake Nicaragua. Therefore, in order to outwit British schemes, he asked for power to negotiate transit treaties.[152] In May, 1849, he again wrote, explaining the urgency of the situation. The British agents, he said, were working to produce results the most inimical to American interests, by planning to secure control of the whole interoceanic line of transit.[153] Because of the slowness of means of communication, no word was received from Hise before the end of Polk's administration; consequently no reply or further instructions were sent to him.[154] In view of this fact and of his belief that further delay would be fatal to American interests, it is not to be wondered at that Hise ventured, without instructions,[155] to negotiate a canal treaty with Nicaragua.

The treaty, signed by Hise June 21, 1849, was in keeping with the Polk policy, and was a definite application of the Monroe doctrine to the situation in Central America. Through it, Nicaragua granted to the American government, or its citizens, in perpetuity, the right of way for transit purposes across Nicaragua, and permitted the fortification of such a route. In return, the United States pledged herself to protect Nicaragua in all territory rightfully hers.[156] By means of this treaty, the Nicaraguan commissioner believed

---

[152] Hise to Buchanan, Dec. 20, 1848, *ibid.*, vol. 1.

[153] Hise to Buchanan, May 25, 1849, *ibid.*

[154] " Letters of Bancroft and Buchanan ", in *Am. Hist. Rev.*, V, 99; Buchanan, *Works*, VIII, 380.

[155] *U. S. Docs.*, ser. no. 579, doc. 75, pp. 105-106.

[156] *Ibid.*, pp. 110-117.

that Nicaragua had gained a protector in the United States, and that her case against Great Britain was consequently secure.[157]

While Hise had been thus cut off from his government, important changes were taking place in the United States. The Polk Democrats had given way to a Whig administration under Taylor. The gold discovery in California, becoming known throughout the country, had created a popular demand for more satisfactory means of transportation to the West than that afforded by ox-team journey across the plains or by the long voyage around Cape Horn. This demand attracted general attention to Nicaragua, where the British were in control of the eastern terminus of what was considered the best transisthmian route. The successful termination of the Mexican War had excited enthusiasm and increased the self-confidence of the nation; the conviction of " manifest destiny " still influenced a large portion of the population.[158] England must not be permitted to monopolize a route so valuable to American prosperity. Public opinion demanded that the government take measures to prevent such a possibility.[159]

At this juncture a group of American citizens formed a transportation company with the object of constructing a canal. In March, 1849, this association made a contract with the Nicaraguan government for the use of the San Juan route across the isthmus. When looking more fully into the subject connected with their

[157] Chatfield to Palmerston, May 17, 1849, F. O., Guat., vol. 58, no. 42.
[158] *Dem. Rev.*, XXV, 3-11.
[159] Travis, *Mosquito History*, 15; Henderson, *American Diplomatic Questions*, 111; Grahame, " The Canal Diplomacy ", in *N. Am. Rev.*, CXCVII, 35-36.

contract, the members of the company learned of the extensive British claims in the name of the Mosquito king,[160] and were much concerned by the discovery. Meanwhile their movements had not escaped the jealous watchfulness of Chatfield, who, through the British consuls in Nicaragua, promptly notified the Nicaraguan government and the company that the whole of the San Juan River from its mouth to Machuca Rapids belonged to Mosquito, and could not be disposed of or used without the consent of the British government.[161] Chatfield also reported the situation to his government;[162] and in response to instructions from the Foreign Office,[163] Barclay, the British consul at New York, published a warning notice to the grantees not to begin work on the proposed canal, inasmuch as the British government was the protector of the Mosquitos, whose territory would be bisected by it.[164] Before this, however, the American company had reported conditions in Central America to the United States government and had asked protection for its undertaking.[165]

The new administration at Washington possessed a definite Central American policy, and promptly upon accession proceeded to execute it. Accordingly, letters were addressed by President Taylor and by Clayton, his secretary of state, to the Nicaraguan government, replying to the appeals for aid made to the Polk administration. These letters expressed the sympathy of the

[160] Keasbey, *Nicaragua Canal,* 193.
[161] Inclosures in Chatfield to Palmerston, May 5, 1849, F. O., Guat., vol. 58, no. 38.
[162] Chatfield to Palmerston, April 14, and 21, 1849, *ibid.,* vol. 57, nos. 33, 35, and May 5, 1849, *ibid.,* vol. 58, no. 38.
[163] Inclosure in Palmerston to Crampton, June 28, 1849, F. O., Am., vol. 497, no. 37.
[164] *Dem. Rev.,* XXV, 406.
[165] *U. S. Docs.,* ser. no. 579, doc. 75, p. 119.

American government and the promise of its friendly interposition for the purpose of adjusting the Mosquito controversy.[166]

At the same time Hise, who had not yet been heard from,[167] was recalled,[168] and Ephraim George Squier was appointed as his successor.[169] Through his instructions Squier was made acquainted with the history of British encroachments in Nicaragua, and was directed to inform the Nicaraguan government that the United States would employ any moral means in its power " for the purpose of frustrating the apparent designs of Great Britain in countenancing the claims of sovereignty over the Mosquito coast, and the Port of San Juan, asserted by her ally the alleged monarch of that region ".[170] The new chargé d'affaires was empowered to make treaties of commerce with the Central American republics, and particularly one with Nicaragua in the interest of the transportation company,[171] which had become absorbed into the American Atlantic and Pacific Ship-Canal Company of New York.[172] This treaty was to secure to American citizens a right of way across the isthmus [173] for a transit line open to all nations, with exclusive benefits to none.[174] No objection would be made by the United States to the employment of foreign capital, which might be necessary to the success of the undertaking.[175] In anticipation of the price which Nicaragua might ask for such a concession, Clayton directed

---

[166] U. S. Docs., ser. no. 579, doc. 75, p. 132.
[167] Ibid., pp. 120-121.   [168] Ibid., p. 117.   [169] Ibid.
[170] Dept. of State, Inst., Am. States, vol. 15, p. 69.
[171] U. S. Docs., ser. no. 579, doc. 75, pp. 120-121.
[172] Keasbey, Nicaragua Canal, 197.
[173] U. S. Docs., ser. no. 579, doc. 75, p. 121.
[174] Ibid., p. 130.   [175] Ibid., p. 129.

that no guarantee of territorial independence should be given in compensation for the grant of right of way.[176] When Squier reached Central America, he found the usual confusion in most of the states.[177] The three republics which favored the American government regarded his coming as an occasion for great rejoicing.[178] Their satisfaction was increased when Squier held out high hopes of American interference to drive out British power.[179] In consequence of Squier's promises, Nicaragua took a defiant stand against the British, strongly denouncing the Mosquito protectorate and expressing a determination to uphold the Monroe doctrine.[180]

The terms of the Hise treaty, still unknown to the United States, had been revealed to Chatfield, and had evidently thoroughly aroused his suspicions.[181] Consequently, he was on the alert when Squier arrived. At once there began between the two a struggle for the supremacy of their governments in Central America, which did not terminate until the recall of Squier a year later. Each important move of Squier was met by an act from Chatfield calculated to checkmate it. Squier's promises of American aid brought forth articles of a counteracting nature by Chatfield, published in the press of Costa Rica and Guatemala.[182] When

[176] *Ibid.*, p. 121.

[177] Inclosure in Squier to Clayton, July 20, 1849, Dept. of State, Des., Guat., vol. 2.

[178] Chatfield to Palmerston, July 27, 1849, F. O., Guat., vol. 59, no. 64.

[179] Squier to Clayton, June 3, 1849, Dept. of State, Des., Guat., vol. 2; Chatfield to Palmerston, July 27, 1849, F. O., Guat., vol. 59, no. 64, and Dec. 15, 1849, *ibid.*, vol. 60, no. 119; Squier, *Travels in Central America*, I, 251-256.

[180] Chatfield to Palmerston, Oct. 25, 1849, F. O., Guat., vol. 60, no. 98; Inclosures in Chatfield to Palmerston, Oct. 29, 1849, *ibid.*, no. 100.

[181] Chatfield to Palmerston, May 17, 1849, *ibid.*, vol. 58, no. 42.

[182] Chatfield to Palmerston, Dec. 15, 1849, *ibid.*, vol. 60, no. 119.

Squier tried to induce the three states friendly to the American government to form a union, the better to resist British encroachments,[183] Chatfield, perceiving his purpose, proceeded to frustrate it by inducing Honduras to form a treaty permanently detaching her from the contemplated league.[184] When a commission came to ask Costa Rica to become a member of the union,[185] the British consul again stepped forward to prevent her consent,[186] and in order the better to dominate Costa Rica, formed a new treaty with her,[187] after which he intimated to Nicaragua that Costa Rica was under British protection, and therefore her boundary rights must be respected.[188]

Notwithstanding the opposition of British agents and the existence of a rival British canal company,[189] Squier succeeded in inducing Nicaragua to grant the American company a favorable concession for the construction of a canal along the line of the San Juan.[190] Following this, the Nicaraguan government granted the company a charter of incorporation.[191]

These arrangements being made, Squier experienced little difficulty in forming a treaty for interoceanic communication based upon the general terms outlined

[183] Squier to Clayton, Aug. 20, 1849, Dept. of State, Des., Guat., vol. 2; Chatfield to Palmerston, Nov. 7, 1849, F. O., Guat., vol. 60, no. 107.

[84] Chatfield to Palmerston. Dec 31, 1849, ibid., no. 126; Squier, Travels in Central America, II, 180-181.

[185] Chatfield to Palmerston, Dec. 24, 1849, F. O., Guat., vol. 60, no. 123.

[186] Ibid.; Chatfield to Palmerston, Dec. 15, 1849, ibid., no. 116.

[187] Chatfield to Palmerston, Nov. 28, 1849, ibid., no. 114.

[188] Chatfield to the Principal Secretary of the Government of Nicaragua, Dec. 1, 1849, ibid., no. 21.

[189] Travis, Clayton-Bulwer Treaty, 65.

[190] Parl. Papers, 1856, Coms., LX, " Correspondence with the United States respecting Central America ", 19-24.

[191] Keasbey, Nicaragua Canal, 198.

in Clayton's instructions. The treaty engaged the two contracting parties to defend the canal company in its enterprise, secured from the American government a recognition of the rights of sovereignty and property possessed by Nicaragua in the canal route, and guaranteed its neutrality as long as it should be controlled by American citizens. The rights and privileges given by the treaty were open to any other nation willing to enter into an agreement with Nicaragua for the protection of the contemplated canal.[192]

As Squier discovered soon after his arrival, Hise's suspicions regarding the designs of British agents upon the termini of the proposed canal line were well founded. Not content with the British claims to San Juan on the Atlantic, Chatfield, as early as January, 1847, had written to Palmerston suggesting that Great Britain, in anticipation of the Americans, obtain a hold on the " Port of the Union " and on Realejo on the Pacific. The Central American states had long been in debt to the British; therefore he thought that an island in the bay might be accepted in part payment.[193] Palmerston displayed but little interest in the scheme,[194] but in the following March the British consul wrote again, this time asking for authority to obtain the cession to Great Britain of the port of San Carlos on Lake Nicaragua and three islands in the Bay of Fonseca, in return for which the British government should assume the payment of all claims against the states concerned.[195] Palmerston promptly replied that the government did

---

[192] *Parl. Papers*, 1856, *Coms.*, LX, " Correspondence with the United States respecting Central America ", 18-19.

[193] F. O., Cen. Am., vol. 45, no. 4.

[194] Palmerston to Ward, April 16, 1847, F. O., Cen. Am., vol. 49.

[195] Palmerston to Chatfield, June 17, 1848, F. O., Guat., vol. 50, no. 15.

not consider such a measure expedient;[196] Chatfield, nevertheless, urged the subject repeatedly,[197] and finally decided to secure Tigre Island, which commanded the Bay of Fonseca, as guarantee for the payment of British claims against Honduras, to which state the island belonged. He therefore wrote to the Honduran government pressing the payment of debts, and stating that if Honduras did not respond promptly a lien might be put upon Tigre until the claims should be paid.[198] In May, 1849, Palmerston again wrote in opposition to Chatfield's plans, stating that the government much preferred that the claims be met by proper payments, as Parliament would be very little disposed to take upon the public the payment of the claims in return for the islands in question.[199] Chatfield, however, still cherished the hope of securing at least the island of Tigre for his government, which, he felt, did not fully appreciate the situation.

The hearty welcome extended to Squier caused the British consul to believe, or at least to pretend to believe, that the three states unfriendly to England were seeking the protection of the American government in order to escape a direct payment of British claims.[200] Therefore, he pressed for settlement more vigorously

---

[196] Palmerston to Chatfield, June 17, 1848, F. O., Guat., vol. 50, no. 15.

[197] Chatfield to Palmerston, Nov. 24, 1848, F. O., Guat., vol. 53, no. 8; Jan. 5, 1849, *ibid.,* vol. 57, no. 4; April 14, 1849, *ibid.,* no. 33; July 24, 1849, *ibid.,* vol. 59, no. 63; July 27, 1849, *ibid.,* no. 67.

[198] Chatfield to the Principal Secretary of the Honduran Government, Jan. 26, 1849, *ibid.,* vol. 57, no. 2. In writing of the proposed lien on Tigre, Chatfield said: " I have partly been made to make it from a desire to anticipate an attempt in any other quarter, to get possession of a spot so valuable in a naval point of view on this side of the Continent." Chatfield to Dundonald, Feb. 24, 1849, *ibid.,* no. 1.

[199] Palmerston to Chatfield, May 1, 1849, *ibid.,* vol. 56, no. 7.

[200] Chatfield to Palmerston, Oct. 17, and Nov. 14, 1849, *ibid.,* vol. 60, nos. 95, 112.

than ever.[201] Upon learning of Chatfield's designs on Tigre, Squier became fearful that, if executed, they would embarrass all efforts to form a canal treaty and construct a canal, for he believed that the canal must terminate on the Bay of Fonseca.[202] Therefore, although unauthorized to do so, he determined to form a treaty with Honduras for the purchase of the island by the United States, or for its temporary cession until the canal arrangements should be completed.[203] Accordingly, at his request a Honduran commissioner came to Guatemala and formed a treaty ceding Tigre to the American government for a period of eighteen months.[204] Squier then promptly notified the British agents of the transaction.[205]

Chatfield thereupon hastened the execution of his plans, and, on October 16, a week after its cession to the United States, at his orders [206] Captain Paynter of the British navy seized the island and hoisted the British flag.[207] Squier protested and demanded its evacuation,[208] Chatfield refused and called attention to the lien which he had placed upon the Tigre in the preceding January. The proprietary rights thus established, he declared, no subsequent arrangement without cognizance of England could undo.[209]

[201] Chatfield to Palmerston, Oct. 17, 1849, *ibid.*, no. 95.

[202] Squier to Clayton, Oct. 10, 1849, Dept. of State, Des., Guat., vol. 2.

[203] Squier to Clayton, Aug. 20, 1849, Dept. of State, Des., Guat., vol. 2.

[204] *Parl. Papers*, 1856, *Coms.*, LX, " Correspondence with the United States respecting Central America ", 31-32.

[205] *Ibid.*, 33.

[206] Inclosures in Chatfield to Palmerston, Oct. 17, 1849, F. O., Guat., vol. 60, no. 95.

[207] Paynter to Hornby, Oct. 25, 1849, *ibid.*, vol. 68, no. 41.

[208] *Parl. Papers*, 1856, *Coms.*, LX, " Correspondence with the United States respecting Central America ", 33.

[209] *Ibid.*

Admiral Hornby, commander of the British fleet in the West Indies, was familiar with Palmerston's view of Chatfield's plans,[210] and, therefore, upon hearing of the seizure, he promptly ordered the restoration of the island to Honduras.[211] Later, both Chatfield[212] and Squier[213] were rebuked by their governments for the parts which they had played in the affair.

But the seizure of Tigre Island produced much excitement in the United States; and suspicion against the British government, which had been somewhat allayed by negotiations then pending, was again aroused, and a peaceful settlement of the canal question endangered. Clayton, through Lawrence, the American minister at London, demanded a disavowal of the act,[214] which, after some delay, was given,[215] though not in an altogether satisfactory manner.

---

[210] Hornby to Chatfield, Dec. 12, 1849, F. O., Cen. Am., vol. 64.

[211] *Ibid.*; Hornby to Parker, Dec. 12, 1849, *ibid.*, vol. 68, no 100.

[212] Palmerston to Chatfield, Jan. 17, 1850, *ibid.*, vol. 63, no. 1.

[213] Dept. of State, Inst., Am. States, vol. 15, pp. 100-101.

[214] *U. S. Docs.*, ser. no. 579, doc. 75, pp. 313-315.

[215] *Parl. Papers*, 1856, *Coms.*, LX, "Correspondence with the United States respecting Central America ", 34-35.

CHAPTER III.

THE CLAYTON-BULWER TREATY, APRIL 19, 1850.

While the British and American agents were manipulating the weak Central American states in the interest of the country each represented, a movement, initiated at Washington, had begun towards effecting, through negotiation, a peaceful settlement of the matter in dispute. But the problem was an unusually hard one because of the peculiar nature of the situation itself; and the difficulty was made greater by the suspicion and jealousy with which each government had long viewed the other; moreover, this mutual distrust was further stimulated by the rash acts of the agents in Central America, and the negotiations were embarrassed accordingly.

George Bancroft was American minister at London when San Juan was seized by the British, but for many months he received no instructions upon the subject, because his government had decided to investigate the situation before determining upon a course of action. The investigation was to be made by Hise, whose report, as has already been stated, was not received before Polk's administration ended. But Bancroft informed the American government of whatever came to his notice with reference to the dispute between England and Nicaragua. When Castellon, accompanied by Marcoleta, the Nicaraguan chargé d'affaires in Belgium, arrived in England for the purpose of trying to settle the Greytown dispute, Bancroft apprised Buchanan of the fact and expressed the belief that Palmerston would not recede.[1] Later he reported the unsatisfactory reply which had been given Castellon, remarking that Aberdeen agreed with Palmerston in the stand which the latter had taken.[2]

Bancroft's last-mentioned report reached Washington very shortly before the inauguration of President Taylor and probably hastened the action of the new administration, which, while it had no schemes for territorial aggrandizement, was interested in dislodging the British from their position in Central America, and very desirous of securing a neutral transisthmian route. On April 30, 1849, Clayton, the new secretary of state, directed Bancroft to notify Castellon that the President had determined to grant Nicaragua's request by trying to induce the British government to abandon its pretensions to Nicaraguan territory. Bancroft was also directed to advise the Nicaraguan minister to "continue firm in asserting the rights of his government and not to do any act which might either weaken or alienate these rights".[3]

Two days later Clayton again wrote to Bancroft stating that for some time the President had anxiously viewed the acts of the British in Central America, but had not asked for an explanation, in the hope that the measures of the British government might still prove consistent with the treaties made between that government and Spain; or, if otherwise, that the differences between Great Britain and the Central American authorities might be settled in a manner satisfactory

[1] *U. S. Docs.*, ser. no. 579, doc. 75, p. 222.
[2] *Ibid.*, p. 224.
[3] Dept. of State, Inst., Gt. Brit., vol. 15, pp. 385-386.

to all parties. That hope, however, had apparently been vain. Therefore, since Nicaragua had requested the interposition of the United States with reference to the seizure of San Juan, the American government had investigated the Mosquito claims asserted by the British and had decided these claims to be without reasonable foundation, consequently the President had decided to present the American views upon the question to the friendly consideration of Great Britain.[4]

But before entering into any written correspondence upon the subject, it seemed best that Bancroft sound Palmerston in conversation as to the views and intentions of the British government regarding the Mosquito coast, and ascertain whether that government intended to set aside for its own use any portion of the territory; if so, for what reason, and on what principle. Clayton also suggested that Bancroft find out if the British government claimed a right as ally and protector of the Mosquito king to " control or obstruct the commerce of the river San Juan de Nicaragua, or *to keep forts or establishments of any kind on its banks* ". Further, Bancroft was instructed to intimate to Palmerston the inexpediency of any great commercial power claiming a right to the river, in case it should become a world highway. He was to inform Palmerston in the most friendly manner that while the United States would look upon the exclusive possession or command of such a river by themselves as a great evil, which would draw upon the nation the jealousy and ultimately the hostility of the rest of the commercial world, yet they ought not to consent to its obstruction by any other power. If, after the subject had been thus presented,

---

[4] *U. S. Docs.,* ser. no. 579, doc. 75, pp. 230-231.

Palmerston was still unwilling to abandon the British
and Mosquito claim, or retire from the river and the
command of its harbor, Bancroft was to express to him
the views of the President regarding the Mosquito
claim, assuring him that the United States was not actu-
ated by ambitious motives or by any feeling in the least
unfriendly to Great Britain. If this failed to move
Palmerston, then Bancroft was to present a formal
written protest to the British government. Bancroft
was also directed to obtain from the Costa Rican minister an assurance that he would not commit the rights
of his state by any convention with Great Britain. A
cession to Great Britain of the territory south of the
San Juan River, which was claimed by Costa Rica as
well as by Nicaragua, might be a serious embarrassment to the United States. No British forts or possessions of any kind should exist on either bank of the
river. Therefore, Clayton stated, it was desirable to
warn Costa Rica against ceding her territory to Great
Britain, for the safety of every American state would
require that it yield to no further foreign aggression.[5]

Bancroft had no opportunity to present the subject
to Palmerston for some time, but he had an interview
with Molina, the Costa Rican minister, who assured
him that the relation existing between his country and
Great Britain was one of friendship, and nothing more.
However, Bancroft suspected from Molina's manner
that, in case war occurred with Nicaragua over the
boundary question, Costa Rica meant to ask protection
of England.[6] Therefore, in reporting the interview to
Clayton, Bancroft suggested that the American agent
in Central America try to get the two states to reach an

[5] *U. S. Docs.,* ser. no. 579, doc. 75, p. 232.
[6] *Ibid.,* p. 233.

agreement over their boundaries; meanwhile, he himself would endeavor to induce the Costa Rican minister to await the outcome of such an effort, before appealing to England.[7]

But Bancroft was decidedly slow in grasping the intentions of Costa Rica. This was evidently due to his inclination to credit Molina with more frankness and friendliness towards the United States than the latter really felt.[8] A note in the Public Record Office in London shows that in December, 1848, five months previous to Bancroft's interview with him, Molina had distinctly asked that the British government take Costa Rica under its protection, as that state feared trouble with New Granada and Nicaragua over boundary questions.[9] The terms offered by the Costa Ricans, in return for the protecting power of the British, practically amounted to a surrender of their country to the latter.[10] Thus it is evident that Clayton's fears of Costa Rican plans for British protection were far from groundless. Palmerston, however, refused the offer, though just at what time is not clear.[11] Buchanan, writing in April, 1850, expressed the belief that but for the determination to resist European colonization on the North American continent, shown by Polk's administration, the offer would have been accepted.[12] Yet this is by no means certain. To be sure, Great Britain, even at this early date, did not think it wise to run counter to the Monroe doctrine, but there were stronger reasons for not con-

---

[7] *Ibid.,* p. 233.   [8] *Ibid.,* p. 223.
[9] Molina to Palmerston, Dec. 23, 1848, F. O., Costa Rica, vol. 1.
[10] *Ibid.*
[11] Molina to Palmerston, Mar. 23, 1850, *ibid.,* vol. 3. This letter of Molina simply refers to the refusal as having been made " on considerations of too great a weight to be controverted."
[12] Buchanan, *Works,* VIII, 379.

sidering Molina's proposal. At this time the British government had come to feel strongly that the country was overburdened with colonies, and it was even believed that Canada must soon become independent.[13] By the seizure of San Juan and the extension of the Mosquito boundary to the Colorado, England had gained all that she desired at the time, in the vicinity of the proposed canal; therefore, all regard for American wishes aside, there could be no object in burdening herself with a Costa Rican protectorate.

Meanwhile the outlook for Nicaragua had grown more discouraging. The British government was plainly determined not to restore San Juan.[14] Palmerston's plan to settle all of the questions in dispute by an agreement between Mosquito, Costa Rica, and Nicaragua would not be considered by the Nicaraguans, who did not recognize the Mosquito kingdom.[15] Therefore, in despair, Nicaragua again turned to the United States. On July 12, Castellon addressed a note to Bancroft asking whether Honduras, Salvador, and Nicaragua, or the last-named only, would be admitted to the American Union. In case the American government were willing, upon what terms could the admission take place, and what steps were necessary to effect it? If the United States were opposed to annexation, could the Nicaraguans count, at least, on American aid in defending the integrity of their territory? If so, upon what terms would the aid be given?[16]

Bancroft, who was entirely without instructions upon this subject, cautiously replied that the United States had no selfish purpose in its policy towards Central

[13] U. S. Docs., ser. no. 579, doc. 75, p. 223.
[14] Ibid., p. 235.   [15] Ibid., p. 236.   [16] Ibid., pp. 301-302.

America; it desired only the welfare of the Central American states. The American government, he said, had hoped to see San Juan returned to Nicaragua, but intervention for that purpose had been delayed by the dissensions within Central America itself. In order that a more sympathetic regard from the outside might be secured, he advised that the boundary dispute be settled peaceably with Costa Rica, and that the latter be permitted to carry on commerce through the port of San Juan, duty free.[17]

After the receipt of this reply, Castellon once more turned to Palmerston and proposed arbitration.[18] " Should this be refused ", Bancroft wrote Clayton, " Nicaragua must submit, unless she can rely on the prompt exertion of the influence of the United States." [19] But Palmerston would not arbitrate; [20] and, indeed, acquiescence in a plan to refer her claims to Mosquito to an international court was hardly to be expected of Great Britain.

Clayton's instructions on Central American affairs had reached Bancroft in May, but it was not until July that he succeeded in securing an interview on them with Palmerston, and even then the latter was called away before the interview was concluded.[21] Bancroft believed, and reported to Clayton, that Palmerston was purposely delaying in order to shut the United States out of the Central American discussion and thereby bring the Central American states to an acquiescence in British arrangements.[22] The British correspondence

---

[17] *Ibid.*, pp. 303-304.   [18] *Ibid.*, 236.   [19] *Ibid.*
[20] Inclosure in Lawrence to Clayton, April 19, 1850, Dept. of State, Des., Eng., vol. 60, no. 45.
[21] *U. S. Docs.,* ser. no. 579, doc. 75, p. 235.
[22] *Ibid.*

indicates the correctness of Bancroft's surmise; the plan was to frighten Nicaragua into yielding, and thus avoid any cause for American interference.

At the interview Bancroft asked whether the British government intended to appropriate to itself the town of San Juan or any part of the " so called Mosquito territory", to which Palmerston replied, " No; you know very well we have already colonies enough." When asked in whose hands San Juan then was, the Foreign Secretary replied, " For the present, in those of English commissioners." He acknowledged that this was an occupation by England, but stated that the occupation was only temporary. Thereupon Bancroft expressed the opinion of his government that there was no such body politic as the kingdom of the Mosquitos; that if there were any, its jurisdiction did not reach to San Juan; and that, even if it did, no right of exercising a protectorate belonged to Great Britain. In his response to this, Bancroft reported to his government, Palmerston " did not in the least disguise his strong disinclination to restore the port, insisting, however, that any purposes the United States might have in reference to connecting the two oceans by a commercial highway, would be better promoted by the policy which he is pursuing than in any other way. And in reference to the whole subject, his words were, ' You and we can have but one interest '." [23]

Bancroft was not reassured by Palmerston's concluding remarks, because of the attitude towards the restoration of San Juan, displayed in this interview, as well as by the reports of Castellon and Marcoleta. Moreover, Palmerston did not invite a renewal of the inter-

[23] *U. S. Docs.,* ser. no. 579, doc. 75, p. 235.

rupted discussion, and when Bancroft learned that the Foreign Secretary had given a long interview to Castellon and Marcoleta, he decided that it was time to present the protest, as directed by Clayton.[24] But he had not quite finished writing the paper when notice of his recall came, and in view of this he thought it best not to present the protest to the British government.[25]

Before Bancroft's report of his interview reached Washington the American government had learned that a contract had been secured from Nicaragua by the Atlantic and Pacific Ship-Canal Company. As he knew that the completion of this contract was to be followed by a canal treaty, drawn up between Squier and the Nicaragua government, Clayton became uneasy over Bancroft's delay. Therefore, on August 16, he wrote to Rives, the newly-appointed minister to France, regarding the situation, and pointed out how important it was that Great Britain become acquainted with the views of the United States government upon the Mosquito question. " We are deeply anxious ", he wrote, " to avoid any collision with the British government in relation to this matter; but that collision will become inevitable if great prudence be not exercised on both sides." With reference to the arrangement between Nicaragua and the canal company, he said: " We view the title of the state of Nicaragua, which entered into this contract, as irrefragable, and are about to make a treaty with her on the subject. When Great Britain shall ascertain the real objects that we have in view, she cannot, I think, fail to see the propriety of aiding instead of obstructing us in securing, for all commercial nations on the same terms, the right of passage by

[24] *Ibid.,* pp. 235-236.   [25] *Ibid.,* p. 234.

the Nicaragua route from ocean to ocean, if that route should prove to be practicable." Consequently, Rives was instructed to pass through London on his way to Paris and perform the duty enjoined upon Bancroft, if, upon his arrival in London, it had not yet been performed. If Palmerston showed himself determined to maintain the Mosquito title, Rives was not to present the protest, but to leave that to Lawrence, Bancroft's successor.[26]

Palmerston was absent from London when Rives arrived,[27] but he soon returned, and on September 24, Rives had an interview with him. Palmerston received the American minister cordially, saying that he had returned to London solely for the purpose of seeing and conversing with him.[28] Rives stated the object of his errand as instructed, explaining the views of the American government and its intention to support the canal company in the rights granted it by Nicaragua. He then pointed out to Palmerston the peculiar interest which the United States must have in the canal route because of her possessions on the Pacific coast, assuring him, however, that the United States "sought no exclusive privilege or preferential right of any kind in regard to the proposed communication " but wished to see it " dedicated to the common use of all nations, on a footing of perfect equality for all." Yet, while possessing no selfish designs on the transisthmian route, the American nation " could never consent to see so important a communication fall under the exclusive control of any other great commercial power." *Mosquito* possession at the mouth of the San Juan could be

[26] *U. S. Docs.*, ser. no. 660, doc. 27, p. 13.
[27] *Ibid.*, p. 15.   [28] *Ibid.*, p. 18.

considered in no other light than *British* possession, and must necessarily cause dissatisfaction and distrust on the part of other commercial powers. In view of these facts, Rives suggested to Palmerston that the governments which they represented come to a " frank and manly understanding with each other, and unite their influence for the accomplishment of an object of the highest importance to both of them as well as the rest of the world, instead of hazarding the final loss of so great an object by jarring and divided councils." [29]

Palmerston replied that he was very glad to have full and free conversation upon the subject. He had conversed to some extent with Bancroft regarding it, he said, but as Bancroft was soon to leave, it had not seemed necessary to enter into much detail. He then reviewed the controversy with Nicaragua, stating that from a very early time the Mosquito Indians had been treated by the British as forming a sovereign state. For more than a century, the British government had given them tokens of recognition and protection. The Nicaraguans, according to the Foreign Secretary, had taken forcible possession of the port of San Juan to which they had no right. The British, as protectors of the Mosquitos, had driven them out, but the Nicaraguans, while not in possession, had fraudulently granted a right of way to American citizens in order to draw the United States into their quarrel. In this connection Palmerston assured Rives, however, that there was not the slightest foundation for the suspicion, which existed in the United States, that the British government wished to plant a new colony on the San Juan, for they already had more colonies than they could manage;

[29] *Ibid.*, pp. 18-19.

" that, as to any idea of their holding exclusive posses-
sion of the mouth of the San Juan as the Key of the con-
templated communication between the Atlantic and the
Pacific, nothing could be further from their minds." [30]

Later Palmerston spoke of the dissension and strife
which distracted the Central American states and prevented the development of their natural resources. In
the interest of humanity and of the general commerce
of the world, he declared, it was desirable to promote
the civilization and improvement of those countries.[31]

When the conversation again reverted to the Mosquitos, Rives called attention to the fact that " the
ultimate property or high domain of Indian territory
was always considered as vested in the nations colonizing the country by the mere fact of discovery or settlement anywhere within the limits declared to be assumed
by them ", and pointed out that this principle had been
acted upon by Great Britain herself in various international pacts. The Foreign Secretary fully admitted
the general doctrine stated by Rives, and said that this
was the principle on which the British relations with
the Indian tribes in Canada were conducted. But he
insisted that the case of the Mosquitos was " *sui generis*
and stood upon its own peculiar circumstances ". However, he declared that the question of Mosquito title
need not prevent the consummation of the plan for
interoceanic communication.[32]

Throughout the interview Palmerston's conversation
was marked by " a tone of perfect frankness and the
most conciliatory and friendly spirit towards the United
States ", which led Rives to feel that the way had been

[30] *U. S. Docs.*, ser. no. 660, doc. 27, p. 20.   The italics appear in
Rives's report to Clayton.
[31] *Ibid.*   [32] *Ibid.*, p. 22.

opened for a better understanding and final co-operation.[33] In conclusion, Rives suggested, that " if Great Britain would do what she had the unquestionable power to effect with the Mosquitos, and exert her influence with Costa Rica, while the United States employed their good offices with Nicaragua, every political impediment to the execution of the great work they both desired to see accomplished would be speedily removed." This done, the benefits of the highway could be secured to all by an international guarantee. Palmerston received the suggestion very favorably and left the American minister with the impression that he was desirous of co-operating with the United States in promoting the accomplishment of the object in which both nations were interested, the construction of an interoceanic highway.[34]

When Lawrence arrived two or three weeks later he had interviews with Palmerston [35] and Russell,[36] both of whom repeated substantially what had been said to Rives. In consequence, Lawrence, like Rives, was led to believe that the British government would join with the United States in the guarantee of a transisthmian highway.[37]

A comparison of the attitude displayed by Palmerston towards Bancroft, with his manner of meeting and answering Rives and Lawrence, plainly reveals a shifting of British policy. The fact of such a change makes desirable at this point a more definite consideration of British motives as well as an investigation into the causes which made the English government show greater willingness at this time to discuss the Central

[33] *Ibid.*, p. 21.   [34] *Ibid.*, p. 23.   [35] *Ibid.*, p. 23-24.
[36] *Ibid.*, p. 24.   [37] *Ibid.*

American question, and particularly the strictly canal phase of it, with the American government.

In the first place, it should be said that the aggressive movement of the United States towards the southwest, accompanied by the talk of " manifest destiny ", had given the British good reason to suspect the Americans of designs upon the territory of the isthmus, and to fear that they might attempt to monopolize the Nicaragua route.[38] Should this fear be realized, the control of commerce in the Pacific would pass from English to American hands. To prevent such a monopoly of the interoceanic highway and to secure a share in any arrangement with regard to it, Palmerston directed the seizure of San Juan. That this was the Foreign Secretary's main and perhaps only motive is evident from a study of his conduct previous and subsequent to the seizure. Moreover, Rives after his interview expressed the belief that Palmerston's aim had been to prevent exclusive control of the interoceanic route by the Americans, and not to monopolize it for the British.[39] A *Times* editorial of a later date took the same view.[40] Indeed, the British government must have clearly realized that the American people would not peacefully permit the establishment of such a foreign monopoly.

After San Juan had come under Anglo-Mosquito control, there was a double British reason for avoiding all discussion with the United States government. Complicated with the old fear of American designs on the route, was the knowledge that since American

[38] Chatfield to ,Palmerston, Mar. 8, 1848, F. O., Guat., vol. 51, no. 30; Sept. 15, 1849, *ibid.*, vol. 59, no. 87; Manning to Green, Oct. 4, 1849, C. O., Hond. vol. 77.

[39] *U. S. Docs.,* ser. no. 660, doc. 27, p. 21.

[40] London *Times,* June 13, 1850.

interests had focussed attention upon the region the Monroe doctrine might be applied to the situation in an attempt to drive out the intruders. This explains the attitude towards Bancroft as well as the attempt to force Nicaragua to acquiesce in British-made boundaries for the Mosquitos.

But despatches containing the purport of the Hise treaty [41] and outlining the terms of the canal contract of the New York company,[42] as well as reports of Squier's reception in Central America and the policy followed by him,[43] must have reached Palmerston a little before Rives's arrival. These would all be strongly influential towards convincing the British government that the United States must be reckoned with eventually in connection with Central America, and that further evasion would be useless, if not distinctly unwise. To lend emphasis to this view there was the fact that Castellon had departed without an agreement regarding Mosquito boundaries, and, in consequence, the Nicaraguans would undoubtedly again turn to the Americans, whose feelings had been strongly enlisted on their side. In the opinion of the *Times,* Nicaragua had gained a position that it was " most unwise to treat with violence and contumely ". [44] Therefore, that newspaper advised a pacific and conciliatory policy.[45] However, this policy was not to be directed towards the weak state of Nicaragua, but towards the power believed to be behind that state—the American govern-

[41] Chatfield to Palmerston, May 17, 1849, F. O., Guat., vol. 58, no. 42.
[42] Chatfield to Palmerston, April 21, 1849, *ibid.,* vol. 57, no. 35; May 5, 1849, *ibid.,* vol. 58, no. 38; Crampton to Palmerston, June 25, 1849, F. O., Am. vol. 499, no. 61.
[43] Chatfield to Palmerston, July 27, 1849, F. O., Guat., vol. 59, no. 64.
[44] London *Times,* Nov. 1, 1849.
[45] *Ibid.*

ment and the American people. These various considerations which have been mentioned seem to furnish ample explanation of the British change in attitude.

After Rives's frank and friendly statement of the American canal policy, practically all remaining suspicion of American intentions concerning Central America seems to have vanished. With its disappearance came a change of attitude towards Central America itself. Since the aim of the United States was really the establishment of a great commercial highway for the benefit of all nations, weakness and disorganization in Central America was no longer an advantage but a handicap to British interests; hence Palmerston's expression of a desire for the quieting of dissension in those countries, and the promotion of civilization.

One further matter requires attention in this connection. By the seizure of San Juan the British government had, for the time, insured the Nicaragua route against foreign monopoly; but in order to give some shadow of legality to the act, it had committed itself to an assertion of the Mosquito title to the port, as well as revived the British protectorate over the Indians and renewed the claim of full sovereignty and independence for them. This unfortunate proclamation of Mosquito sovereignty placed Great Britain in a position from which she could not easily withdraw. This attitude, in reality outworn, but forced on England as consistent with her past stand, consequently became the source of virtually all future trouble between the British and Americans over Central America, for it proved an obstacle in all negotiations and made difficult a free discussion of the matters taken up, with the result that misunderstandings arose which complicated the Cen-

tral American question and delayed its final settlement
for more than half a century.

Lawrence's full instructions did not reach him until
some time following his arrival in London.[46] After a
long discussion showing the fallacy of the Mosquito
claim,[47] they directed Lawrence to suggest to Palmerston that the two governments form a treaty guaranteeing the independence of Nicaragua, Honduras, and
Costa Rica, with provisions for extinguishing the title
of the Mosquitos to any lands assigned to them in
carrying out the terms of the treaty, should the proposed interoceanic canal pass through those lands.[48] A
copy of the part of the Squier treaty pertaining to the
canal was inclosed by Clayton with instructions to
Lawrence to call Palmerston's attention to the terms of
this and express to him the desire of the United States
that the British government enter into a similar treaty
with Nicaragua.[49] The whole negotiation with Great
Britain should be placed on the " broad basis of a great
highway for the benefit of mankind, to be dedicated
especially by Great Britain and the United States, to
the equal benefit and advantage of all the nations of
the world that would join them in entering into the
proper treaty stipulations with Nicaragua." [50] Should
Great Britain desire any further guarantees of American good faith than those already given, Clayton added,
the American government would gladly enter into a
treaty with her binding both nations " never to colonize, annex, settle, or fortify any part of the ancient

<hr>

[46] The instructions were dated October 20, and were written after the
receipt of Bancroft's and Rives's reports of their interviews. *U. S. Docs.,*
ser. no. 660, doc. 27, p. 24.

[47] *Ibid.,* pp. 24-29.   [48] *Ibid.,* pp. 29-30.   [49] *Ibid.,* p. 30.   [50] *Ibid.*

territory of Guatemala, embracing Nicaragua, Costa Rica, Honduras, and, indeed, the whole Mosquito coast." [51]

In case the British rejected these overtures and refused to cooperate, Lawrence should present the terms of Hise's treaty which had recently been received, informing Palmerston that the treaty was made without authority from the United States, and assuring him that no step would be taken towards ratifying it, if, by an arrangement with England, American interests could be placed upon a " just and satisfactory foundation ". Should the efforts to this end fail, however, the President would not hesitate to present it, or some other treaty which might be concluded by Squier, to the Senate for ratification, in which action he would be supported by the American people. [52]

Should the British government refuse all propositions made by Lawrence, the latter was directed to enter the protest which Bancroft was to have presented, and immediately notify his government of the fact. [53] If, on the other hand, Palmerston showed a willingness to co-operate, but should be still tenacious about the protection of the Indians, Lawrence was to suggest that the Nicaraguan government pay them an annuity in order to extinguish their title. Lawrence should strive to produce a withdrawal from all pretensions to the whole Mosquito coast. [54] " I shall await the result of your negotiation with no little anxiety ", Clayton concluded. " Bring it to a speedy close one way or the other. We are ready for either alternative. If we

[51] *U. S. Docs.,* ser. no. 660, doc. 27, p. 31.
[52] *Ibid.*   [53] *Ibid.,* p. 33.   [54] *Ibid.,* p. 34.

must have a collision with Great Britain about this matter, the sooner we understand it the better for us. The President is firm in his purpose and will never consent that Great Britain shall, under any pretext, enjoy any exclusive possession within the territory of Nicaragua. If we adopt the treaty negotiated by Mr. Hise and Great Britain should persevere in her assertion of the Mosquito title, I know not how we can avoid a collision consistently with our national honor." [55]

After the receipt of his instructions, Lawrence promptly secured an interview with Palmerston, and opened the subject in a general way, but avoided a discussion of the rights of the Mosquitos, explaining to the Foreign Secretary that he hoped it would not become necessary to do so.[56] After his interview he addressed a note to Palmerston, asking whether Great Britain intended to occupy or colonize Nicaragua, Costa Rica, the Mosquito coast, or any part of Central America, and also whether the British government would join with the United States in guaranteeing the neutrality of a " ship-canal, railway or other communication to be open to the world and common to all nations." [57]

Lawrence's object in avoiding agitation of the Mosquito title and in narrowing the discussion to the two questions was to make more possible a prompt reply, and thus relieve the popular mind in America. Moreover, he believed that if the points covered by his inquiries could be settled, an amicable arrangement of the Mosquito question would follow.[58]

Palmerston's reply, written on November 13, stated that the British government did not intend to " occupy

[55] *Ibid.*   [56] *Ibid.,* pp. 43-44.   [57] *Ibid.,* p. 45.   [58] *Ibid.,* p. 44.

or colonize Nicaragua, Costa Rica, the Mosquito coast, or any part of Central America." In regard to Lawrence's second inquiry, the Foreign Secretary wrote that the British government would feel great pleasure in combining with the United States to effect the establishment of such an interoceanic highway as was suggested and would fully undertake to obtain the consent of Mosquito to such arrangements as would render the port of Greytown applicable for the purpose.[59]

In a private letter to Lawrence of the same date Palmerston protested against the terms of the Squier treaty. He had as yet received no copy of that document, he said, but if he had been correctly informed with reference to it, one object of the treaty was to engage the United States to endeavor to compel the British government to return Greytown to Nicaragua. Such an engagement would involve the United States in an unprovoked aggression towards Great Britain.[60]

Lawrence replied by pointing out that no maritime nation ought to desire or to be permitted to have exclusive foothold on the isthmus. On the contrary, the aims of such a nation should be confined to guarantees of neutrality. He hoped, therefore, that the Mosquitos might be properly provided for, that other causes of difference might be satisfactorily arranged, and the two governments thus be spared a discussion which could only defer matters, and perhaps lead to serious results. The Squier treaty, while it rested upon the validity of Nicaragua's claim of sovereignty from ocean to ocean, sought to secure nothing exclusively to

[59] *U. S. Docs.,* ser. no. 660, doc. 27, p. 46.

[60] *Parl. Papers,* 1856, *Coms.,* LX, " Correspondence with the United States respecting Central America ", 8.

the United States, and contemplated an invitation to the world to join in its provisions. " I have reason to believe ", Lawrence concluded, " that the United States are as firm as they are sincere on this point." [61]

It was now clear that the negotiations would not proceed as smoothly as was at first hoped. Clayton saw an obstacle in the Foreign Secretary's promise to obtain the consent of Mosquito to arrangements regarding Greytown; consequently he declared that British withdrawal from the port was essential to the success of the enterprise.[62] Lawrence was accordingly instructed to press the matter so as to leave no doubt in Palmerston's mind of the American convictions regarding it.[63]

Lawrence also quickly saw the difficulty and soon became convinced that discussion of the Mosquito question could not be avoided. On December 14 he wrote to Palmerston that unless the views of the two governments upon the subject could be harmonized the desired cooperation would be prevented; and he asked definitely whether the British government was willing to transfer the Mosquito protectorate to other hands under provisions for the humane treatment of the Indians, and to let such parts of the territory, said to be occupied by them, as might be necessary, be dedicated to the transit route.[64] On the same date Lawrence wrote to Clayton expressing a determination to insist upon the abandonment of the Mosquito protectorate, even if Lord Palmerston gave up everything else.[65]

No reply was made to Lawrence's last-mentioned note to Palmerston, and with this note negotiations on

[61] *Ibid.*, 24-25.
[62] *U. S. Docs.*, ser. no. 660, doc. 27, pp. 51-52.
[63] *Ibid.*   [64] *Ibid.*, pp. 54-58.   [65] *Ibid.*, pp. 53-54.

the British side of the Atlantic terminated. The reason for this cessation was perhaps Lawrence's insistence upon discussing the Mosquito question with the purpose of forcing the British to retreat from the stand they had taken.

Some time in the autumn of 1849, probably when Lawrence began to direct his attention to the Mosquito title, the British government seems to have carefully investigated the history of the question. As a result it evidently concluded that the rights previously contended for were not easily reconcilable with the terms of the treaties with Spain.[66] Moreover, it discovered that the mouth of the San Juan was fortified by the Spaniards long before the establishment of the Mosquito protectorate.[67] The results of this investigation, and the fact that Nicaragua had won the sympathy of the United States, evidently caused the cabinet to abandon any intention it might have had to assume a defiant stand on the question,[68] which, with the existing temper of the American people, would have made war very probable.

On the other hand, the English government did not intend to give up the claims hitherto maintained for the Mosquitos if it could possibly avoid doing so. Besides, the British protectorate was not easily disposed of. Yet, from the present evidence it seems pretty certain that had Great Britain been squarely confronted with an American war as the only other alternative, a method of relinquishing Mosquito claims without too great damage to British pride would have been found.

[66] London *Times,* June 13, 1850.
[67] *Ibid.* [68] *Ibid.*

As it was, the British government determined to proceed cautiously and, if possible, to remove all cause of jealousy regarding the canal route, while still maintaining the protectorate. Evidently with this in view the cabinet concluded to attempt negotiations in Washington. There were reasons for believing that better terms might be made with Clayton than with Lawrence. The former had shown nervousness when speaking to Crampton just after the receipt of the Hise treaty and had expressed great anxiety that the British government should not think that the treaty was in accordance with the wishes of the American government.[69] Besides, both Whig and Democratic press in America were violently attacking the British claims and calling upon the administration for action on the matter.[70] This situation also might have been expected to incline Clayton, embarrassed by a refractory Democratic Senate, to an early compromise settlement. Be these speculations as they may, the fact remains that some time previous to November 14 [71] Sir Henry Bulwer was appointed British agent to Washington, presumably for the purpose of determining what chance there was of making a favorable arrangement with Clayton.[72] But hope of reaching terms with Lawrence was not entirely given up;[73] the aim was to satisfy the United States without forsaking the protectorate, and if Law-

[69] *U. S. Docs.*, ser. no. 1991, doc. 194, pp. 55-56.
[70] Crampton to Palmerston, Nov. 4, 1849, F. O., Am., vol. 501, no. 95.
[71] Bulwer sailed for America on November 14, the day after Palmerston wrote to Lawrence complaining of the terms of the Squier treaty. *U. S. Docs.*, ser. no. 660, doc. 27, p. 45.
[72] The British Public Record Office is singularly lacking in any correspondence giving reasons for taking up the discussion of the question at Washington.
[73] *Parl. Papers*, 1856, *Coms.*, LX, " Correspondence with the United States respecting Central America ", 35.

rence showed any sign of yielding, there was no reason why negotiations with him should not be resumed.[74]

Bulwer received no detailed instructions before his departure, but in his last conversation with the Foreign Secretary, Palmerston pointed out that an unforeseen difficulty had arisen about an unimportant matter, and that while the question itself would have to be solved in a manner that comported with British honor, the matter out of which the difficulty had grown would admit of adjustment.[75] This view of the situation indicates that the British government was prepared to arrange its relations with Central America to suit whatever were the ultimate demands of the United States, should these demands be in any way reasonable.

Bulwer reached Washington some time in December, but for some weeks no attempt at negotiation was made. Indeed, for a short time it appeared that there would be no further effort to settle the question with England. This was when the British seizure of Tigre Island became known at Washington, and excitement ran high as a result.[76] Just at this crisis Carcache, a representative of the Nicaraguan government, arrived to solicit ratification of the Squier treaty.[77] Clayton, partaking of the general increase in suspicion of British aims in Central America, promptly stated, on January 5, in response to a note from Carcache, that the Presi-

---

[74] Lawrence did not receive word until April, 1850, that the negotiations had been entirely transferred to Washington. Appleton, " Memoir of Hon. Abbott Lawrence ", in Mass. Hist. Soc., *Proc.*, III (1855-1858), 76.

[75] Bulwer to Palmerston, April 28, 1850, " Private ", F. O., Am., vol. 512.

[76] *Parl. Papers*, 1856, *Coms.*, LX, " Correspondence with the United States respecting Central America ", 28-29.

[77] *U. S. Docs.*, ser. no. 579, doc. 75, pp. 312-313.

dent would submit the Squier treaty to the Senate and would cheerfully ratify it if it received the approval of that body.[77] Bulwer, however, seems to have come to the rescue, and succeeded in allaying the suspicions of the American government to such a degree as to alter its intentions regarding the Squier treaty. Consequently, when, a little later, a call came from the Senate for the Squier correspondence and treaties,[79] it was met with a refusal from President Taylor.[80]

After his arrival in Washington, Bulwer carefully studied the situation and saw that the chief interest of the American people regarding Central America lay in the need for an interoceanic route, and that the broader question of Mosquito claims had for the time a secondary place. He therefore concluded that, in trying to reach an agreement, it would be best to avoid all consideration of the latter question and to concentrate upon the former.[81] This he seemed to believe would make possible a disposal of the difficulty without serious sacrifice of British pride. The situation of the American government at the time favored the idea. When Clayton, his nervousness increased by the discontent of the country and the demand of both houses of Congress for the Squier correspondence,[82] went to him and declared that he " must either deliver up the whole subject to popular discussion and determination, or come to some immediate settlement upon it ",[83] Bul-

[78] *Ibid.,* p. 313.
[79] *Cong. Globe,* 31 Cong., 1 sess., pt. 1, p. 159.
[80] Richardson, *Messages and Papers,* V, 31-32.
[81] *Parl. Papers,* 1856, *Coms.,* LX, " Correspondence with the United States respecting Central America ", 29-30.
[82] *Ibid.,* 35.
[83] *U. S. Docs.,* ser. no 1991, doc. 194, p. 61.

wer saw his chance. He determined to enter into a negotiation for the purpose of forming a treaty, although he was without treaty-making power and even without definite instructions from his government. Clayton's semi-appeal to him gave him an advantage which he was quick to seize. By playing upon the nervousness of the Secretary of State he induced him to avoid the subject of Mosquito claims in the discussion which followed, and to put practically the whole emphasis on securing guarantees of neutrality for the isthmian canal.[84]

Yet, while driven from the bolder stand of a few months before, Clayton by no means gave up hopes of making the British relinquish the Indian protectorate. As a frank promise to withdraw seemed out of the question, he determined to gain his end by a less direct route; this was by securing such a wording of the treaty as would amount to a British agreement to abandon all control in Central America. Bulwer, on the other hand, strove to preserve the protectorate, while giving up all special advantage which might interfere with the security of the interoceanic highway. Even a casual study of the Clayton-Bulwer treaty makes it evident that a severe struggle took place between the negotiators, a struggle as the *Times* put it, " for·generalship in the use of terms " ;[85] and such a study also shows that both contestants were forced to recede from some of the ground which they had hoped to hold. In short, it makes it clear that the treaty was not a victory, but a compromise.

[84] *Parl. Papers,* 1856, *Coms.,* LX, " Correspondence with the United States respecting Central America ", 35-38.
[85] London *Times,* Jan. 19, 1856.

The project of a convention was quickly completed and on February 3 this was sent to Palmerston for his approval, together with a letter explaining the circumstances producing it.[86] But as negotiations had progressed, discontent in the United States had increased. A disavowal of the seizure of Tigre had not yet reached Washington, and just a week after the project was sent off, reports again came from Central America [87] of other violent acts committed by Chatfield and the British naval officers, in their efforts to collect claims against the republics.[88] Probably roused by the fresh suspicions resulting from these reports,[89] certain members of the American cabinet who knew the character of the recent agreement went to Clayton and desired that alterations be made in the project in order to prevent further disputes. Some arrangement, they stated, should be made for the relinquishment of Mosquito claims to territory along the San Juan. As it was, they felt that many would contend that the British meant to do under another name that which they agreed not to do under their own.[90]

Clayton, thereupon, explained the situation to Bulwer, and on February 18 the latter wrote to Palmerston explaining the change of feeling which had taken place. It was his belief, he stated, that if Clayton had not already signed the project he would not do so now. However, having done so, he was bound inevitably to a conciliatory line of policy, if the project should be

[86] *Parl. Papers*, 1856, *Coms.*, LX, " Correspondence with the United States respecting Central America ", 35-40.
[87] Bulwer to Palmerston, Feb. 18, 1850, F. O., Am., vol. 511, no. 31.
[88] Crowe, *Gospel in Central America*, 217-220.
[89] Bulwer to Palmerston, Feb. 18, 1850, F. O., Am., vol. 511, no. 31.
[90] *Ibid.*

approved by the British government, and would omit nothing to make that policy succeed. Though Clayton's colleagues were not so interested, Bulwer believed they would be loath to reject the treaty. But he added, " I ought not to disguise from your Lordship that this question is becoming, the longer it remains in abeyance the more intricate and perplexing, and that it contains within it if not the seeds of actual war, the seeds of such hostile and angry excitement as render war always possible, and very often produce many of the evils of war even when war itself is not produced." He therefore suggested that Palmerston add to the project, if approved by him, an explanation or clause that would quiet to some extent the suspicions of British intentions. In conclusion, he wrote: " I am bound to add my opinion that if nothing is done, and even that if nothing is done speedily, to set this business at rest, and bring it to an amicable conclusion, the tone of opinion on this side of the Atlantic will raise it ere long into very serious importance." [91]

While negotiations remained in this uncertain state the situation grew more tense. Rumors again reached the American government that British protection was to be extended to Costa Rica; [92] and before fear of this could be allayed by word from Palmerston,[93] there arrived from Lawrence the announcement regarding the evacuation of Tigre Island and a disavowal of its seizure, qualified by the declaration: " Her Majesty's

[91] Bulwer to Palmerston, Feb. 18, 1850, F. O. Am., vol. 511, no. 31. Part of this despatch is given in *Parl. Papers, 1856, Coms.*, LX, " Correspondence with the United States respecting Central America ", 40-42.
[92] *Parl. Papers, 1856, Coms.*, LX, " Correspondence with the United States respecting Central America ", 46.
[93] *Ibid.*, 46-47.

Government must not on that account be considered as giving up in any degree the claims which it has made on the Government of Honduras, and must hold itself free to use whatever means the Law of Nations may allow for obtaining the redress which it demands if that redress should continue to be withheld." [94]

Such a statement, closely following reports of blockades and seizures in Central America, seemed to the American government utterly inconsistent with Palmerston's declaration that the British government had no intention of occupying or colonizing the region; [95] consequently it roused all the old suspicion of British good faith, [96] and caused the American government almost to despair of reaching an agreement. [97] As a result, the administration decided to pursue its own course, with the intention of continuing it should Great Britain prove herself determined not to act honorably. Accordingly, the American government seems to have worked in anticipation of a later struggle, diplomatic or military, with the British. In 1847 Christopher Hempstead had been appointed United States consul at Belize, [98] securing his exequatur from Great Britain. [99] On March 1, 1850, Clayton sent him a letter of recall, explaining that as the appointment might have been made " without full consideration of the territorial rights of Great Britain in that quarter ", it was deemed advisable under existing circumstances to discontinue the consulate. [100] Although, before negotiations had begun, Bulwer, at least, had understood that the Squier treaty would not be presented to the Senate before the

[94] *Ibid.*, 34-35.   [95] *Ibid.*, 48-49.   [96] *Ibid.*   [97] *Ibid.*, 53.
[98] *U. S. Docs.*, ser. no. 579, doc. 75, pp. 310-311.
[99] *Ibid.*, p. 311.
[100] *Ibid.*, ser. no. 660, doc. 12, p. 2.

treaty which it was hoped would result from the negotiations, or except in connection with it,[101] on March 19 it was nevertheless transmitted " for the advice of the Senate in regard to its ratification ".[102]

A few days after this, Bulwer received his government's approval of the treaty project, and was empowered to sign it. In order to remove the suspicions of the Americans, Palmerston directed that at the time of signing Bulwer give to Clayton a note stating that the British government had no intention of making use of the protection which it afforded to the Mosquitos, for the purpose of doing under cover of that protection any of the things the intention to do which was disclaimed in the letter to Lawrence [103] of November 13, 1849.[104] This greatly eased the situation. Moreover, a little later a letter was received from Palmerston disavowing any intention on the part of the British government of establishing a protectorate over Costa Rica.[105] Consequently, the negotiations proceeded, and after a few minor changes in the body of the treaty Clayton agreed to sign it. He added, however, that upon receiving the statement which the Foreign Secretary had directed Bulwer to make, he should be obliged to present a counter-declaration on the part of the United States government to the effect that it in no wise recognized the Mosquito title or sovereignty.[106] Thereupon, Bulwer, desiring to omit such an allusion

---

[101] Parl. Papers, 1856, Coms., LX, " Correspondence with the United States respecting Central America ", 52-53.
[102] Richardson, Messages and Papers, V, 23-34.
[103] See above, pp. 85-86.
[104] Parl. Papers, 1856, Coms., LX, " Correspondence with the United States respecting Central America ", 45-46.
[105] Ibid., 46-47.
[106] Bulwer to Palmerston, April 28, 1850, F. O., Am., vol. 512, no. 67.

to a difference between the two governments and feeling it desirable to bind the United States also as to American protection over any part of Central America, decided to omit the statement suggested by Palmerston, and instead to embody in the treaty the substance of the statement, but without direct mention of the Mosquito protectorate.[107] This being arranged, the convention was signed by the two negotiators on April 19, 1850.[108]

Since the fame and notoriety of the Clayton-Bulwer treaty resulted almost entirely from the peculiar wording of the first article, that article is here quoted in full:

The Governments of Great Britain and the United States hereby declare that neither the one nor the other will ever obtain or maintain for itself any exclusive control over the said Ship-Canal; agreeing that neither will ever erect or maintain any fortifications commanding the same, or in the vicinity thereof, or occupy, or fortify, or colonize, or assume or exercise any dominion over Nicaragua, Costa Rica, the Mosquito Coast, or any part of Central America; nor will either make use of any protection which either affords or any may afford, or any alliance which either has or may have, to or with any State or people, for the purpose of erecting or maintaining any such fortifications or of occupying, fortifying or colonizing Nicaragua, Costa Rica, the Mosquito Coast, or any part of Central America, or of assuming or exercising dominion over the same. Nor will Great Britain or the United States take advantage of any intimacy, or use any alliance, connection, or influence that either may possess with any State or Government through whose territory the said canal may pass, for the purpose of acquiring or holding, directly or indirectly, for the subjects or citizens of the one, any rights or advantages in regard to commerce or navigation through the said canal,

[107] *Ibid.* Part of this despatch is given in *Parl. Papers, 1856, Coms.,* LX, " Correspondence with the United States respecting Central America ", 55-56.
[108] *Ibid.,* 52.

which shall not be offered, on the same terms, to the subjects or citizens of the other.[109]

By the fourth article the two governments engaged to use their good offices to " procure the establishment of two free ports, one at each end of the said canal ", and the eighth stated that the two contracting parties desiring not only " to accomplish a particular object, but also to establish a general principle ", agreed to extend their protection, by treaty, to any other practicable communications, whether by canal or railway, across the isthmus connecting North and South America. The remainder of the treaty referred to the more obvious provisions necessary for securing the construction and neutralization of the canal.[110]

Before signing the agreement, Clayton, fearing opposition from the Democratic majority of the Senate, with the aid of King, the chairman of the Committee on Foreign Relations, obtained the approval of the leading members to the measure.[111] Therefore, he submitted it with a fair hope of securing ratification. Nevertheless, the treaty had a stormy time in the Senate, the members of which were distinctly divided on the question of what should be accomplished by the arrangement. Some were primarily interested in securing the guarantee for the proposed canal; others were bent upon driving the British completely out of Central America.[112] Stephen A. Douglas was leader of the latter faction, and was bitterly opposed to the treaty.[113]

[109] *Parl. Papers*, 1856, *Coms.*, LX, " Correspondence with the United States respecting Central America ", 50.

[110] *Ibid.*, 50-52.

[111] Buchanan, *Works*, VIII, 382; *Cong. Record*, XXII, 2981.

[112] *Cong. Globe*, 32 Cong., 2 sess., 237-238; 34 Cong., 1 sess., pt. 2, p. 1072.

[113] *Ibid.*, 34 Cong., 1 sess., pt. 2, p. 1072; *Cong. Record*, XXII, 2971.

It took the best efforts of Clayton and King to persuade the opposition that the agreement was a practical application of the Monroe doctrine, and required the abandonment of the Mosquito protectorate.[114]

In the discussion of the treaty the uncertain wording of the first article was criticised, but King explained that the obscurity was due to a wish on the part of Bulwer to protect his nation's pride, and the desire of Clayton to indulge him in this. England, it was explained, felt that she was being forced into a sort of backward step, and it was expected that the Americans would not insist upon any expression that might wound her sensibilities.[115] These explanations, evidently given with perfect sincerity by King[116]—though up to this time neither Bulwer nor Palmerston had acknowledged a retreat on the part of their government—so convinced some of the senators that they wished to retain in the Squier treaty the clause recognizing the right of Nicaragua over the proposed canal route. They argued that this recognition was now of no real importance,

[114] Buchanan, *Works*, VIII, 381-382.

[115] *Cong. Globe*, 32 Cong., 2 sess., 253. In a letter to Squier describing the new treaty, Clayton added, "But let there be no exultation on our side at the expense of British pride or sensibility ", and cautioned Squier to deal kindly with both British subjects and British agents. Dept. of State, Inst., Am. States, vol. 15, p. 108.

[116] On May 8, 1850, King wrote to Buchanan in reference to the Clayton-Bulwer treaty: " I saw no objection to entering into a Treaty stipulation not to occupy or colonise any portion of Central America, when by so doing we are practically enforcing the Monroe doctrine, by requiring of England the abandonment of her claim to the protectorate of the King of the Mosquitos . . . The Treaty as I conceive accomplishes all that we ought to desire, while it strengthens the position we have heretofore taken, and avowed before the world. I may be mistaken in the views I have expressed; but if so, four-fifths of the Democratic Senators whom I consulted before the signature of the Treaty, were equally in error." Buchanan, *Works*, VIII, 382.

and that it would be satisfactory to Nicaragua and, in view of the terms of the Clayton-Bulwer treaty, could not be obnoxious to Great Britain.[117] Bulwer, however, pointed out to Clayton that this policy would destroy the harmony so necessary to the construction of the canal.[118] Clayton agreed with him; and the Senate as a whole showed the same desire for friendly action.[119] As a result of the efforts of Clayton and King, aided by Bulwer,[120] considerable temporary favor was created for the treaty in the Senate, and it was ratified without modification by a vote of forty-two to eleven.[121] In view of the temper of the Senate a few weeks before, the fact that the treaty passed by such a large majority, or even that it passed at all, seems ample proof that the Senate as a whole believed the arrangement to be in harmony with the Monroe doctrine and felt that it would force the British out of Central America.

Shortly before the treaty was sent to the Senate, an instruction of far-reaching significance was received by Bulwer from his government. It had been reported, Palmerston wrote, that some Americans were about to establish themselves in the island of Ruatan. The islands of Ruatan and Bonacca were not only English *de jure* but were actually occupied by British settlers

[117] Bulwer to Palmerston, May 6, 1850, " Private and confidential ", F. O., Am., vol. 512.

[118] When the treaty was signed on April 19, Clayton had assured Bulwer that should the Senate ratify it, care would be taken that any other treaty also confirmed by the Senate should conform with it. *Parl. Papers,* 1856, *Coms.,* LX, " Correspondence with the United States respecting Central America ", 52-54.

[119] Bulwer to Palmerston, May, 6, 1850, " Private and confidential ", F. O., Am., vol. 512.

[120] Bulwer to Palmerston, Aug. 6, 1850, " Secret and confidential ", vol. 514, no. 157.

[121] *Cong. Globe,* 32 Cong., 2 and 3 sess., Appendix, 267.

who were governed by a British magistrate appointed by the Belize superintendent. Moreover, in 1841 the governor of Jamaica had been instructed that if any other power should take possession of Ruatan he was to demand the removal of the intruder, and, should the demand be disregarded, he was authorized to resort to forcible means for compelling withdrawal without further instructions.[122]

In a note to Clayton, dated April 15, Bulwer made known this view of his government, adding, " should any persons attempt to locate themselves therein and resist his [the governor of Jamaica's] request for their withdrawal, I deem it advisable to report to you at once the intelligence which H. M. Govt. has received knowing that you will take all the steps in your power to prevent the aggression of wh. H. M.'s Govt. has been informed." [123]

Clayton was much disconcerted by this communication which seemed to threaten disaster to the treaty just negotiated with Bulwer. For several days he delayed action, during which time the treaty was signed and sent to the Senate, but when it was under discussion by that body he called upon the British minister and asked that he cancel his note. An official message like the note, he explained, if permitted to stand, must be sent to Congress, and should this be done, some of the members would very possibly imagine that Great Britain was at that moment laying claim to new territories in America—a belief which, however erroneous, would affect the passing of the treaty now under their

[122] Palmerston to Bulwer, Mar. 14, 1850, F. O., Am., vol. 509, no. 25. See above, p. 39.
[123] Inclosure in Bulwer to Palmerston, April 16, 1850, F. O., Am., vol. 512, no. 63.

consideration. The reports of American designs upon Ruatan, Clayton stated, he believed were entirely incorrect.[124]

In consequence of Clayton's representations, Bulwer agreed to cancel his note of April 15,[125] and to accept from Clayton as satisfactory a private note to the effect that the American government had never desired to occupy, fortify, or settle any of the Bay Islands, that he, Clayton, had no knowledge, information, or belief that Americans desired to establish themselves there and that no attempt of American citizens to do so would receive countenance from their government.[126]

This indirection on the part of the American secretary of state, though it probably saved the treaty, played an important part in complicating English-American isthmian relations, as will appear later.

The treaty as altered by Bulwer met the approval of Palmerston, who stated that the government would ratify it.[127] But a suspicion that it was intended by the Americans to apply to Belize and the Bay Islands seems to have risen in Palmerston's mind—evidently in consequence of Clayton's attitude towards Bulwer's note of April 15—and made him anxious to guard against such a contingency. The sole object of the British in wishing to retain the Mosquito protectorate was to save the dignity of the government and perhaps to do their duty by the Indians ; but with Belize it was different ; the population there was almost wholly composed

---

[124] Bulwer to Palmerston, April 27, 1850, " Private and confidential ", F. O., Am., vol. 512.

[125] *Ibid.*

[126] Clayton to Bulwer, April 24, 1850, " Private ", *ibid.*

[127] *Parl. Papers*, 1856, *Coms.*, LX, " Correspondence with the United States respecting Central America ", 58.

of British subjects, the territory was desirable, and the full title to it was almost their own. The attempts to place it entirely under British sovereignty have been described. The Bay Islands also were prized by the British because of the fine harbors of Ruatan. Consequently, Palmerston was roused to precautionary measures. He instructed Bulwer to deliver to Clayton, at the time of exchanging ratifications, a declaration that "Her Majesty's Government do not understand the engagements of that Convention as applying to Her Majesty's settlement at Honduras, or to its dependencies."[128] Should the United States government object to receiving and assenting to this declaration, Bulwer was not to proceed to the exchange of ratifications without further instructions.[129]

Palmerston's declaration was regarded with much dissatisfaction by Clayton, to whom the treaty was already much less than he had hoped for and desired.[130] Consequently, for a time it was resolved to abandon the arrangement entirely.[131] Besides, the doubt regarding the efficacy of the treaty, for a time overcome in the Senate, had returned very strongly immediately after the vote was taken,[132] and King declared that if the document should be resubmitted for reconsideration in connection with Palmerston's statement, it would not receive a single vote.[133] But King seems to have convinced Clayton that the Senate did not regard the treaty as applying to Belize.[134]

[128] *Ibid.*, 59-60.   [129] *Ibid.*, 60.
[130] *U. S. Docs.*, ser. no. 694, doc. 13, p. 16.
[131] *Ibid.*
[132] Bulwer to Palmerston, Aug. 6, 1850, " Secret and confidential ", F. O., Am., vol. 514, no. 157.
[133] *Cong. Globe*, 32 Cong., 2 sess., 237.
[134] *Ibid.*, 250.

King suspected, however, that the object of the declaration was to obtain from the American government an acknowledgment of British title to the Belize territory,[135] and he was determined that no such admission should be made. Clayton also suspected the British of this design ; but, in view of his evasive arrangement with Bulwer to prevent British pretensions to the Bay Islands from defeating ratification of the treaty by the Senate, he was especially concerned over the elastic possibilities of the term " dependencies ", and believed that by this wording the British government aimed to insure its claims to the Bay Islands.[136]

After considerable discussion the American government decided to proceed with the ratification, but to present a counter-declaration, calculated to annul any effect intended to be produced by the statement of the British government.[137] This counter-declaration was carefully drawn up by Clayton, who consulted Johnson, the United States attorney-general, with regard to its phraseology.[138]

[135] *Cong. Globe,* 33 Cong., 1 sess., Appendix, 96.
[136] Bulwer to Palmerston, Aug. 6, 1850, " Secret and confidential ", F. O., Am., vol. 514. According to Bulwer, in a conversation during the period of negotiation Clayton had acknowledged Belize " with its dependencies, including two islands called Ruatan and Bonaca ", to be excluded from the terms of the treaty. Extract of memorandum inclosed by Bulwer in a private note to Webster, Aug. 17, 1850, Dept. of State, Notes to Dept., Gt. Brit., vol. 27. This statement appears inconsistent with some of Clayton's other statements and actions, but a knowledge of his equivocal conduct regarding the islands when the treaty was before the Senate makes it seem not unlikely that Bulwer reported the conversation correctly. Clayton possessed a wavering and contradictory disposition, qualities which were fully recognized by Bulwer. Bulwer to Palmerston, Mar. 2, 1850, " Private and confidential ", F. O., Am., vol. 512, no. 43; " Letters of Bancroft and Buchanan ", in *Am. Hist. Rev.,* V, 98. *Cf.* Crampton to Clarendon, Mar. 31, 1856, F. O., Am., vol. 642, no. 77; May 19, 1856, *ibid.,* vol. 643, no. 128; May 27, 1856, *ibid.*
[137] *U. S. Docs.,* ser. no. 694, doc. 13, pp. 16-17.
[138] *Ibid.,* p. 16.

On July 4, the day upon which the ratifications were exchanged, Clayton wrote to King with reference to the proposed counter-statement and asked for his permission to state that the true meaning of the treaty had been explained by him, King, to the Senate before the vote was taken.[139] To this King replied that the Senate " perfectly understood that the treaty did not include British Honduras ".[140]

Consequently, before the ratifications were exchanged that night Clayton handed to Bulwer a document which declared that the treaty was not understood by the British or American governments or by the negotiators—

to include the British settlement in Honduras (commonly called British Honduras, as distinct from the State of Honduras) nor the small islands in the neighborhood which may be known as its dependencies. To this settlement, and these islands, the treaty we negotiated was not intended by either of us to apply. The title to them it is now and has been my intention, throughout the negotiation, to leave, as the treaty leaves it, without denying, affirming, or in any way meddling with the same, just as it stood previously. The chairman of the Committee on Foreign Relations of the Senate, the Hon. William R. King, informs me that " the Senate perfectly understood that the treaty did not include British Honduras". It was understood to apply to, and does include all the Central American States of Guatemala, Honduras, San Salvador, Nicaragua, and Costa Rica with their just limits and proper dependencies.[141]

To this Bulwer replied in substance, that he understood Clayton's answer to the declaration of the British government as meaning that he, Clayton, fully recog-

[139] *Cong. Globe*, 32 Cong., 2 sess., 250.
[140] *Ibid.*
[141] *U. S. Docs.*, ser. no. 660, doc. 12, pp. 2-3.

nized that it was not the intention of the treaty to include the British settlement at Honduras, whatever might be included under the term, nor its dependencies, whatever they might be; and that British title to the settlement would not in any way be altered in consequence of the treaty.[142] Exchange of ratifications followed.[143]

Thus the treaty was concluded without the consent of the Senate to the declaration, and, in consequence, that declaration was obviously not an alteration of the treaty but was merely understood by the two negotiators as a " just specification of its meaning and intentions ".[144] However, the President and his cabinet,[145] as well as individual senators who were consulted, knew of the existence of the declaration before the treaty was ratified. Furthermore, the interpretation of the treaty held by the government must have become pretty well known to the Senate as a whole within a few days after it was concluded, for, on July 8, the *National Intelligencer* stated that the treaty neither recognized nor altered in any way the British title to Belize;[146] and the message of the President, of the fourteenth of the same month, transferring the treaty to the House of Representatives, contained more detailed expressions to the same effect.[147]

Although no discussion appears to have arisen at the time, in consequence of these post-ratification announcements, the Clayton-Bulwer treaty from the

[142] *Parl. Papers*, 1856, *Coms.*, LX, " Correspondence with the United States respecting Central America ", 63-64.

[143] *U. S. Docs.*, ser. no. 660, doc. 12, p. 4.

[144] Bulwer to Palmerston, Aug. 6, 1850, F. O., Am., vol. 514, no. 157.

[145] *Cong. Globe*, 32 Cong., 2 sess., 248.

[146] *Ibid.*, 249.   [147] *Ibid.*

first was unpopular in America. Its phraseology was vague and it did not directly abolish the Mosquito protectorate; hence it failed to convey the full assurance desired by the nation that British influence in Central America was absolutely obliterated. However, the American government believed that the peculiar wording of the first article had rendered the protectorate null; it felt that the agreement not to occupy, colonize, fortify, or exercise dominion was equivalent to an agreement to withdraw, for without the ability to do these things protection was impossible. To be sure, a nominal protectorate could exist under the treaty, but it was hoped that as the protectorate was utterly shorn of its power, the British government would entirely abandon it. This general view of the treaty was reflected in a letter written by Clayton to Squier when the treaty was before the Senate. He wrote:

I trust that means will speedily be adopted by Great Britain to extinguish the Indian title with the help of the Nicaraguans or the Company [148] within what we consider to be the limits of Nicaragua . . . Having always regarded an Indian title as a mere right of occupancy, we can never agree that such a title should be treated otherwise than as a thing to be extinguished at the will of the discoverer of the country. Upon the ratifying of the treaty, Great Britain will no longer have any interest to deny this principle which she had recognized in every other case in common with us. Her protectorate will be reduced to a shadow, "*Stat nominis umbra*," for she can neither occupy, fortify, colonize or exercise dominion or control in any part of the Mosquito coast or Central America. To attempt to do either of those things after the exchange of ratifications, would inevitably produce a rupture with the United States. [149]

[148] The canal company.
[149] Dept. of State, Inst., Am. States, vol. 15, pp. 105-106.

Reverdy Johnson, the attorney-general, interpreted the agreement in the same manner. On December 30, 1853, he wrote in a letter to Clayton:

> As one of the advisers of the President, I unhesitatingly gave him my opinion, that the treaty did effectually, to all intents and purposes, disarm the British protectorate in Central America and the Mosquito coast, although it did not abolish the protectorate in terms, nor was it thought advisable to do so *"in ipsissimis verbis"*. All that was desired by us was to extinguish British dominion over that country, whether held directly or indirectly—whether claimed by Great Britain in her own right, or in the right of the Indians.[150]

The correspondence upon the subject makes it clear that at the time of negotiation the British government agreed pretty closely with the United States as to the influence of the treaty upon the Mosquito protectorate[151]—an influence, however, which, strange to say, Bulwer, the British negotiator of the treaty, did not recognize as existing.[152] Though there was no feeling

[150] *U. S. Docs.,* ser. no. 694, doc. 13, p. 15. Though Johnson's letter was written more than three years after the ratification of the treaty, and during a controversy between the British and American governments over its interpretation, there is no reason to believe that the opinion of the Attorney-General here expressed differed in any degree from that held by him when the treaty was concluded.

[151] This will be brought out in the following chapters.

[152] On April 28, 1850, after the treaty was signed, Bulwer wrote to Palmerston: " I need not say that should your Lordship wish to make any further statement as to the views of Her Majesty's Government with regard to the protectorate of Mosquito, that statement can still be made; nothing in the present Convention is affirmed thereupon, but nothing is abandoned." *Parl. Papers,* 1856, *Coms.,* LX, " Correspondence with the United States respecting Central America ", 56.

In a memorandum of the negotiations kept for his own use Bulwer wrote: " The treaty, indeed, was intended to apply to future and not to present possessions in Central America; so that without any question as to what Central America is, H. M.'s settlement in Honduras and its dependencies are not included in the said treaty." Extract of Memorandum inclosed by Bulwer in a private note to Webster, Aug. 17, 1850, Dept. of State, Notes to Dept., Gt. Brit., vol. 27.

that the protectorate over the Mosquitos had been abandoned, it was fully realized that the relations with the Indians had been decidedly weakened.[153] Through the persistence of Clayton the substance of the protectorate had been taken away, though the form, with the pride of the British, had been preserved by Bulwer's shrewd diplomacy.

Just what either government thought would be the effect of the treaty upon British occupation of Belize and the Bay Islands, it is impossible to say, for no expression of opinion upon this point seems to have been recorded at this time. It seems fair to presume, however, that, after the British declaration regarding Belize had been exchanged for the American counter-declaration, both governments were uncertain as to what had actually been lost or won by the transaction; but that both were determined to get the most possible out of the arrangement in the execution of their respective policies. The effect of this procedure will appear later.

[153] During the negotiation of the Clayton-Bulwer treaty, Chatfield endeavored to form a treaty with Honduras regarding the Mosquito boundary at the north. The first draft of the agreement bore the Queen's name as one of the parties to the agreement. Inclosure in Palmerston to Chatfield, Mar. 30, 1850, F. O., Cen. Am., vol. 63, no. 11. Later, in June, this was changed by order of the British government, and the name of the Mosquito king was substituted, on the ground that the other form was not consistent with the language of the treaty with the United States, which engaged both parties not to " assume or exercise any dominion over Mosquito coast ", etc. Palmerston to Chatfield, June 20, 1850, and inclosure, *ibid.*, no. 21, and Foreign Office notes of June 6 and 7, 1850, *ibid.*, vol. 63.

CHAPTER IV.

Attempts at Readjustment Under the New Treaty, 1850-1852.

The negotiation of the Clayton-Bulwer treaty was brought to a successful conclusion by careful concentration upon the points of agreement between the two contracting parties, and studied avoidance of the larger Central American question, regarding which differences were well known to exist. To carry out the spirit of the treaty in its application to the Mosquitos was far more difficult, but it was a task which the British government honestly planned to attempt, even before ratifications were exchanged.

When the treaty was under consideration of the Senate, Bulwer wrote to Palmerston:

> You will best judge if anything, and if anything what, is to be done as to the remaining difference between Nicaragua and Mosquito, on which the Government of Her Majesty and that of the United States still entertain opposite opinions, although these opinions are, by our Treaty, restrained or withdrawn from the necessity of being carried out into any act of hostility.[1]

Though the British government, he added, no longer had any interest in maintaining the Mosquitos where they were or in protecting them in that particular locality, still they could not give up the protectorate or

---

[1] *Parl. Papers,* 1856, *Coms.,* LX, "Correspondence with the United States respecting Central America ", 56.

change the condition of things on which it existed if pressed to do so in a disagreeable way; yet the question might be finally settled with a friendly power on general and friendly grounds. If the pending treaty with the United States, and that between the latter and Nicaragua could be completed without any assertion of the right of Nicaragua over the Mosquito territory, a friendly arrangement might be made with the United States for the withdrawal of the Mosquitos from the vicinity of the canal. The Mosquito title might be purchased and the Indians reorganized in a particular district.[2]

In reply to these suggestions, Palmerston wrote:

Her Majesty's government feel that the present state of things in regard to the Mosquito Territory, and especially with regard to the Port of Grey Town, is in many respects inconvenient, and not entirely in conformity with the true spirit and meaning of the Convention just concluded between Great Britain and the United States. The British government is bound in honor to protect the Mosquitos, but her Majesty's government are of the opinion that the protection of Great Britain might be afforded to that nation as effectually in a different way, and without any direct interference of any agent of the British Government in the internal affairs of that country.

In accordance with this idea, he explained, the boundaries of the Mosquito territory might be adjusted by Great Britain in co-operation with the United States. In order to meet the terms of the treaty, and yet to secure for Greytown a well-organized government, the boundary dispute between Mosquito and Costa Rica might be so arranged as to give the port, with a suffi-

[2] *Ibid.*, 56-57.

cient district to the north of it, to the latter.[3] In return for the cession, Palmerston wrote, the Mosquitos should be given some suitable and adequate compensation.[4] In combination with these arrangements, he thought that the general differences between Costa Rica and Nicaragua might be settled by the good offices of the British and American governments.[5] The basis of such arrangement might be the decision in favor of Nicaragua of some of the disputed questions of boundary on the western side of the isthmus.[6]

Bulwer knew that the American government was interested in securing a favorable canal treaty from Nicaragua, and therefore would not be likely to make any disagreeable suggestions to her while the Squier treaty was in abeyance. Consequently, he approached Clayton cautiously, remarking that if the American government would agree to the transfer of Greytown to Costa Rica in return for some cession of other disputed territory he would suggest such an arrangement to Palmerston.[7] However, as he suspected would be the case, Clayton was opposed to such a disposal of the question.[8] Bulwer therefore became convinced that the most urgent need at that time was to prevent the United States from recognizing by treaty the rights of

[3] F. O., Am., vol. 509, no. 58. Though Costa Rica did possess a more stable government than Nicaragua, the fact that Great Britain was a friend of the former, while bad feeling existed between herself and the latter, which looked towards the United States for protection, undoubtedly also influenced Palmerston in considering the disposal of Greytown.

[4] *Parl. Papers,* 1856, *Coms.,* LX, " Correspondence with the United States respecting Central America ", 58-59.

[5] F. O., Am., vol. 509, no. 59.

[6] *Ibid.*

[7] Bulwer to Palmerston, July 1, 1850, " Private and confidential ", F. O., Am., vol. 513.

[8] *Ibid.*

Nicaragua over the San Juan, and worked with that end in view.[9]

With the accession of President Fillmore, Daniel Webster became secretary of state, and as the Clayton-Bulwer treaty was by this time ratified, discussions more to the point regarding the disposal of affairs in Central America seemed possible. Shortly after the ratification, Molina, the Costa Rican representative, informed Palmerston that his government was willing to submit the boundary dispute with Nicaragua to the joint mediation or arbitration of the United States and Great Britain,[10] and would be bound by the decision of those governments.[11] Thereupon Palmerston communicated Molina's message to Bulwer with instructions to submit the proposal to the United States government.[12] The matter was made known to Webster by Bulwer,[13] who at the same time suggested the desirability of speedily settling by joint mediation all of the territorial differences between Mosquito, Costa Rica, and Nicaragua.[14]

Webster replied that it would be necessary to know what the Nicaraguans would consent to before the United States government, which was in some degree compromised with respect to their claims by the expression of its opinions, could decide what would be the best course. He added, however, that he entirely agreed in the spirit of the plan suggested by Palmerston, and stated that he would recommend the Senate to do nothing for the time being with regard to the

[9] *Ibid.*
[10] This was in reply to an offer made by Palmerston. *Parl. Papers,* 1856, *Coms.,* LX, " Correspondence with the United States respecting Central America ", 65.
[11] *Ibid.,* 65-66.   [12] *Ibid.,* 67.   [13] *Ibid.,* 68.   [14] *Ibid.,* 67.

Squier treaty,[15] to which Bulwer had called attention because it contained certain points objectionable to the British government.[16]

But the situation in Central America was such as to make a prompt settlement very difficult, if not impossible. Political conditions in Nicaragua had grown worse and the government had been brought very much under the influence of the canal company,[17] an agent of which was reported as trying to induce the Nicaraguans to recapture San Juan.[18] This town[19] was at the time nominally under Mosquito sovereignty, but really governed by the British consul, who was virtually dictator[20] and, as representative of the arch-enemy, was cordially hated by the Nicaraguans. To avert danger of an attack, British war ships were ordered to visit the port,[21] and after a time one or two vessels were kept constantly in the harbor.[22] The boundary dispute between Costa Rica and Nicaragua had also grown more bitter, and war between the two threatened to increase the confusion.[23]

More serious still was the fact that communication with the British and American agents in Central Amer-

---

[15] *Parl. Papers*, 1856, *Coms.*, LX, " Correspondence with the United States respecting Central America ", 68-69.

[16] *Ibid.*, 70-72.

[17] Bulwer to Palmerston, Sept. 29, 1850, " Private and confidential ", F. O., Am., vol. 515, no. 189.

[18] *Parl. Papers*, 1856 *Coms.* LX, " Correspondence with the United States respecting Central America ", 90.

[19] In the autumn of 1850 the place contained fifty or sixty houses with a population of about three hundred. Squier, *Nicaragua*, I, 72-73.

[20] Froebel, *Seven Years' Travel in Central America*, 14; Squier, *Nicaragua*, I, 79.

[21] *Parl. Papers*, 1856, *Coms.*, LX, " Correspondence with the United States respecting Central America ", 90-91.

[22] Squier, *Nicaragua*, I, 79.

[23] *Parl. Papers*, 1856, *Coms.*, LX, " Correspondence with the United States respecting Central America ", 95.

ica was so difficult that it was almost impossible for
their governments to keep in touch with or control
them. The actions of Chatfield and Squier in particular, both of whom were lacking in tact and judgment
and were exceedingly jealous of each other's intentions,
often threatened to cause trouble for the countries
which they represented. Apparently unaware of the
opinion held at Washington regarding his treaty for
the cession of Tigre, Squier seized the island shortly
after its evacuation by the British,[24] and for many
months the American flag floated over it, regardless of
the fact that the Honduras legislature had disavowed
the treaty of cession.[25] Chatfield, on the other hand,
seemed finally to lose all interest in making Tigre British territory, but busied himself with various other
violent acts calculated to force the Central American
states to pay their long-standing debts. His efforts
with Nicaragua and Costa Rica availed little, however,
for both states united in refusing payment until the
British acknowledged their rights to Mosquito Shore.[26]
Furthermore, scarcely had the terms of the Clayton-
Bulwer treaty become known before the two agents
began to rouse irritation by their extreme and contradictory interpretations of that instrument, as to the
peculiar advantages conferred by it upon their respective governments.[27] As a result of his unsatisfactory

---

[24] *Ibid.*, 61.   [25] *Ibid.*, 94-95.
[26] Hall to Macdonald, Dec. 8, 1841, F. O., Cen. Am., vol. 25; Chatfield
to Palmerston, Nov. 6, 1850, *ibid.*, vol. 66, no. 104. Spain, by a treaty
with Nicaragua, made July 25, 1850, acknowledged the exclusive claims
of the latter to the sovereignty of Mosquito coast. Chatfield to
Palmerston, Oct. 9, 1850, *ibid.*, vol. 65, no. 87.
[27] Inclosure in Chatfield to Palmerston, July 1, 1850, *ibid.*, vol. 64;
Chatfield to Palmerston, Aug. 20, 1850, *ibid.*, vol. 65, no. 58; Bulwer to
Palmerston, Mar. 10, 1851, F. O., Am., vol. 528, no. 49.

conduct, Squier was recalled in the autumn of 1850,[28] and was succeeded by Kerr,[29] who was of a less pugnacious disposition.[30] This change relieved matters but little, however, for Chatfield remained and kept up the condition of semi-warfare in Central America,[31] and consequently created ill-feeling in the United States against England. But he too was removed, in January, 1852,[32] presumably in consequence of repeated complaints by the American government,[33] and after his departure more pacific relations prevailed between British and American representatives on the isthmus.

Notwithstanding these various obstacles, Bulwer tried to keep the question of a Central American settlement to the front, for he felt that better and fairer terms, from a British viewpoint, could be obtained from Webster than from any other secretary of state.[34] But in consequence of Webster's determination to consider Nicaragua's wishes in the matter, no progress was made for several months. The Nicaraguan government had promised to send a representative to Washington, but none had arrived.[35] Should none be sent, Webster assured Bulwer, it was the intention of the American government to establish diplomatic relations

[28] Bulwer to Palmerston, Oct. 7, 1850, *ibid.*, vol. 515, no. 208.

[29] *U. S. Docs.*, ser. no. 819, doc. 25, pp. 47-48.

[30] Chatfield to Palmerston, Oct. 25, 1851, F. O., Cen. Am., vol. 72, no. 126.

[31] Bulwer to Palmerston, Jan. 28, 1851, F. O., Am., vol. 527, no. 20; Bulwer to Palmerston, Mar. 10, 1851, *ibid.*, vol. 528, no. 49.

[32] Granville to Chatfield, Jan. 15, 1852, F. O., Cen. Am., vol. 76, no. 2; Bulwer to Palmerston, June 22, 1851, F. O., Am., vol. 529, no. 112.

[33] Bulwer to Palmerston, Jan. 28, 1851, *ibid.*, vol. 527, no. 20; Mar. 10, 1851, *ibid.*, vol. 528, no. 49.

[34] White to Palmerston, Nov. 12, 1851, *ibid.*, vol. 537; Bulwer to Palmerston, May 19, 1851, *ibid.*, vol. 528, no. 98.

[35] *Parl. Papers*, 1856, *Coms.*, LX, " Correspondence with the United States respecting Central America ", 95.

with Nicaragua by appointing an agent to that government at once.[36]

While the American government waited to hear from Nicaragua, Bulwer resumed the discussion of terms of settlement, and finally persuaded Webster to agree not to recognize the exclusive right of Nicaragua over the San Juan River or to make more than a commercial treaty with that government; but Webster would not consent to the cession of Greytown to Costa Rica.[37] Bulwer therefore suggested to Palmerston that the town be given to Nicaragua, in return for compensation to the Mosquitos and to Costa Rica ;[38] and Palmerston agreed to this plan, provided insurmountable difficulties prevented the transfer of the port to Costa Rica.[39]

Finally Marcoleta arrived as representative of the Nicaraguan government and expressed a desire to form commercial treaties with Great Britain and with the United States.[40] Shortly afterwards he began negotiations for the latter purpose with Webster.[41] Meanwhile the discussion of the disputed points in connection with Mosquito was vigorously pursued by Webster and Bulwer, and the latter began to hope for a speedy termination of the whole question.[42] However, when the two negotiators had almost reached an agreement regarding Greytown,[43] Marcoleta displayed a sudden change of mind,[44] and declared himself unwilling to sign any commercial treaty with England, or even with

[36] *Ibid.*   [37] *Ibid.,* 96-97.   [38] *Ibid.*   [39] *Ibid.,* 98.
[40] *Ibid.*   [41] *Ibid.*   [42] *Ibid.*   [43] *Ibid.,* 98-99.
[44] The change in Marcoleta was evidently due to criticism from his government because of a willingness to make concessions, which he had at first shown, and to a correspondence which he had recently carried on with Senator Douglas, who was an enemy of any compromise with England. Bulwer to Palmerston, July 28, 1851, F. O., Am., vol. 529, no. 132.

the United States unless something respecting Greytown and the Mosquito territory was at the same time settled.[45]

This stand of the Nicaraguan agent produced a change in Webster, who, while still expressing adherence to his former opinions, seemed reluctant to act upon them.[46] Bulwer, desirous of securing some definite result, drew up a statement of the opinions expressed by himself and Webster, which the latter after some reflection finally refused to sign.[47] Then Bulwer proposed a meeting of Marcoleta, Molina (the Costa Rican minister), Webster, and himself for the purpose of trying to reach satisfactory terms. The meeting was held July 11, but it resulted in nothing, as the Nicaraguan minister refused to accept any arrangement suggested by Bulwer, and offered instead proposals from his own government,[48] which Bulwer in turn refused to consider.[49] This change in affairs again brought negotiations to a standstill, for Marcoleta had no powers to go beyond the proposals he had made.[50] Some time before, Crampton had arrived at Washington for the purpose of relieving Bulwer, but at Webster's request the latter had consented to remain longer

[45] *Parl. Papers*, 1856, *Coms.*, LX, "Correspondence with the United States respecting Central America ", 99.

[46] *Ibid.*

[47] *Ibid.* Webster's reluctance was certainly produced to some extent by the change in Marcoleta; but public criticism of his foreign policy may also have caused him to hesitate. Bulwer to Palmerston, April 7, 1851, F. O., Am., vol. 528, no. 69.

[48] *Parl. Papers*, 1856, *Coms.*, "Correspondence with the United States respecting Central America ", 99. Marcoleta's proposals differed from those of Bulwer in that they provided for no compensation to the Mosquitos in return for Greytown, which, by both projects was to go to Nicaragua; and the boundary dispute between the latter and Costa Rica was to be settled by arbitration. *Ibid.*, 100.

[49] *Ibid.*, 98. [50] *Ibid.*, 100.

in order to try to settle the Mosquito difficulty.[51] Now, as no progress could be made until the Nicaraguan government was again heard from, Bulwer returned home in August, 1851.[52]

During the period of delay an event occurred which created considerable feeling against England in the United States, and seriously threatened the friendly relations which the Clayton-Bulwer treaty had temporarily established. On November 21, 1851, the *Prometheus,* a vessel belonging to the Atlantic and Pacific Ship-Canal Company, was in Greytown harbor, about to leave for New York.[53] For some time harbor dues[54] had been levied by the municipal authorities upon all vessels entering the port except the English steamers which carried the mail. All had fulfilled the requirement except the *Prometheus,* which had made several trips, each time steadily refusing to meet the demands of the port officials, on the ground that the company did not recognize the Mosquito authorities.[55] On the occasion in question, after the usual bill of charges, plus

[51] Bulwer to Palmerston, May 25, 1851, F. O., Am., vol. 528, no. 100.
[52] *Dic. Nat. Biog.,* XIII, 6.
[53] *Parl. Papers,* 1856, *Coms.,* LX, " Correspondence with the United States respecting Central America ", 111.
[54] This was a port charge levied solely by the local officials in order to meet expenses connected with the harbor. *U. S. Docs.,* ser. no. 618, doc. 30, p. 5. In accordance with the provisions of the Clayton-Bulwer treaty, Palmerston, in the autumn of 1850, had instructed the Mosquito authorities to make Greytown a free port. Palmerston to Bulwer, Nov. 15, 1850, F. O., Am., vol. 510, no. 150. These instructions had been obeyed, and since January 1, 1851, no duties had been levied by the representatives of the Mosquito government upon vessels or goods. *U. S. Docs.,* ser. no. 618, doc. 30, p. 5.
[55] It should be remembered that the canal company had obtained its charter and contract from the Nicaraguan government. The contract had granted the company the use of the river and harbor " free of all duties or charges of any kind whatsoever ". *Parl. Papers,* 1856, *Coms.,* LX, " Correspondence with the United States respecting Central America ", 22.

arrears, had been presented and payment refused, a warrant was issued for the arrest of Churchill, the captain of the vessel, for the debt. Local officials went aboard and served the warrant, but Churchill still resisted. The officials, after giving notice that the vessel would not be permitted to leave until the debt was paid, went ashore. The captain, however, ignored the threat and in a few minutes his vessel was dropping down the harbor.[56] The British brig-of-war *Express* happened to be in the port at the time and its captain, Fead, had been requested by Green, the British consul, to detain the *Prometheus* in case the dues were not paid.[57] Accordingly the *Express* immediately followed the departing vessel and at Green's orders two shots were fired across her bows. The *Prometheus* then returned to her place of anchorage, and the president of the canal company, Cornelius Vanderbilt, who happened to be aboard, went ashore and paid the debt. The vessel was then permitted to proceed on her voyage.[58]

On December 1, the board of directors of the canal company met and drew up resolutions regarding the affair, in which they claimed the interference and protection of the United States government.[59] White, the counsel for the company, sent resolutions, accompanied by a letter calling attention to Green's share in detaining the vessel, to the United States government.[60] Promptly upon receiving intelligence of the matter, the Navy Department ordered Commodore Parker,

---

[56] *Parl. Papers*, 1856, *Coms.*, LX, " Correspondence with the United States respecting Central America ", 111.

[57] *Ibid.*, 113.

[58] *Ibid.*, 111; *U. S. Docs.*, ser. no. 614, doc. 6, pp. 2-3.

[59] *Ibid.*, p. 3.   [60] *Ibid.*, p. 2.

commander of the home squadron, to leave as soon as possible for San Juan in order to protect American interests there.[61] Parker was instructed to assure the authorities of the port, however, that the American government would not justify the non-payment of any lawful and proper port dues on the part of merchant vessels.[62] On the same date Webster sent a despatch to Lawrence calling his attention to the action of the British officials at San Juan and directing him to inquire of Palmerston whether the captain of the *Express* had acted under orders from his government, and whether his course was approved. Should Palmerston's reply be in the affirmative, Lawrence was to state that the President would consider the proceeding a violation of the treaty of April 19, 1850.[63]

The resignation of Palmerston just when Lawrence presented his communication prevented a prompt reply from the British government,[64] but on December 30, immediately after his installation in the Foreign Office, Granville wrote to Lawrence stating that Fead's act was not in consequence of any orders from his government, and that as soon as word should be received from Greytown a further statement would be made. In the meanwhile Lawrence might rest assured that it was " far from the intention of her Majesty's government to authorize any proceeding at variance with the stipulations of the treaty of Washington of the 19th of April, 1850." [65] Upon receipt of this note Lawrence expressed his regret that the British government had not yet received the official intelligence which would enable it to disavow the act of the *Express*.[66] To this

[61] *Ibid.*, p. 4.   [62] *Ibid.*   [63] *Ibid.*, ser. no. 618, doc. 30, pp. 1-2.
[64] *Ibid.*, p. 4.   [65] *Ibid.*, pp. 5-6.   [66] *Ibid.*, p. 6.

Granville replied that should the circumstances of the affair be shown to be such as were described by the American minister, the British government would at once disavow it.[67]

During this period of suspense the affair was taken up in an angry manner in the United States by the Democratic party and the press, and matters were becoming serious [68] when Crampton received a letter from Vice-Admiral Seymour of the British navy, which relieved the situation.   Seymour stated that his instructions to the commander of the Jamaica division of the navy did not sanction such an act as Fead had committed, and that therefore he had sent word to Fead to desist from enforcing the payment of dues at Greytown until further orders.   Seymour also stated that Green, too, had apparently acted without instructions.[69]   Crampton greatly relieved Webster's anxiety by reading portions of this timely letter to him, and he, Webster, asked Crampton to inform Seymour that the United States government highly appreciated the friendly and considerate spirit in which he had acted.[70]

On December 20, Seymour had written to the Admiralty of the affair and explained the instructions which he had given regarding Greytown.[71]   Through this letter Granville received his first official information regarding the matter.[72]   On January 10, 1852, immediately upon the receipt of it, he wrote to Lawrence making known the attitude taken by the Vice-Admiral, and stating that the British government entirely ap-

[67] U. S. Docs., ser. no. 618, doc. 30, pp. 6-7.
[68] Parl. Papers, 1856, Coms., LX, " Correspondence with the United States respecting Central America ", 122.
[69] Ibid., 121.   [70] Ibid., 122.   [71] Ibid., 121.
[72] U. S. Docs., ser. no. 618, doc. 30, pp. 7-8.

proved of the latter's conduct, and disavowed the acts of Green and Fead.[73]

Lawrence expressed his gratification at the promptness with which the disavowal had followed the receipt of Seymour's report and stated that he had no doubt but that the apology would be received by his government in the same spirit which had dictated it on the part of Great Britain.[74] Lawrence's earlier report of the attitude taken by Granville had been received by Webster with much satisfaction,[75] and after notice of the disavowal and apology had reached him he expressed his belief that the British government had "behaved with great honor and justice in the affair of the *Prometheus*".[76] Thus the matter ended peaceably, and with friendly feelings between the two governments.

But the excitement growing out of the affair showed the constant danger in delaying a settlement regarding the Mosquito question and created greater anxiety on both sides for a resumption of negotiations.[77] Webster now, apparently for the first time, showed a real interest in effecting an adjustment. While writing to Lawrence shortly before the news of the disavowal was received, he expressed his fears for the future should the arrangement of matters in dispute with England much longer be postponed.[78] Moreover, Palmerston's withdrawal from the government was considered as particularly favorable to American interests, and hence to an adjustment.[79] It was now believed that England

[73] *Ibid.* [74] *Ibid.*, pp. 8-9.
[75] Webster, *Writings and Speeches*, XVI, 635.
[76] Curtis, *Daniel Webster*, II, 596.
[77] *Parl. Papers*, 1856, *Coms.*, "Correspondence with the United States respecting Central America", 117, 123-124.
[78] Webster, *Writings and Speeches*, XVI, 634-635.
[79] *Ibid.*, XVIII, 504, 510.

had a strong desire to settle all pending questions [80] and that she would never be in a better humor for the purpose.[81] A strong effort was made to have Bulwer return to the country for the purpose of resuming the negotiations,[82] but circumstances prevented,[83] so that duty fell to Crampton.

Matters, however, were in such confusion in Nicaragua that it seemed impossible to make the diplomatic connections necessary for consulting her with reference to terms. It was just at this time that the three states of Honduras, Nicaragua, and Salvador were making an effort to federate, but affairs were so unstable as to force Marcoleta to acknowledge that there was no government which he could properly represent, or which could properly give him instructions; [84] and Kerr, the American minister, who had been in Nicaragua for several months, reported that he had not yet been able to find any authority to which he could present his credentials.[85]

But upon reflection the American government had decided that until the boundary dispute between Nicaragua and Costa Rica was settled, and until it was determined just where the proposed canal should run, no guarantee of sovereignty over the canal line could be given to Nicaragua; for such a guarantee, should the route run on the south side of the river—which was claimed by Costa Rica—would only complicate diffi-

---

[80] Curtis, *Daniel Webster*, II, 593.
[81] Webster, *Writings and Speeches*, XVIII, 525.
[82] Curtis, *Daniel Webster*, II, 593.
[83] *Ibid.*, 593-596.
[84] Webster, *Writings and Speeches*, XVI, 636; *U. S. Docs.*, ser. no. 819, doc. 25, p. 55.
[85] *Ibid.*

culties.[86] Hence, as a canal treaty with Nicaragua must be an arrangement of the indefinite future, the friendship of that nation was not now so eagerly sought. This fact, as well as the urgency for the settlement of the Mosquito question and the hopelessness of early restoration of diplomatic relations with Nicaragua, made Webster willing to consider terms, independently of that state. The idea now was to reach an agreement satisfactory to the British and American governments, which could become the basis for a quadripartite treaty.[87]

After Webster had expressed a desire to come to an understanding over the question,[88] Granville, on January 23, 1852, instructed Crampton to enter into a discussion with him, and outlined various plans of settlement to be proposed to the American secretary of state. It was the desire of the British government, Granville wrote, that the whole Mosquito question should be settled, and especially that it should be settled in such a manner as to secure the cordial assent and good will of the United States. The only stipulation upon which the government insisted was that the settlement be consistent with British honor.[89]

But the change which almost immediately again took place in the Foreign Office, as well as the preoccupation of Webster with other matters,[90] prevented any definite progress from being made before events at Greytown once more attracted attention to that place.

[86] *U. S. Docs.*, ser. no. 819, doc. 25, pp. 47-48.
[87] Webster, *Writings and Speeches*, XIV, 480.
[88] *Parl. Papers*, 1856, *Coms.*, LX " Correspondence with the United States respecting Central America ", 117.
[89] *Ibid.*, 124-126.
[90] *Ibid.*, 131, 143, 144, 146.

The difficulty this time rose from the instructions given Commodore Parker before his departure for Greytown. These had stated that the United States acknowledged no right in the government or vessels of Great Britain to exercise any police or supervision over American merchant vessels in Nicaragua or elsewhere, out of British dominions; on the contrary, the first article of the convention between the United States and Great Britain relative to Nicaragua, signed April 19, 1850, excluded each of the contracting parties from assuming or exercising any dominion over Nicaragua, Costa Rica, the Mosquito coast, or any part of Central America.[91]

This view of the matter was presented by Parker to Captain Fead, who in turn reported it to his government. Upon receipt of Fead's letter, Granville wrote in an injured tone to Crampton with regard to Parker's language:

Her Majesty's Government cannot admit such an interpretation of the Convention of the 19th of April, by which, as understood by Her Majesty's Government, Great Britain is not precluded from protecting the Mosquitos but is only restricted from occupying, fortifying, or colonizing, or of assuming or exercising any dominion over the Mosquito Coast or any part of Central America; and Her Majesty's Government will therefore resist any attempt on the part of Nicaragua or any other Power to take possession of Greytown, or of any portion of the Mosquito territory, until some arrangement is concluded between Great Britain and the United States.[92]

With his letter Granville inclosed a report from Seymour, showing matters to be in a critical condition at Greytown. The language of some of Parker's officers

[91] *U. S. Docs.,* ser. no. 614, doc. 6, p. 4.
[92] *Parl. Papers,* 1856, *Coms.,* LX, " Correspondence with the United States respecting Central America ", 127.

was of so unfriendly a nature as to cause the British
officers at the place to fear that they would further a
threatened attack on the port by the Nicaraguans. In
consequence of these demonstrations, Seymour had
ordered an additional vessel to Greytown.[93]

With reference to this situation, Granville stated that
in order to maintain a good understanding between the
two countries it was desirable that, until a final settlement could be reached, a provisional agreement be
made, by which, without entering into any question of
right of possession, both parties should recognize the
existing government of Greytown as a merely *de facto*
body, existing there for the benefit of commerce and
the maintenance of order; and that in accordance with
this agreement British subjects and American citizens
at Greytown be enjoined to respect the local laws and
pay the local port dues, and the commanders of British
and American vessels stationed or arriving at the port
be instructed to enforce respect to these laws and regulations.[94]

The view given by Granville as to the bearing of the
Clayton-Bulwer treaty upon the Mosquito protectorate
is of interest because it is the first expression of opinion
upon the subject exchanged between the two governments and is a slight hint of the long and bitter discussions over the interpretation of the treaty which were
to come with more aggressive administrations in England and the United States. But at this time no discussion resulted, for when Crampton called Webster's
attention to the matter, the Secretary of State replied
that he by no means held the doctrine, which, from the
terms of the Foreign Secretary's letter, the British

[93] *Ibid.*, 128. [94] *Ibid.*, 127-128.

government seemed to infer was that held by the American government. On the contrary, he said, he was " well aware that each Government still held its own opinion as to the rights of Nicaragua and Mosquito to Greytown " and that it was for the purpose of removing and reconciling these recognized differences of opinion that he was engaged in negotiations upon the subject with the British minister.[95] Furthermore, Webster received with favor Granville's proposal to recognize the *de facto* government at Greytown.[96] Therefore, in accordance with a suggestion from Webster, identical instructions, with full power to come to an agreement and execute the details of the arrangement, were sent to Parker and Seymour by their respective governments.[97]

But before the instructions for this mutual arrangement were given, another event took place at the storm-center, which threatened further to embarrass the situation. On February 28 there met in San Juan a body of men largely composed of Americans—resident merchants [98] and adventurers, pausing on their way to California.[99] This assemblage passed resolutions expressing a desire for a more satisfactory government than that existing under the Anglo-Mosquito authorities, and indicating the determination to establish a new government based upon power to be obtained from Nicaragua, which was declared to be the rightful owner of the territory. In accordance with the resolutions, a committee of fifteen was appointed with instructions to

[95] *Parl. Papers*, 1856, *Coms.*, LX, " Correspondence with the United States respecting Central America ", 134.
[96] *Ibid.*   [97] *Ibid.*, 134-137.   [98] *Ibid.*, 110-112, 139.
[99] *Ibid.*, 137, 151.

proceed to Nicaragua and secure a charter of incorporation.[100]

Crampton, upon learning of these proceedings, immediately realized that the plans of the Americans could not be carried into effect without the violent expulsion of the existing authorities at Greytown—an event likely to cause misunderstandings or collisions between the British and American naval officers at the port, and, consequently, bad feeling between their governments.[101] Therefore, he promptly communicated with Webster, and the two agreed upon a set of instructions which was sent to the British and American naval officers stationed at Greytown.[102] These instructions were similar to those recently furnished to Parker and Seymour,[103] who were at the time so far apart that it would be long before they could meet and come to an agreement.[104] This prompt action and the good judgment of the acting British consul at Greytown [105] apparently convinced the disaffected Americans that they could not count on any support from their government, and caused their plans to come to nothing.[106]

But the increase of immigration to the California gold fields and the popularity of the Nicaragua route had in four years' time quite changed the character of the population of Greytown, as well as greatly added to its numbers.[107] The American residents, who were the most numerous,[108] complained of British influence and attributed the difficulties which constantly rose in the town, not to Mosquito, but to British interference.[109] Therefore, Green, who acted as British consul and agent for the Mosquito king, and was in the latter capacity

[100] *Ibid.*, 138-139.   [101] *Ibid.*, 137.   [102] *Ibid.*   [103] *Ibid.*, 140-142.
[104] *Ibid.*, 137.   [105] *Ibid.*, 150-152.   [106] *Ibid.*, 151-152.   [107] *Ibid.*, 169.
[108] *Ibid.*, 168.   [109] *Ibid.*, 168-169.

chairman of the town council,[110] decided to remove the cause of friction by withdrawing from all direct interference with the management of the local government.[111] He was very probably also moved to this resolve by fear of another attempt such as that made in February to overthrow Mosquito sovereignty at Greytown and establish that of Nicaragua. Consequently, on April 1, he called a meeting of the inhabitants and transferred to them the power of self-government.[112] The result was the establishment of a free town corresponding in a small way to the German cities of Hamburg or Bremen.[113] A new constitution was formed, and under it new officers were elected.[114] The inhabitants, who preferred a government of their own to being under the dominion of Nicaragua, now unanimously expressed a dislike for that state and declared their intention of forcibly resisting any attempt of the Nicaraguans to occupy the place.[115] However, they had no objection to the nominal supremacy of the Mosquito king, and permitted his flag to fly over the town.[116]

While the accidental discovery of gold in the California Sierras was thus causing the cessation of active British interference at Greytown, negotiations for the final disposal of the Mosquito question had made some headway. At Webster's request, Crampton had outlined a plan for the settlement of the dispute, to which the British government would agree. This provided for the cession of Greytown and a district to the north of it to Nicaragua, in return for a sum of money to be paid to the Mosquitos; for the establishment of a

[110] *Parl. Papers,* 1856, *Coms.,* LX, " Correspondence with the United States respecting Central America ", 168-169.
[111] *Ibid.*   [112] *Ibid.,* 169.   [113] *Ibid.,* 168, 169.
[114] *Ibid.,* 169-173.   [115] *Ibid.,* 169-170.   [116] *Ibid.,* 168, 188.

definite boundary for the remainder of the Mosquito territory wherein the rights of the Indians were to be respected; and for the settlement of the boundary dispute by giving to Costa Rica the district of Guanacaste and all territory south of the San Juan, together with a limited right of navigation of the river.[117] After a conference upon the matter, Webster failed to approve of the arrangement, and seemed inclined to the cession of Greytown to Nicaragua without an equivalent, as Nicaragua was without funds; and he proposed the recommendation of union between the Nicaraguans and Mosquitos, the latter becoming Nicaraguan citizens. Crampton on his part objected to this plan as inadvisable and inconsistent with the position which the British had always held in regard to Mosquito, a position from which, he said, Webster must feel they could not honorably recede.[118] Finally Webster again told him to draw up the articles in a manner acceptable to the British government, and to add such improvements and conditions as should occur to him.[119] Crampton did this,[120] modifying his project in the hope of meeting the most serious objections of the United States.[121] This project he sent to his government, which, after making some slight modifications, returned the articles with its approval.[122] The document then became the basis of a plan of settlement.

There is no evidence that in the negotiations which followed Webster made any attempt to force the British out of Central America. The Fillmore administration restricted its interest in that region almost wholly

[117] *Ibid.*, 142-143.   [118] *Ibid.*, 143.   [119] *Ibid.*, 144.
[120] *Ibid.*, 144-146.   [121] *Ibid.*, 144.   [122] *Ibid.*, 147-150.

to gaining protection for the transisthmian canal,[123] though it had no intention of recognizing the Mosquito kingdom.[124] The British, on the other hand, took the same attitude as during the negotiation of the Clayton-Bulwer treaty. The aim was to effect a settlement entirely satisfactory to the United States, and at the same time to save what the British government called its "honour", in connection with the Mosquito protectorate and the Mosquito claims. Great Britain no longer harbored selfish designs in connection with her former allies; but it was necessary that the Indians be secured from the possible tyranny of Nicaragua. The object of the supplementary project was to effect this, and there is no reason to doubt that the British intended to withdraw all of their officials from the Mosquito territory, should the treaty, of which the project was meant to become a basis, be ratified.[125] However, out of regard for British pride no concession could be made to the Nicaraguan government which could possibly be interpreted as an acknowledgment that the seizure of San Juan had been unjustifiable, or that the claims of Mosquito sovereignty and independence on which it had been based were a mere convenient pretense. With these objects in view, the articles were worked over, and, after various changes had been made, they were signed by the negotiators, on April 30, 1852.[126] The substance of the arrangement was as follows:

(1) Definite boundaries should be established for the Mosquitos, who were to relinquish Greytown and a

[123] Webster, *Writings and Speeches,* XIV, 636.
[124] *Ibid.,* 471.
[125] See above, p. 108.
[126] *Parl. Papers,* 1856, *Coms.,* LX, "Correspondence with the United States respecting Central America ", 158.

tract of territory to the north of San Juan River to Nicaragua. In return for this cession, the Mosquitos were to have for three years the net receipts of all duties levied and collected at Greytown, at the rate of ten per cent. *ad valorem* on all goods imported into the state. The protection of the Indians was to be secured by an agreement on the part of Nicaragua not to molest them within their territorial reserve.

(2) Nothing in the preceding article should prevent the Mosquitos from voluntarily incorporating themselves with the Nicaraguans, in which case they were to be on the same basis as other citizens of Nicaragua. Greytown was to be established as a free port.

(3) Boundaries were to be defined between Nicaragua and Costa Rica, giving to the latter all of the territory south of the San Juan, and limited privileges of navigation in this river.

Articles four to seven contained provisions intended to facilitate the construction of the canal or to govern its use.[127]

As neither Molina nor Marcoleta had been consulted regarding this last plan of arrangement,[128] the negotiators attached to it a statement that the propositions, so far as they pertained to the governments of Costa Rica and Nicaragua, were merely advisory and recommendatory; but their immediate consideration by those governments was earnestly invoked. Furthermore, unless these states promptly agreed to the general basis

[127] *Ibid.*, 155-158.
[128] Molina had been ignored because the terms he demanded for land on the Costa Rican side of the San Juan, to be used by the canal company, were considered unreasonable by Webster. Marcoleta had remained without powers or instructions until the project was practically complete. *U. S. Docs.*, ser. no. 819, doc. 25, pp. 64, 66.

of the arrangement and adopted proper measures for carrying it into effect, the British and American governments would immediately agree between themselves upon such measures as they should deem advisable to carry into full execution the terms of the treaty of April 19, 1850.[129]

Since it was very desirable that the whole affair be terminated before the American Congress adjourned, Webster suggested that the proposals be sent directly to Central America for submission to the governments concerned. Crampton agreed to this, although the revised draft had not yet been approved by his government. Accordingly, it was decided that Kerr, who was at Nicaragua, should present the project to that government, and that a special agent, Robert Walsh, should be sent to Costa Rica to obtain her consent. In behalf of the British government, the proposals should be presented to both Costa Rica and Nicaragua by Wyke, the successor of Chatfield, who had some time before arrived in Washington on his way to his post. At the suggestion of President Fillmore, he had awaited the completion of the project in order that he might proceed to Central America in company with the American special agent, and thus make apparent to the Nicaraguans that the British and American governments were in harmony regarding the matter.[130] The plan was carried out, and Walsh and Wyke sailed from New York on May 10, intending to proceed first to Costa Rica.[131]

Some time before this Webster had sent Kerr careful instructions for the presentation of the subject to the

[129] *Parl. Papers,* 1856, *Coms.,* vol. LX, " Correspondence with United States respecting Central America ", 157-158.
[130] *Ibid.,* 146.   [131] *Ibid.,* 159.

Nicaraguan government. In anticipation of probable objection to payment for the return of Greytown, Kerr was directed to point out that the port had not been in Nicaraguan possession since January, 1848, when Nicaraguan authority was forcibly expelled. The hopelessness of inducing the British government to agree to the cession without equivalent was also to be hinted at; but Kerr was to assure Nicaragua that by agreeing to pay the compensation the Nicaraguan government would by no means be chargeable with inconsistency or dishonor, but would only be yielding to the stronger party, a frequent occurrence in the world's history.[132] Such arguments were not likely to appeal to the proud Nicaraguans, but they were the strongest that Webster had to offer.[133]

Kerr used his best efforts, but the Nicaraguans looked upon the project with anything but favor. Various reasons prompted their attitude. Naturally, they objected to giving any sort of compensation for the return of the port which they had repeatedly and emphatically declared to be their own. To make this objection more decided was the fact that Castellon, who had won prominence by his stand on the claims regarding Greytown, was now secretary of foreign affairs.[134] Moreover, the Nicaraguans had begun to feel that they had been betrayed by the American government,[135] which seemed to have gone over to the enemy. The hopes held out by the Monroe doctrine, reflected in the speeches of Hise and Squier, had not been fulfilled. Instead, the American government had united with the British in recommending settlement on

---

[132] U. S. Docs., ser. no. 819, doc. 25, pp. 77-79.
[133] Ibid., 97-99.   [134] Ibid., p. 93.   [135] Ibid., pp. 100-101.

terms humiliating to Nicaraguan pride; and the recommendation had been reinforced by a threat.[136] Furthermore, American citizens had been guilty of high-handed conduct in Nicaragua. The canal company had usurped powers not granted by the contract;[137] San Juan had been converted into a free city, through the influence of North Americans; and the United States, in co-operation with Great Britain, continued to protect the place.[138] As an indication of its feelings, the Nicaraguan government on July 20, a few days after the proposals were presented, issued a decree which contained a refusal to consider such an arrangement as that recommended, an expression of a desire for settlement by impartial arbitration, and a declaration that the state of Nicaragua solemnly protested against all foreign interference in matters of her administration and against the use of force to restrain her will and her rights.[139]

Wyke, having promptly secured the consent of the Costa Rican government to the project,[140] proceeded to Managua, the Nicaraguan capital, which he reached on July 26,[141] but a few days after the decree had been issued. Kerr informed him of his lack of success;[142] Wyke nevertheless presented the proposed arrangement in the name of his government, but was met with the answer that "the sacrifices demanded of Nicaragua were too great for that Government ever to make, and that they were ready to take the consequences, whatever they might be, of refusing to come to the proposed arrangement." [143]

---

[136] *U. S. Docs.*, ser. no. 819, doc. 25, p. 123.
[137] *Ibid.*, pp. 100-101.   [138] *Ibid.*, pp. 100-101, 104-106.
[139] *Ibid.*, pp. 103-104.   [140] *Ibid.*, pp. 91-92.
[141] *Parl. Papers*, 1856, *Coms.*, LX, " Correspondence with the United States respecting Central America ", 191.
[142] *Ibid.*   [143] *Ibid.*

Thus, after negotiations extending over a period of two years, all attempts to carry out the terms of the Clayton-Bulwer treaty had proved failures. Yet it is by no means certain that at this time any arrangement based upon that ambiguous document could have been made which would have been acceptable to all of the parties concerned. Though the British were anxious for a definite settlement, in view of the concessions which they had gained from the United States by means of the Clayton-Bulwer treaty, it seems likely that even a much more aggressive administration than that in power would have found it difficult to induce them at this time to give up Greytown without compensation to the Mosquitos. England most probably would have met any American attempt to secure such terms by a studied policy of evasion.

Yet it seems clear that the American negotiator did not do his best to effect a speedy and satisfactory settlement, which would secure for Nicaragua such an arrangement as that state had at an earlier date been led to expect. Though Webster for a time firmly insisted upon being guided in the negotiations by the wishes of Nicaragua, he later, as has been seen, retreated from this stand, though probably from justifiable reasons, and negotiated a project of arrangement which was a virtual disavowal of the earlier attitude of the American government. The project went further than the much-criticised treaty, the spirit of which it was intended to carry out; for while the Clayton-Bulwer treaty tacitly recognized the existence of a protectorate in Central America, the Webster-Crampton arrangement was, by its terms, practically an acknowledgment of Mosquito sovereignty.[144] This project marks the low tide of American interest in Central America during the period between 1850 and 1860, and the Webster-Fillmore administration which made it possible covers the period when British influence most nearly dominated the policy of the United States in that region.[145]

[144] After the departure of Walsh and Wyke for Central America, word came from Malmesbury directing various changes in the project. Upon learning that these modifications could not be introduced before the proposals should be submitted to Costa Rica and Nicaragua, the Foreign Secretary wrote: " If I were not conscious of the great difficulties which you must have encountered in inducing the United States Government to enter into any agreement at all by which they should admit the independence of the Mosquitos, whose very existence as a nation the United States, as well as the Central American States, have hitherto constantly denied, I should be unable to conceal the regret I feel that so wide a departure had been admitted from the original Project." *Parl. Papers,* 1856, *Coms.,* LX, " Correspondence with the United States respecting Central America ", 165.

[145] An effort was made to keep secret the terms of this project, but Marcoleta, to whom a copy was loaned, angry at being left out of the discussion, permitted them to be published in a newspaper. *U. S. Docs.,* ser. no. 819, doc. 25, p. 79; Dept. of State, Inst., Am. States, vol. 15, p. 59. They appeared in the *North American and United States Gazette* of June 28, 1852, by which they were severely criticised. The Clayton-Bulwer treaty, said the article, was made for the express purpose of driving the British out of Central America, and of compelling the relinquishment of the Mosquito protectorate. The present scheme of settlement was a surrender of the American policy on this continent; it admitted England as protector of the Mosquito Indians. Let the Senate look to it.

CHAPTER V.

THE BAY ISLANDS COLONY AND THE NEW INTERPRE-
TATION OF THE CLAYTON-BULWER TREATY,
1852-1854.

While the English and American negotiators, in a spirit of friendly understanding, had been vainly trying to settle the Mosquito question, trouble was brewing in another quarter. On March 20, 1852, by royal proclamation, Ruatan, Bonacca, and four neighboring islands were erected into the British "Colony of the Bay Islands"; and thus Clayton's fears regarding the evil possibilities of the word "dependencies" in the Belize declaration were realized. This act eventually led both the British and American governments to assume extreme and decided attitudes towards the Clayton-Bulwer treaty and caused the Mosquito question to develop into the more complicated and dangerous Central American question. In view of this fact, it is desirable to determine, if possible, the motives of the British government in its relations with the Bay Islands.

The later interest of the British government in the islands, like its interest in the port and river of San Juan, rose chiefly from a fear that they might be monopolized by some other government in connection with a transisthmian highway, and, in consequence, British commercial and political power be crippled. The most dangerous rival, obviously, was the United States; and the bold and rapid advance of that nation towards the southwest gave very valid grounds for suspicion. The aggressions of the British upon the Bay Islands previous to 1850, it will be remembered, kept pace with American territorial expansion.

There were two important differences, however, between the attitude of the British government towards the San Juan route and towards Ruatan, with its desirable harbors. The former could be made neutral and of equal benefit to all nations; but this could scarcely be done in the case of the latter. After the dissolution of the Central American confederation, it seemed hardly likely that, should the canal be built, the island would remain under the sovereignty of the weak Honduran republic. Instead, it was almost certain to be seized by some strong commercial power. Moreover, though the British government realized that the United States would never permit any foreign monopoly of the canal route, there was no particular reason to believe that a similar stand would be taken with regard to the Bay Islands, especially as they had been kept pretty well out of the early discussion preceding the formation of the Clayton-Bulwer treaty. Some such thoughts probably determined the British government quietly to maintain its hold upon the islands; and the statement which Bulwer handed to Clayton at the time of ratification, containing as it did the reference to "dependencies",[1] was undoubtedly meant to save the islands from the terms of the treaty.

But in view of the unwillingness of the nation to undergo further expense for the protection of new

[1] It will be remembered that the Bay Islands were governed to some extent from Belize.

colonies,[2] the British government had discouraged the settlement of British subjects on the islands.[3] The aim of the cabinet seems to have been to hold the islands, more especially Ruatan, against all intruders until the canal should be built, when they should be declared a British possession, and become an important commercial station on the way to the Pacific. But in spite of discouragement from their government, many British subjects took up their residence on the islands, and, evidently at the instigation of British agents in Central America,[4] sent repeated petitions to London, asking for protection.[5] This situation, as well as the compromising attitude of Clayton towards the Bay Islands while the Clayton-Bulwer treaty was before the Senate, and the fact that the Webster-Fillmore administration had been primarily interested in guaranteeing the canal route and had seemed indifferent to British aggressions in other parts of Central America, led directly to the proclamation of the Bay Islands colony.

What would have been the American attitude towards this act had the Whigs won in the election of 1852 may well be left to conjecture; but it was very evident from the first that the Democrats, whose ambitious plans had been interrupted by a Whig administration, would not passively acquiesce in such an arrangement. Harbingers of coming difficulty appeared before the old administration went out. A newspaper announcement regarding the new British

[2] Colonial Office to Greaves, Jan. 18, 1849, C. O., Hond., vol. 78.
[3] Lord Grey to Sir Charles Grey, April 14, 1851, *ibid.*, vol. 80, no. 111.
[4] Squier, *Notes on Central America*, 375-376; Michell, "Island of Ruatan", in *United Service Magazine*, 1850, II, 544-545.
[5] Colonial Office to Greaves, Jan. 18, 1849, C. O., Hond., vol. 78; Sir Charles Grey to Lord Grey, Dec. 11, 1850, *ibid.*, vol. 80, no. 33; Lord Grey to Sir Charles Grey, April 14, 1851, *ibid.*, no. 111.

colony had attracted attention in the United States;[6] consequently, shortly after Congress met in December, the Senate carried a resolution, offered by Cass of Michigan, requesting the President to communicate any information which he might possess respecting the establishment of a new British colony in Central America, together with a statement of what measures, if any, had been taken by the Executive to prevent the violation of the treaty between the United States and Great Britain, which provided that neither party should " occupy, or fortify, or colonize, or assume dominion over Nicaragua, Costa Rica, the Mosquito Coast, or any part of Central America ".[7]

The President stated in his reply of a few days later that no information of the character requested had been received by the State Department.[8] But with the message were inclosed Palmerston's declaration regarding Belize and the notes exchanged by Clayton and Bulwer with regard to it.[9] Thus, for the first time, the declaration became known to the Senate as a whole.

This at once produced an attack on Taylor's administration in general, and particularly on his secretary of state, who was charged with willfully concealing the correspondence. Cass and other Democrats now declared emphatically that had they understood that the treaty was not meant to apply to Belize they would never have voted for it. His object in voting for the treaty, Cass stated, had been to free Central America

---

[6] Travis, *Clayton-Bulwer Treaty*, 141. A very caustic article upon the subject, written by Squier, appeared in the *Democratic Review* for November-December, 1852.

[7] *Parl. Papers*, 1856, *Coms.*, LX, " Correspondence with the United States respecting Central America ", 201-202, 205.

[8] *Ibid.*, 205.   [9] *Ibid.*, 206-207.

from all British influence. In view of the declaration, the British government had far better grounds for its supposed actions than he had at first believed.[10]

The defense of the administration was assumed by Seward, among others, and he defended Clayton from the charges brought against him, showing that the opposition could hardly have been so ignorant of the intentions of the treaty, immediately after ratification, as they pretended. The main object of the treaty, the defense declared, had been the building of the canal, and the aim had been merely to limit the encroachments of the British within the five republics of Central America, of which Belize was not a part.[11]

This debate, and those following Clayton's election to Congress as senator from Delaware, were of a very bitter nature; and from an attack upon the Whig administration they soon changed to a denunciation of Great Britain. They pointed out that though more than two years had elapsed since the ratification of the treaty, British relations in Central America had undergone practically no change, and charged the British government with violating the terms of compact.[12]

Throughout the debates, the extreme Democrats maintained that the intention of the treaty had been to remove all British influence from Central America, Belize included. These claims, though not without foundation in the words of the treaty itself, were evidently more extravagant than those held by the same members at the time when the treaty was completed. The change was probably due partly to the fact that

[10] *Cong. Globe,* 32 Cong., 2 sess., 237-238; 33 Cong., 1 sess., Appendix, 61-72.

[11] *Ibid.,* 32 Cong., 2 sess., 247, 266-272, 414-416.

[12] *Ibid.,* 2 and 3 sess., Appendix, 245, 247-256, 257-279, 284-290.

the canal company had failed to fulfill its contract;[13] and thus the building of the canal, which it had been hoped would be begun immediately, was indefinitely postponed. Naturally, therefore, interest was shifted from the theoretical canal to the actual British encroachments. The bitterness of feeling in the Senate, caused by the reported British colonization of the Bay Islands, was undoubtedly also increased by the recent revelation of British efforts to thwart American designs in Cuba. While extending her own territory by direct violation of treaty engagements, Great Britain, in co-operation with France, had tried to induce the United States to enter into a tripartite treaty, guaranteeing Cuba to Spain. The proposal had been emphatically refused by the Fillmore administration, but resentment at British interference lingered.[14]

The President's message in reply to the Senate resolution was referred to the Committee on Foreign Relations, which was also instructed to determine what measures, if any, should be taken regarding the Belize declaration.[15] In its report the committee stated that it had obtained unofficial information, which appeared to be true, regarding the supposed new British colony in Central America, and had proceeded with its investigation as if the information were official. The committee accordingly reported that the Bay Islands formed a part of the republic of Honduras, and hence were a part of Central America; consequently, any occupation or

---

[13] *Parl. Papers,* 1856, *Coms.,* LX, " Correspondence with the United States respecting Central America ", 214-216.

[14] Schouler, *History of the United States,* V, 251-252.

[15] *U. S. Docs.,* ser. no. 671, doc. 407, p. 1.

colonization of them would be a violation of the treaty of April 19, 1850.[16]

As regarded Belize, the committee offered the decided opinion that the settlement, as defined by the treaties with Spain, lay within the territory of the Guatemalan republic, and therefore also formed a part of Central America. And it further stated that, should this opinion be correct, while it was not prepared to say that the treaty of 1850 would require the abandonment of those settlements by Great Britain, yet the United States government would have just cause of complaint against any extension of the boundaries beyond those prescribed by Spain, or as further allowed by the republic where they might be found; and that in any manner to enlarge or change the character of the settlements by any mode of jurisdiction would be a violation of the treaty.[17] Furthermore, even should the settlements be found later to be outside of Central America, and thus not come within the strict engagements of the treaty, yet any colonies or other permanent establishments erected there by Great Britain or any other European power must necessarily excite the most anxious concern of the American government, and would, if persisted in, "lead to consequences of most unpleasant character".[18]

As to the resolution of the Senate with reference to Belize, the committee reported that the declaration of the British government and the reply made to it by the American secretary of state imported nothing more than an admission on the part of the two governments, or their functionaries, at the time of the exchange of ratifications, that nothing contained in the treaty was

[16] *Ibid.*, p. 17.   [17] *Ibid.*   [18] *Ibid.*

to be considered as affecting the title or existing rights of Great Britain to the English settlements in Honduras Bay, and, consequently, that no measures were necessary on the part of the Senate because of such declaration and reply.[19]

This report was plainly a sharp return to Monroe-doctrine principles with reference to Central America, and it was a strong indication of the policy to be pursued by the incoming administration.

The stir created in Congress by the rumors of a new colony in Central America and by the presentation of the Belize correspondence quickly became known to the British government, but that government seemed unmoved by the attack upon it, and determined to pursue a conciliatory policy. In fact, it rather appears as if the policy became more conciliatory in consequence of American criticism, for two days after the receipt of a despatch from Crampton, reporting the Cass resolution,[20] Russell, now foreign secretary, wrote to Crampton offering terms for the settlement of the Mosquito question. Conditions had so changed, he explained, since the assumption of the Mosquito protectorate that the British now no longer had any interest in the Indians other than that derived from an honorable regard for their old connection with them. In consequence of this change, the British government had for several years vainly tried to suit its engagements to the altered circumstances. Now he suggested that an agreement be made by the British and American governments with the authorities at Greytown, making that

---

[19] *U. S. Docs.*, ser. no. 671, doc. 407, p. 17.
[20] *Parl. Papers*, 1856, *Coms.*, LX, " Correspondence with the United States respecting Central America ", 200-201, 204-214, 217, 222-235.

place a free and independent port, after the payment
of proper indemnity to the Indians. Plans for the protection of the Mosquitos were also offered. In conclusion, the Foreign Secretary added that though it was
the intention of the British government to do all that
honor and humanity demanded in behalf of the Mosquitos, it intended to adhere strictly to the treaty of
1850, and not to assume any sovereignty, directly or
indirectly, in Central America.[21]

In a letter written later on the same day Russell
referred to the plans already outlined and expressed
the desire of the British government to make Mosquito
a reality instead of a fiction. He acknowledged that
while Greytown was virtually a possession and Mosquito a dependency of Great Britain, it was not un-
natural that the United States should have looked upon
that state of things with jealousy and aversion, and
should have sided with Nicaragua; this, however, had
all been changed by the Clayton-Bulwer treaty, and the
great question now was how to turn the Mosquito
country to the best account for the whole world.
Therefore Crampton was instructed to present the
matter in this light to the American secretary of state,
explaining that honor required the British government
to provide liberally and permanently for the Indians,
but that, this point being secured, it had no objection
to arranging with the United States for insuring the
more rapid settlement and colonization of the Mosquito
territory, and for establishing its future administration.
Once established, the new state would soon become
independent of both Great Britain and the United
States, and probably soon be able to protect itself.[22]

[21] *Ibid.*, 202-203.   [22] *Ibid.*, 203-204.

These proposals, it will be noted, utterly disregarded the rights of Nicaragua and were in conformity with the threat contained in the Webster-Crampton project, to ignore the Central American states concerned, should they refuse to accept the project as a basis of settlement.

But the suggestions of Russell met with no favor from Everett, who upon Webster's death had become secretary of state. In a communication to the President, Everett declared it more advisable to attempt to secure Nicaragua's acceptance of the Webster-Fillmore arrangement, than to resort to terms less favorable to her.[23] However, as the Fillmore administration was almost ended, no measures were taken, in consequence of Russell's proposals, to settle the dispute at that time.

The character of the claims made in the Senate for the Clayton-Bulwer treaty soon convinced the British government that in order to avoid serious misapprehension it was very desirable that the American government be given clearly to understand the British view of the treaty, and the conduct which the British government intended to pursue in regard to it. Consequently, on May 27, Clarendon, who as Russell's successor was again in the Foreign Office, wrote to Crampton with reference to the matter. Great Britain, he declared, intended to observe religiously all of the engagements of the treaty, but she had nowhere in that agreement renounced, and never had intended to renounce, the full and absolute right which she possessed over her own lawful territories in Central America. Neither had she renounced the protection which she had for

---

[23] *Parl. Papers,* 1856, *Coms.,* LX, " Correspondence with the United States respecting Central America ", 218-222.

centuries afforded, and still afforded, to the Mosquito territory. The Foreign Secretary then reverted to the efforts which had been made by the British government to adjust matters in Central America, asserting that it was still ready and desirous to effect a settlement. He added, however, that until such arrangement was made his government could not abandon its present position, nor permit either Nicaragua or Honduras to assert or attempt to establish by force a right of possession which the British government had always denied, and still denied.[24]

Crampton made known this attitude to Marcy, Pierce's secretary of state, who replied that he was not yet able to say what would be the opinion of the American government in regard to the interpretation of the treaty, but that the matter was then being considered by the cabinet. He added that Buchanan, who had recently been appointed United States minister to England, would probably be instructed upon the subject and empowered to discuss it with the British foreign secretary.[25]

Buchanan, who as Polk's secretary of state had taken much interest in the Mosquito question, now shrewdly planned for the settlement of the larger Central American question into which it had grown. On May 29 he wrote to Marcy and revealed his plan. It provided that the treaty with Great Britain regarding the Canadian fisheries and reciprocity be perfected at Washington, where it had been begun, with the exception of its final execution, which should be made to await the result of the negotiation to be carried on by Buchanan in London.[26] Buchanan believed that if the reciprocity

[24] *Ibid.*, 247-249.   [25] *Ibid.*, 252.
[26] Buchanan, *Works,* IX, 1.

treaty, which England was anxious to conclude, were held in suspense, she might be induced to abandon her pretensions in Central America.[27] Should such a plan as he mentioned not prove feasible, he suggested that the Central American question be settled in connection with the others at Washington.[28]

Pierce, however, opposed the first plan, because he believed that the delay necessary to the completion of a Central American treaty might lead to actual collision between the two countries upon the fishing grounds;[29] the second plan he found equally objectionable, for he felt that to attempt to settle all of the questions at Washington would simply be to complicate difficulties.[30] In consequence of the President's disapproval of his suggestions, Buchanan declined the mission, for he believed that without some such arrangement as he had proposed the settlement of the Central American question would be delayed for years.[31] He was finally induced to accept the post, however, and agreed to do his best towards effecting a settlement;[32] but it was only with great reluctance that he gave up his idea of making the reciprocity treaty wait upon a settlement with reference to Central America.[33]

Marcy's instructions to Buchanan were written July 2, 1853. Since the acquisition of California, he stated, Great Britain had manifested a more deliberate design to change the Belize settlement into a British dominion. Such a design would not be disregarded by the American government. Acts passed by Great Britain in 1817 and 1819, as well as the treaty made with Mexico in

---

[27] Buchanan, *Works*, VIII, 511; IX, 19.
[28] *Ibid.*, IX, 2-3, 23-24.   [29] *Ibid.*, VIII, 511; IX, 1, 10, 19.
[30] *Ibid.*, IX, 23-24.   [31] *Ibid.*, IX, 1-2.   [32] *Ibid.*, 2, 24.   [33] *Ibid.*, 3.

1826, clearly showed that Belize was not within British dominion; therefore, while the American government conceded that Great Britain had rights in Belize, it positively denied that Belize was a British province, and it was bound to resist any attempt to convert the settlement into a colony.[34]

Though the direct object of the Clayton-Bulwer treaty, Marcy continued, was ostensibly to guarantee the transisthmian canal route, the stipulation in the treaty most regarded by the United States was that for the discontinuation of Great Britain's assumed protection over the Mosquito Indians, and with it the removal of all pretext for interfering with the territorial arrangements which the Central American states might wish to make among themselves. It was the intention, as it was obviously the import, of the treaty of April 19, 1850, to place Great Britain under an obligation to cease her interposition in the affairs of Central America, and to confine herself to the enjoyment of her limited rights in Belize. In spite of her agreement not to occupy, colonize, or exercise dominion over any part of Central America, Great Britain still asserted the right to hold possession of and to exercise control over large districts of that country and important islands in the Bay of Honduras, the unquestionable appanages of the Central American states. The object which it was hoped that Buchanan would be able to accomplish, Marcy pointed out, was to induce Great Britain to withdraw from all control over the territories and islands of Central America, and, if possible, to abstain from

[34] Dept. of State, Inst., Gt. Brit., vol. 16, no. 2.

intermeddling with the political affairs of the governments and people of that region.[35]

The policy of the new administration with reference to Central America was quite in harmony with Buchanan's own ideas; it was, in fact, a reversion to the old Monroe-doctrine principles of the Polk administration, which, according to Buchanan, aimed to sweep geographic Central America clear of all British influence which had developed since 1786;[36] and the basis of the demands to be made for British evacuation was to be the Clayton-Bulwer treaty.

The wording of this document is so ambiguous that any discussion, at the present time, for the purpose of getting at its full meaning would be of little profit. However, an impartial examination of the first article in connection with the statements in Marcy's letter leads to the conclusion that, on the whole, such an interpretation of the article as he made was not so unreasonable as might at first appear, though it was in strong contrast to that which the Fillmore administration seemed willing to accept.

It is true that the Belize settlement was originally in Mexico, but the encroachments of the settlers had been to the south, into what was plainly Guatemalan territory; therefore the district between the Sibun and Sarstoon rivers would evidently come under a strict application of the treaty terms. Moreover, though Marcy's intimation that the treaty required the discontinuation of British protection over the Mosquitos was rather sweeping, it is nevertheless true that a strict

---

[35] Dept. of State, Inst., Gt. Brit., vol. 16, no. 2.   Most of this instruction is printed in *U. S. Docs.,* ser. no. 840, doc. 1, pp. 42-49.

[36] " Letters of Bancroft and Buchanan " in *Am. Hist. Rev.,* V, 99.

observance of the other terms would have made such protection a virtual impossibility.

On September 2, some time after Buchanan's arrival in London, Marcy sent him full powers to negotiate a treaty with regard to Central America. In his letter of that date Marcy stated that though the United States could not claim as a matter of right that Great Britain should altogether withdraw from Belize, still it was a very important object to prevail on her to do so. As to the Bay Islands, he believed that Great Britain had never defined the character of her claim to possess the so-called colony; but whatever rights she may have had to the islands were all relinquished by the Clayton-Bulwer treaty. However, it seemed wisest to give the British government a chance to explain its views upon the matter before presenting a formal protest against her further occupancy of the colony.[37] The President, he added, expected Buchanan so to treat the subject as to leave no doubt in the minds of the British ministers that the United States would insist upon the abandonment of the islands.[38]

As the Crimean War was impending when Buchanan reached London, it was some time before he was able to secure an interview with Clarendon, and he thought it indiscreet under the circumstances to press the matter,[39] but in the last part of October he met Clarendon by appointment at the Foreign Office and had an interview which he considered highly satisfactory. The Foreign Secretary on his own account introduced the

[37] Such a protest had been previously suggested by Buchanan and was apparently a favorite idea of his. Buchanan, *Works*, IX, 29, 65.

[38] *U. S. Docs.*, ser. no. 840, doc. 1, pp. 49-50.

[39] Buchanan, *Works*, IX, 70, 77.

subject of the Bay Islands and of the general Central American question, which led Buchanan to express the wish of his government that the questions be settled without unnecessary delay. After touching on the best method of procedure in regard to the negotiations, the conversation returned to the Bay Islands, and Clarendon remarked that he believed Ruatan to be a " miserable little Island " which had been occupied for many years by British subjects whose request for some kind of government had been granted. This, he declared, was an entirely different case from what it would have been had the British but recently first occupied the island.[40]

Buchanan replied that he believed it would appear that the British, far from having occupied Ruatan for many years, had taken the island by force from Honduras as recently as 1841 ; but, in any event, the Clayton-Bulwer treaty had disposed of the question, for the island was unquestionably a part of Central America. He concluded by averring that the United States had no idea of acquiring any territory in Central America ; it desired only that the Central American states be permitted to enjoy in peace what belonged to them, and that the British and American governments interpose their good offices to settle the boundary disputes between them. Neither Great Britain nor the United States, he believed, had any real interest to pursue a different course; moreover, in America all had expected that the Clayton-Bulwer treaty would produce that happy result. To Buchanan's wish for the welfare of Central America Clarendon heartily agreed, and with that the conversation on the subject ended.[41]

40 Buchanan, *Works,* IX, 77, 80-81.   41 *Ibid.,* 81-82.

On November 12, a second interview took place. In the early part of it the Foreign Secretary asked if the Webster-Crampton project would do for a basis of settlement; and Buchanan promptly replied that that agreement was now at an end and could not be considered. That project, he stated, " both recognized and constituted the Mosquito Indians as an Independent Power; which could never be assented to by the United States. That these Indians were incapable of governing themselves; and the consequence would be that they must continue to be under the dominion of the British government." However much the American government liked Great Britain, it desired her withdrawal from Central America as quickly as possible. It was to effect this withdrawal that the United States had concluded the Clayton-Bulwer treaty; but unfortunately the object had not yet been accomplished. Besides, the United States could never recognize the right of Great Britain to a protectorate over the Mosquito Indians. Clarendon replied that the British government earnestly desired to get rid of its protectorate, but British honor required that this be done with a proper regard for the interest and well-being of the Mosquitos.[42]

The plan suggested by Russell in the preceding January was also mentioned by Clarendon, but Buchanan objected to such an arrangement on the ground that it would deprive the Central American states of territory to which they were justly entitled; furthermore, this arrangement would perpetuate strife in Central America, because the states would never cease trying

[42] *Ibid.*, 88-90.

to have the injustice redressed; in short, it would make confusion worse confounded.[43]

At this second interview Clarendon showed a desire to avoid mention of the Bay Islands, and the subject was finally introduced by Buchanan, whereupon Clarendon, as before, tried to minimize the importance of the colonization of the islands, and intimated that the Americans were making " a Mountain out of a Mole Hill ".[44] To this Buchanan answered—to quote from his despatch to Marcy:

> Whatever you may suppose, I can assure you that this is the dangerous question; because we firmly believe that the establishment of this Colony is a direct violation of the Clayton and Bulwer Treaty . . . Even if it were a fact that you had always been in possession of Ruatan, still your obligation to withdraw from it would, in my opinion, be imperative, under the Clayton and Bulwer Treaty . . . Let me assure you that this will be considered a most important question by the Congress and people of the United States; and I have no doubt they will arrive at the same conclusion with the Committee of Foreign Relations of the Senate.[45]

At the conclusion of this interview, Buchanan asked Clarendon for an official document regarding the colonization of the Bay Islands which Clarendon had previously promised him, and the Foreign Secretary gave him a copy of the proclamation, by the lieutenant-governor of the islands, erecting them into a colony in the name of the Queen. Buchanan sent this paper—which contained the first official information regarding the new colony in Central America to be received by the American government—to Marcy with his report of the interview.[46]

[43] Buchanan, *Works*, IX, 91.   [44] *Ibid.*, 94.   [45] *Ibid.*, 94-95.
[46] *Ibid.*, 96, 97. *Cf. Parl. Papers*, 1856, *Coms.*, XLIV, " Bay Islands ", 1-5.

Clarendon was so preoccupied with the Russo-Turkish question that Buchanan did not secure a chance to resume the discussion until the first part of January. During the interview which then took place the Foreign Secretary astonished Buchanan by presenting a new interpretation of the Clayton-Bulwer treaty. That arrangement, he declared, was entirely prospective in its operations and did not require an abandonment of any British possessions in Central America.[47] Bulwer, it will be remembered, took this view of the treaty from the first,[48] but a study of the previous correspondence upon the subject leaves no doubt that the British government itself had but recently adopted this interpretation.[49] Though it had hoped that possible American indifference and the declaration of Palmerston regarding Belize and its dependencies might limit attention to the Mosquito Shore, still the British government clearly understood the treaty to apply to existing as well as to future relations.

The change of attitude seems to have been due to several causes. Among these might be mentioned the temper which the Pierce administration had shown in reference to the Belize declaration and the colonization of the Bay Islands; congressional criticism of the British failure to withdraw from Mosquito Shore; and the actual difficulty of an honorable withdrawal which England had experienced in her attempts of the last two years. The fact that the canal company had

---

[47] Buchanan, *Works,* IX, 117, 134-135.

[48] See above, p. 108; also below, p. 163, note 59.

[49] See above, pp. 108-109, 111, 146-147; also below, p. 161. *Cf.* Buchanan, *Works,* IX, 341-342.

not carried out its contract very probably was also influential in producing this new stand; for now no early commercial gain, as a result of a transisthmian world highway, seemed likely to appear as compensation for relinquishing special interests in Central America.

Thus, after this interview of January, 1854, the general position of each of the parties on the Clayton-Bulwer treaty was clear to the other: in the opinion of the American government, the treaty was meant to be retrospective as well as prospective, and demanded British withdrawal from Central America; to the British government it was only prospective and merely prohibited further territorial and political extension in the region.

At this meeting in January Buchanan gave Clarendon a memorandum containing the views of the American government on the whole Central American question. The paper was temperately and logically worded and was a shrewd defense of the American attitude. The object of the Clayton-Bulwer treaty, it declared, had been to place the two nations on exact equality with regard to the interoceanic highway; consequently, both had agreed never to occupy, fortify, or exercise dominion over any portion of Central America. As the United States held no land in the region, she was simply restrained from making future acquisitions; but in the case of Great Britain the language applied to the present as well as to the future, because when the treaty was made she was exercising dominion over a large portion of the eastern coast of Central America. Notwithstanding the agreement, the

British government had not taken the first step towards withdrawing from Central America. The failure to do so could not result from any obscurity in the treaty itself, for the first article clearly meant that the contracting parties should not exercise dominion over Central America, either directly or indirectly. Great Britain's disregard of treaty obligations was even more palpable in the case of Ruatan; not only had she failed to retire from there, but since the completion of the treaty she had formed Ruatan and five adjoining islands into a British colony. In vain had the self-denying stipulations been made, if Great Britain was to continue to exercise dominion over the Bay Islands.[50]

Some months elapsed after the interview in January before further opportunity was given Buchanan regarding the matter, and before a reply was made to his paper. The reason for this lapse of time is partly to be found in the pressure of the war question with Russia; but a study of the correspondence leads to the suspicion that it was also due to intentional evasion of the subject on the part of the British government. This postponement of discussion may have resulted entirely from a desire to see the outcome of the quarrel between Russia and Turkey before a more determined stand should be taken upon the question in dispute with America; but Clarendon's words as well as his actions give cause for the belief that, as Buchanan suspected,[51] he did not find it as easy as he had at first supposed it would be to defend the British claims in Central America, or to justify the view that the Clay-

---

[50] Buchanan, *Works,* IX, 118-128.
[51] *Ibid.,* 148, 154, 180-181.

ton-Bulwer treaty was intended to be only prospective in its operations.

At the next interview, which was held April 11, Clarendon again announced distinctly that the British government considered the treaty to be entirely prospective, and not as interfering with existing possessions in Central America. This led Buchanan to point out that, in view of such interpretation, Palmerston had put himself to much unnecessary trouble in insisting upon an acknowledgment, before the exchange of ratifications, that the provisions of the treaty did not embrace Belize. To this Clarendon made no satisfactory answer, and he never did supply Buchanan with an explanation which reconciled Palmerston's action with the new interpretation of the treaty. As the Foreign Secretary promised a written statement of British views within a few days,[52] but little more was said regarding the Central American question during this interview.

Yet the paper was not received until the first week in May. The statement was, as Buchanan characterized it, " rambling and inconclusive in its arguments ".[53] Clarendon summarily disposed of the Mosquito question by stating that the United States would scarcely expect Great Britain to enter into an explanation of acts committed by her nearly forty years before, in a matter in which no right or possession of the United States was involved. He added, however, that since the peace of 1815 Spain had never raised a question with respect to the protectorate; and that the Central American republics—if it were to be admitted that the

[52] Buchanan, *Works*, IX, 180.
[53] *Ibid.*, 189.

rights and obligations of Spain were vested in them—
had made no remonstrance against the protectorate for
many years, though they well knew that it existed.
Furthermore, though in 1842 the United States government was informed of the existence of the protectorate,[54] no objection was made up to the end of the year
1849. The protectorate had not been abolished by the
terms of the first article of the treaty; the American
minister had confounded the conditions of a sovereignty
and a protectorate and had treated the agreement " not
to colonize, nor occupy, nor fortify, nor assume, nor
exercise dominion over ", as including an agreement
not to protect. The British government never claimed,
and did not then claim, any sovereignty over Mosquito;
but the treaty of 1850 did not, and was not meant to,
annihilate the protectorate which had long been exercised over it.[55]

The aim in forming the treaty, Clarendon proceeded,
had been to neutralize the proposed canal; and in
deciding upon the terms the object of both negotiators
had been presumably to draw up such a convention as,
without conceding any specific point on which one
party could not in honor yield, would make such concessions on all other points as the other party desired.
An examination of the treaty would show that it was
drawn up in such a manner as to make it a matter of
indifference, so far as the canal was concerned, whether
the port and town of San Juan were under the modified

[54] Macdonald informed Murphy, the American agent in Central America, that the protectorate had been reestablished, and Murphy reported
the fact to his government. Murphy to the Secretary of State, January
20, 1842, Dept. of State, Des., Cen. Am., vol. 2.
[55] *U. S. Docs.,* ser. no. 840, doc. 1, pp. 81-84.

protectorate of Great Britain, or under the government of Nicaragua.[56]

Though, the paper continued, the British government did not pretend that the treaty by implication recognized the protectorate, still it clearly acknowledged the possibility of Great Britain or the United States affording protection to Mosquito, or any other Central American state, and admitted that the intention of the parties was not to prohibit or abolish, but to limit and restrict, such a protectorate. Defending and protecting was a temporary act of friendship; occupying, colonizing, fortifying, or acquiring sovereignty were acts having a permanent result. No one would maintain that the bar to colonization was a bar to all protection.[57]

As to Belize and its dependencies, neither government had ever intended that the treaty should interfere in any way with them; this was shown by the fact that the term " Central America " could only be applied to the territory once included under the term " Central American republic ", and also by the declarations exchanged by Clayton and Bulwer. Moreover, the fact that, in 1847, the United States sent to Belize a consul who received his exequatur from the British government, gave reason to believe that the term " Belize " in the declaration meant the Belize with the limits of 1850, for this act constituted a recognition by the United States government of the settlement of British Honduras, as it then existed. Furthermore, the limits of the settlement established in 1786 were abolished by a subsequent state of war between Spain and England.[58]

[56] *U. S. Docs.,* ser. no. 840, doc. 1, p. 86.
[57] *Ibid.*, p. 87.   [58] *Ibid.*, pp. 89-90.

With reference to Ruatan and the adjoining islands, Clarendon stated, the only thing debatable was whether they were dependencies of Belize, or of some Central American state. An attempt followed to show that the pretensions of Great Britain to consider Ruatan and Bonacca dependencies of Belize were of long standing and existed when the treaty of 1850 was formed, at which time it was not questioned by the American government. In consequence of these facts, the British government could not admit that an alteration in the internal form of government of these islands was a violation of the treaty, or afforded to the United States a just cause of remonstrance.[59]

In reply to the views presented by Clarendon, Buchanan, on July 22, 1854, wrote a long and able paper, emphasizing his former arguments and presenting new ones to meet those of the Foreign Secretary. An agreement on the part of Great Britain not to " occupy " any territory then actually occupied by her, he maintained, clearly was an agreement to withdraw therefrom. If, as the British government held, the treaty was only prospective in its nature it amounted to an American recognition of the British right to territory already held in Central America. Such an interpretation entirely destroyed the mutuality of the convention, for it bound the United States, which held no territory there, not to acquire any. But the British government, at the time of ratification, must have regarded the treaty as applying to the present as well as the future; otherwise, why the Belize declaration?

[59] *Ibid.*, pp. 90-93. Clarendon's paper was based partially upon arguments furnished by Bulwer. Inclosures in Bulwer to Hammond, Sept. 30, 1854, F. O., Cen. Am., vol. 83. See above, p. 108.

The fact that no attempt was made to except any other Central American territory amounted to an admission that the British were bound to withdraw from all of their other possessions there.[60]

As for the Bay Islands, even admitting for the sake of argument that the Belize declaration was binding, these islands were not excluded by it, for the word " dependencies " applied only to the small islands in the neighborhood of the settlement, as stated by Clayton in his note to Bulwer, and not to the large island of Ruatan which was hundreds of miles from Belize. The British statement attached much importance to the fact that Ruatan was occupied by the British in 1850; it was for the reason that not only Ruatan but the whole eastern coast of Central America was occupied by them that the United States was so anxious for a convention requiring British withdrawal. But for this agreement, the United States, in self-defense, would have been compelled to accept cessions of territory in Central America.[61] Then followed an investigation into the British title to Ruatan, which Buchanan showed to rest on very flimsy foundations.[62]

When the treaty was formed, the paper proceeded, Great Britain had merely taken the first step towards possessing the island. Consequently, no mention was made of the matter by the United States government at the time, for, in view of the terms of the treaty, it was not doubted that Great Britain would promptly withdraw. Instead of so doing the British government had erected Ruatan and five adjoining islands into a British colony. Clarendon had failed to assert any-

[60] Buchanan, *Works,* IX, 216-217.
[61] *Ibid.,* 217-220. [62] *Ibid.,* 220-225.

where in his paper that any of these five islands had ever been occupied by the British government previous to their formation into a colony.[63]

The protection of the San Juan route, far from being the only feature of the convention, as the statement of Clarendon seemed to intimate, was only one feature of a policy far more liberal and extended. This policy embraced all routes, whether for railroads or canals, throughout Central America; and the prohibition of occupation was co-extensive with the whole territory over which such canals or railroads might pass. The American government could not become a party to any arrangement whereby Great Britain should merely withdraw from the port and harbor of Greytown and the northern bank of the San Juan, thus leaving the remainder of the Mosquito coast in its present condition; the American government stood upon the treaty, and firmly believed that Great Britain should have abandoned the whole Mosquito territory more than four years before.[64]

The British statement asserted, Buchanan continued, that though, in 1842, the American government knew that the protectorate existed, it did not complain until 1850. The American government had no right under any treaty with Great Britain until 1850. Had it interfered previous to this time it could have done so only under the Monroe doctrine, which the British government did not recognize. But it should not be concluded that without this convention the United States would not have interfered eventually to prevent, if possible, any portion of Central America from being permanently occupied or colonized by Great Britain.[65]

[63] *Ibid.*, 225-226.   [64] *Ibid.*, 230-232.   [65] *Ibid.*, 232-238.

Finally, the American statement declared, whether the term "Central America" appearing in the first article of the treaty was considered in a political or a geographical sense, it applied to the territory between the Sibun and the Sarstoon, for this was a part of the province of Vera Paz in Guatemala. Moreover, Clayton's letter to Bulwer upon exchanging ratifications referred to the convention of 1850 as applying to all of the Central American states, "with their just limits and proper dependencies". Hence, the territory in question, being within the just limits of the state of Guatemala, was expressly embraced by the convention. The United States emphatically denied that the appointment of a consul to Belize was even the slightest recognition of British title to the port. Consuls were mere commercial, and not political, agents. The contention that the territory between the Sibun and the Sarstoon was British by right of conquest, Buchanan proved to be unsound by citing the treaties of 1809 and 1814 with Spain and the treaty of 1826 with Mexico, as well as acts of Parliament pased in 1817 and 1819.[66]

But regardless of the nature of the British claim to this territory, the question, as in the case of the Bay Islands and the Mosquito coast, did not turn upon the validity of the claim, but upon the fact that Great Britain had bound herself not to occupy any portion of Central America, or to exercise dominion over it. As to Belize proper, limited by the treaties of 1783 and 1786, the United States would not for the present insist upon the withdrawal of Great Britain from it, provided all the other questions between the two governments were settled amicably. But it must be distinctly under-

---

[66] Buchanan, *Works*, IX, 238-240.

stood that the United States government acknowledged no British claim there except the right to the usufruct specified in the Spanish treaties, and it recognized the former Spanish sovereignty as now belonging either to Guatemala or to Mexico.[67]

Thus, through Buchanan's second formal statement the attitude of the United States was more clearly revealed, and such arguments were presented against the British view as it seemed hardly likely that the British government would be able to refute. This was the last word between the two governments for some time, directly upon the controversy over the Clayton-Bulwer treaty. Meanwhile events of importance to British-American relations were taking place in Central America, and to these attention is now directed.

[67] *Ibid.*, 241.

CHAPTER VI.

AMERICAN DEFIANCE OF BRITISH CLAIMS, 1853-1855.

At the time when Great Britain and the United States were approaching what appeared to be irreconcilable differences over the meaning of the Clayton-Bulwer treaty, affairs in Central America were assuming a correspondingly serious aspect. Borland, Kerr's successor as United States minister, was one of the earlier causes of discord. He was a man of the school of Squier and worked as assiduously as did the latter to build up American influence and counteract that of Great Britain. Upon arriving in Central America, Borland found the British in the ascendancy in Costa Rica and Salvador, and especially in Guatemala,[1] where the American government was particularly hated and feared because of its recent interference in Mexico.[2] Even Nicaragua was suspicious of the United States, partly because she had come to regard the Clayton-Bulwer treaty as an abandonment of the Monroe doctrine.[3] In fact, Honduras was the only state which was at this time distinctly friendly towards the American

[1] Wyke to Clarendon, Nov. 27, 1853, F. O., Cen. Am., vol. 79, no. 37; Borland to Secretary of State, Dec. 10, 1853, Dept. of State, Des., Nic., vol. 1, no. 11.

[2] Wyke to Clarendon, Mar. 13, 1854, F. O., Cen. Am., vol. 82, no. 9. So fearful of American designs were the Guatemalans that they even talked of a Spanish protectorate. Wyke to Clarendon, Oct. 30, 1853, *ibid.,* vol. 79, no. 33.

[3] Borland to Marcy, Sept. 20, 1853, Dept. of State, Des., Nic., vol. 1, no. 5.

government;[4] and this loyalty was obviously due to the attitude of the United States regarding the British colonization of the Bay Islands.

Borland, however, while complaining vigorously against the actions of the British in Central America,[5] immediately set about improving conditions in that region for his own country. By liberal promises he soon regained Nicaragua's confidence,[6] and, in accordance with his Monroe-doctrine principles, negotiated a commercial treaty with her, by which her territorial claims were again guaranteed on the part of the United States.[7] He went further than this; he criticised the Clayton-Bulwer treaty and urged its abrogation on the ground that Great Britain had violated its terms;[8] and then he proceeded to act as if the treaty had been already set aside. His plan, strongly hinted at in his speeches and letters, was evidently to bring the whole of Central America under the control of the United States for the purpose of annexing the region to the American Union.[9]

While Borland was working, in a manner entirely unauthorized by his government, to strengthen Ameri-

[4] *Ibid.*, Borland to Marcy, Dec. 10, 1853, *ibid.*, no. 11; Wyke to Clarendon, Feb. 27, 1854, F. O., Cen. Am., vol. 82, no. 6.

[5] Borland to Marcy, Dec. 10, 1853, Dept. of State, Des., Nic., vol. 1, no. 11.

[6] Wyke to Clarendon, Oct. 30, 1853, F. O., Cen. Am., vol. 79, no. 33.

[7] Crampton to Clarendon, May 1, 1854, F. O., Am., vol. 595, no. 115; July 3, 1854, *ibid.*, vol. 597, no. 172. This treaty met with no favor from the American government. *Ibid.*

[8] Borland to the Secretary of State, Aug. 28, 1853, Dept. of State, Des., Nic., vol. 1, no. 3.

[9] Inclosure in Borland to Marcy, Aug. 29, 1853, *ibid.*, Borland to Marcy, Nov. 10, 1853, *ibid.*, vol. 1; Dec. 15[?], 1853, *ibid.*, no. 15. In one of his public speeches in Nicaragua Borland stated that his greatest desire was to see Nicaragua forming a bright star in the flag of the United States. Wyke to Clarendon, Nov. 27, 1853, F. O., Cen. Am., vol. 79, no. 37.

can interests in Nicaragua, Squier, as a private citizen, was similarly engaged in Honduras. During his residence in Central America as an agent of the United States government, Squier had contracted an intense hatred of British influence on the isthmus. This feeling was kept alive after his recall, and at about the time of Borland's arrival in Nicaragua Squier also returned to Central America and made his headquarters in Honduras. The ostensible purpose of his visit was to obtain a grant from that republic for the construction of an interoceanic railway,[10] but he was suspected by the British of being primarily interested in "the furtherance of his well-known political views regarding Central America".[11]

Indeed, Squier's actions appear to have given good reason for British suspicion. According to reports, he lost no opportunity of declaring that he staked all of his hopes of success in life on the prospect of annihilating every vestige of British influence in Central America.[12] At this time Honduras and Guatemala were at war, and, as the latter was a British stronghold, Squier was much interested in the contest. He became the chief instigator and adviser of Honduras, and it was said that under his influence a Honduran agent was sent to Washington to secure aid in the war, and possibly also with the idea of bringing about annexation to the United States.[13] Moreover, rumors were afloat

[10] Crampton to Clarendon, July 24, 1854, "Confidential", F. O., Am., vol. 597, no. 195.

[11] *Ibid.*

[12] Crampton to Clarendon, Mar. 6, 1854, "Confidential", *ibid.,* vol. 594, no. 58.

[13] Crampton to Clarendon, June 5, 1854, *ibid.,* vol. 596, no. 147; Seymour to the Secretary of the Admiralty, Mar. 24, 1854, Ad. Sec. In-Letters, 5629, no. 32.

that Squier had secured, or was about to secure, from the United States, men and arms for the purpose of driving the British out of Mosquito territory and Ruatan.[14]

Though Great Britain felt at this time that the American government intended honestly to observe the terms of the Clayton-Bulwer treaty, there was yet a fear that public opinion in the United States might force support of Squier;[15] consequently, Crampton was directed by the foreign secretary to inform Marcy that the British government was convinced that he would give no countenance to the schemes of Squier.[16] As an additional precaution, it was decided to reinforce the British naval station in the West Indies.[17]

While affairs were in this condition, an event occurred which on first appearance seemed likely to produce a rupture between the British and American governments; the famous British protectorate over Mosquito was put to test by the United States. The occurrence originated in a quarrel, begun early in 1853, between the Accessory Transit Company[18] and the

[14] Crampton to Clarendon, Mar. 6, 1854, F. O., Am., vol. 594, no. 58; Seymour to the Secretary of the Admiralty, Mar. 24, 1854, Ad. Sec. In-Letters, 5629, no. 32.

[15] Wyke to Clarendon, Nov. 27, 1853, F. O., Cen. Am., vol. 79, no. 37.

[16] Clarendon to Crampton, Mar. 24, 1854, F. O., Am., vol. 590, no. 64.

[17] Crampton to Clarendon, Mar. 6, 1854, *ibid.*, vol. 594, no. 58; Seymour to the Secretary of the Admiralty, Mar. 24, 1854, Ad. Sec. In-Letters, 5629, no. 32; Hammond to Merivale, April 26, 1854, C. O., Hond., vol. 89.

[18] In order to take advantage of the increase of traffic across the isthmus, in consequence of the discovery of gold in California, the Atlantic and Pacific Ship-Canal Company had secured a modified charter giving it the monopoly of a line of transit across the isthmus. Under this charter it styled itself the Accessory Transit Company. Scroggs, "William Walker and the Steamship Corporation in Nicaragua", in *Am. Hist. Rev.*, X, 793.

authorities at Greytown. Though securing its charter from Nicaragua, the company had obtained from Greytown a concession to build a coal depot on Point Arenas, on the opposite side of the river from the town.[19] The terms of the concession were quickly exceeded by the erection of warehouses, stores, and hotels.[20] This angered the town authorities, and the anger was increased by the company's refusal to deliver its passengers on the town side of the harbor, thus cutting off the inhabitants from all share in the profits from trans-isthmian traffic.[21]

According to the agreement, the land was to be given up upon requisition from the town;[22] the requisition was made, but the company ignored it. The town then ordered the removal of the establishments from Point Arenas within thirty days,[23] but no attention was paid to the notice, and when the time limit had expired the town officials destroyed some of the buildings.[24]

Meanwhile, as a result of appeal from the Transit Company,[25] Captain Hollins of the American navy had been ordered to Greytown with the sloop-of-war *Cyane,* for the protection of American interests.[26] He arrived a day or two before the time set for a second attack on the buildings, and upon learning of the situation notified the town authorities that he would resist by force any attempt to execute the design.[27] However, a body of armed men was sent from Greytown to complete the

[19] *Parl. Papers,* 1856, *Coms.,* LX, " Correspondence with the United States respecting Central America ", 236.
[20] *Ibid.*
[21] *Harper's Magazine,* X, 56.
[22] *Parl. Papers,* 1856, *Coms.,* LX, " Correspondence with the United States respecting Central America ", 236.
[23] *Ibid.*   [24] Ibid., 237.   [25] *Ibid.,* 243-245.   [26] *Ibid.,* 245.
[27] *Ibid.,* 240.

work of destruction; but upon landing they were confronted by marines from the *Cyane,* sent by Hollins. In the face of this resistance the party from the town retired and for a time efforts against the company were abandoned.[28]

This event became the subject of correspondence between Great Britain and the United States; but as this was just when the British government was being sharply attacked by the American Senate, Clarendon very wisely preserved a conciliatory tone, only showing sufficient resentment at Hollins's act to preserve the dignity of his government.[29] Marcy's reply to the complaint of Clarendon contained a hostile note,[30] however, which further roused the Foreign Secretary;[31] but the American government soon learned that the Transit Company had received its concession from Greytown— a fact of which it had previously been ignorant [32]—and therefore assumed a milder tone.[33] The British government quickly responded, and the irritation produced by the affair disappeared.[34]

But the Transit Company's buildings remained on Point Arenas and, in consequence, bad feeling continued between the company and Greytown. At first the feeling was largely on the side of the latter, which bitterly resented the commercial monopoly maintained by the company, but soon the enmity of the Transit Company was increased by the loss of large amounts of goods stolen from their stores, apparently in retaliation, by their neighbors in the community across the river. When the company demanded the return of the goods and the punishment of the offenders, the town

[28] *Ibid.*   [29] *Ibid.,* 246-247.   [30] *Ibid.,* 252-255.   [31] *Ibid.,* 255-257.
[32] *Ibid.,* 257-258.   [33] *Ibid.,* 258.   [34] *Ibid.,* 257-258.

officials refused to take any action.[35] This was the situation in the summer of 1854 just before the second clash came.

The initial act of the second difficulty was the shooting of a negro citizen of Greytown by Captain Smith of the *Routh,* one of the Transit Company's steamers. Smith's vessel ran into a bungo of merchandise belonging to the negro, and in the quarrel that followed the negro met his death.[36] This took place some miles up the San Juan River. Borland, the United States minister to Central America, happened to be aboard the *Routh* at the time, but apparently he made no attempt to interfere.[37]

After the vessel returned to Greytown, the municipal authorities attempted to arrest Smith on the charge of murder. The latter resisted and Borland went to his aid, informing the marshal of the place that the United States government recognized no authority as existing at Greytown to arrest an American citizen. When, a few minutes later, a body of men who had accompanied the marshal in a boat to the steamer's side threatened to board the *Routh* and attack the captain, Borland ordered them off with a gun. This produced quiet, and the marshal withdrew.[38]

But in the evening of the same day an attempt was made to arrest Borland while he was at the home of Fabens, the United States consul at the port. A number of people gathered about Fabens's house, and, during a conversation between Borland and the mayor of the town, some one in the crowd threw a broken

[35] *U. S. Docs.,* ser. no. 734, doc. 126, pp. 19, 20, 22-25.
[36] *Ibid.,* ser. no. 918, doc. 9, p. 8.
[37] *Ibid.,* p. 9.
[38] *Ibid.,* ser. no. 734, doc. 126, p. 16.

bottle at Borland, slightly wounding him. The mayor stated that the second attempt at arrest was made without his authority, so the gathering soon dispersed, but an armed force was stationed between the consulate and the harbor, thus keeping the American minister a prisoner throughout the night.[39]

At a meeting held in the morning aboard the *Northern Light*, one of the company's steamers about to sail for New York, it was decided that the persons and property of American citizens were not safe from aggression.[40] Consequently, Borland made arrangements with fifty of the passengers, who agreed to remain over and afford the necessary protection; and he himself returned to the United States aboard the *Northern Light* for the purpose of laying the whole subject before his government.[41] Fabens also reported the matter to Washington, by letter, expressing the opinion that frequent visits of a United States man-of-war would have a beneficial effect upon all concerned.[42]

In consequence of the reports of Borland and Fabens, and of previous complaints on the part of the Transit Company,[43] the American government determined to send the *Cyane* to the scene of difficulties. In his instructions Hollins was told to consult with Fabens and learn the truth regarding the actions of the Greytown citizens. " It is very desirable ", wrote the secretary of the navy, " that these people should be taught that the United States will not tolerate these outrages, and that they have the power and the determination to check them. It is, however, very much to be hoped that you can effect the purposes of your visit without

[39] *Ibid.*, p. 17.   [40] *Ibid.*   [41] *Ibid.*, pp. 17, 18.
[42] *Ibid.*, ser. no. 702, doc. 85, pp. 10-11.
[43] von Holst, *History of the United States*, V, 12.

a resort to violence and destruction of property and loss of life. The presence of your vessel will, no doubt, work much good. The department reposes much in your prudence and good sense." [44]

On June 9, Marcy wrote to Fabens instructing him to co-operate with Hollins. Goods belonging to the Transit Company, he stated, had been stolen and withheld by the people or authorities of Greytown. It was hoped that the town would have adjusted that matter to the entire satisfaction of the company, and thus would have relieved Hollins from the " disagreeable necessity of taking any action with regard to the subject ". The American minister to Central America had been insulted by the authorities or people of Greytown, Marcy continued, and nothing short of an apology would save the place from the infliction which such an act justly merited. It was expected that this apology would be promptly made, and satisfactory assurances given of future good conduct towards the United States and its agents who might in future be sent to the place. [45]

The peculiar character of the above instructions immediately attracts attention. They implicitly directed that in case of necessity violence should be used against Greytown, but left entirely to Hollins and Fabens the determination of the necessity, as well as of the degree of violence to be employed. Such instructions seem to indicate a desire actually to test the British protectorate over Greytown, as well as a resolve to ignore the agreement, made with Great Britain two years before, to protect the *de facto* government of the place. This defiant attitude of the American govern-

[44] *U. S. Docs.*, ser., no. 734, doc. 126, p. 2.
[45] *Ibid.*, pp. 19-20.

ment seems to have been produced by the unsatisfactory condition of the general Central American question. But two or three weeks before the instructions were sent to Fabens and Hollins, Marcy had received from Buchanan Clarendon's statement of May 2, presenting formally and officially the view that the Clayton-Bulwer treaty was prospective in its operation, and did not apply to existing British possessions in Central America. This unreasonable stand apparently led the American government to use the opportunity offered by the situation at Greytown with the aim of convincing Great Britain that such an interpretation of the treaty would not be tolerated, and that complete abandonment of former claims in Central America was essential to the preservation of friendly relations with the United States.

The instructions to Hollins and Fabens had been made known to the Transit Company and were quite in harmony with its wishes and plans. In fact, judging from a letter written June 16, 1854, by White, counsel for the company, to Fabens, a quiet understanding existed between the American government, Hollins, Fabens, and the company. Much discretion had been given Fabens, White wrote, and he hoped that it would "not be exercised to show any mercy to the town or people. . . . If the scoundrels are severely punished", he continued, " we can take possession and build it up as a business place, put in our own officers, transfer the jurisdiction, and you know the rest. It is of the last importance that the people of the town should be taught to fear us. Punishment will teach them, after which you must agree with them as to the organization of a new Government and the officers of it. Everything now depends on you and Hollins. The latter is all right. He fully understands the outrage, and will not hesitate in enforcing reparation." [46]

The instructions were executed by Fabens and Hollins, aided by Scott, agent of the company at Greytown. Before the arrival of the *Cyane*, Fabens, as directed, notified the inhabitants of the town that the United States government required reparation for the wrongs committed by them, but had received no reply. [47] He learned from private sources, however, that the town neither intended to pay damages nor to apologize for the insult to Borland. [48] As soon as he arrived, Hollins communicated with Fabens and the two decided to renew the demands already made. After consultation with Scott, it was determined to call for $24,000 damages for the loss of goods belonging to the Transit Company, [49] and an apology for the insult to Borland, with an assurance of future good behavior. [50]

Accordingly, on July 11 such a demand was made by Fabens. [51] This demand was likewise unheeded, and Hollins, after consultation with the others, decided to give the town twenty-four hours in which to render satisfaction. Hence, on the following day at Hollins's order a proclamation was posted in public places about

---

[46] Inclosure in Crampton to Clarendon, Sept. 10, 1855, F. O., Am., vol. 623, no. 188. There seems to be no reason for doubting the authenticity of this letter. It was printed in the newspapers and appears not to have been questioned. Moreover, the proposed scheme was quite in harmony with the company's well-known character.

[47] *U. S. Docs.*, ser. no. 734, doc. 126, p. 29.

[48] *Ibid.*

[49] In the opinion of Clarendon, this was an unreasonable sum (Clarendon to Crampton, Aug. 31, 1854, F. O., Am., vol. 591, no. 191), and, though there are no means of verifying this opinion, a knowledge of the circumstances leads to the belief that it was correct.

[50] *U. S. Docs.*, ser. no. 734, doc. 126, p. 9.

[51] *Ibid.*

the town, declaring that if the demands were not met by nine o'clock the next morning the place would be bombarded.[52] A body of marines sent by Hollins secured the arms and ammunition which were at the station house.[53] At the same time Scott invited the women and children and the aged and infirm as well as all who would declare themselves well-disposed towards the United States to take refuge in the river steamers of the company.[54] But only about twelve availed themselves of the offer.[55]

While these things were taking place, the British schooner *Bermuda* with Lieutenant Jolly in charge lay in the harbor. Hollins notified Jolly of his intentions,[56] and the latter entered a solemn protest against the proposed action. The town, he pointed out, was entirely defenseless and the force under his command was totally inadequate to protect the place against the *Cyane.*[57] Hollins expressed regret that Jolly considered a protest necessary, but declared that he, Hollins, must enforce the reparation demanded by his government.[58]

As no attention had been paid to any of the demands made in behalf of the United States government, on the morning of July 13 Hollins opened bombardment. When the bombardment was over, the buildings spared by the guns of the *Cyane* were set afire by Hollins's orders, and the town was thus totally destroyed.[59]

Hollins's action met with strong condemnation from the American press and people.[60] The New York *Times* was particularly bitter, and, assuming that the

[52] *Ibid.*, pp. 6-7, 9-10.   [53] *Ibid.*, p. 10.   [54] *Ibid.*, p. 10, 30.
[53] *Ibid.*, p. 31.   [56] *Ibid.*, p. 7.   [57] *Ibid.*   [58] *Ibid.*, pp. 7-8.
[59] *Ibid.*, ser. no. 702, doc. 85, p. 29.
[60] New York *Times*, July 26, 31, Aug. 1, 2, 1854; New York *Tribune*, Aug. 2, 3, 5, 16, 1854; Boston *Transcript*, July 28, 29, Aug. 3, 1854; Boston *Post*, July 31, 1854; von Holst, *History*, V, 12.

action was directed or approved by the government, intimated that the terms of the Clayton-Bulwer treaty had been broken, and denounced President Pierce for a violation of the Constitution of the United States, on the ground that Congress alone could declare war.[61] The *Times* was an opposition paper, but the best elements of the Democrats themselves felt that they could not honestly defend the deed.[62] The fact that resolutions from both houses of Congress, asking for the correspondence upon the subject, with a copy of Hollins's instructions, were carried by a large majority and in spite of administrative opposition was indicative of the general disapprobation of the country.[63]

The attitude of the British government towards the destruction of Greytown is of decided interest in view of the declaration, which the government had repeatedly made, that the place was under British protection and would remain so until terms could be agreed upon for its disposal. The town had been utterly destroyed by a United States war vessel. The protectorate was thus finally put to a test.

Throughout England the affair was, of course, disapproved, regretfully by those friendly to the United States, and savagely by newspapers like the London *Times*.[64] As usual, this paper reflected the views of the government. Clarendon, writing to Crampton on August 31, 1854, declared the outrage to be " without a parallel in the annals of modern times ",[65] but added that it was a consolation to learn, as he had from

---

[61] New York *Times,* Aug. 1, 1854.
[62] von Holst, *History,* V, 9-10.
[63] Crampton to Clarendon, July 31, 1854, F. O., Am., vol. 598, no. 204; Griffith to Hammond, Aug. 20, 1854, " Private ", *ibid.,* vol. 598.
[64] Buchanan, *Works,* IX, 248.
[65] F. O., Am., vol. 598, no. 191.

Crampton, that the deed had been indignantly repro-
bated by public opinion in the United States, and he had
no doubt that these feelings would be shared by the
American government.[66]

Upon first learning of the matter, Buchanan had
promptly assured the British government of his conviction that Hollins's act was without authority and would
be disavowed by the United States.[67] Marcy, however,
seems to have been placed in a quandary by the situation.
It is possible that Hollins's measures were more extreme than had been desired by the American government,[68] but in view of the instructions furnished him,
they could hardly be disavowed. On the other hand,
American public opinion, which was probably much
more adverse than had been expected, had to be considered; and the British government had to be reckoned with. In this dilemma it was evidently thought
best to avoid discussion as long as possible. Accordingly, when approached by Crampton regarding the
subject, Marcy replied that for the present he must
decline expressing any opinion, as the matter was under
consideration of the American government.[69] A little
later when Crampton broached the subject, Marcy
declared that he could not yet speak officially regarding
it, as he had not heard from the President. But during
this conversation, he tried to make much of the fact

[66] *Ibid.*

[67] Buchanan, *Works,* IX, 248.

[68] On August 8, Marcy wrote in a private letter to Buchanan: " The
occurrence at Greytown is an embarrassing affair. The place merited
chastisement, but the severity of the one inflicted exceeded our expectations. The Government will, however, I think, stand by Capt. Hollins."
Ibid., 242. Marcy may have been perfectly sincere in this statement, but
in view of Buchanan's expectation of a disavowal, in a letter to Buchanan
Marcy would scarcely have commended the act.

[69] Crampton to Clarendon, July 31, 1854, F. O., Am., vol. 598, no. 204.

that the principal ringleaders of Greytown had been received aboard Jolly's vessel, and, as Crampton expressed it, showed an attempt to shift the blame for an unpopular act to the shoulders of a British officer.[70]

On September 21, when more than two months had passed without a disavowal or an explanation from the American government, Clarendon again addressed the British minister at Washington. The British government, he wrote, had confidently expected the outrages and wrongs committed at Greytown to be indignantly disavowed by the United States government as they had been by the American people, but had seen with surprise and regret that the sentiments of the people had not been re-echoed by the cabinet at Washington, and that so long a time had been allowed to elapse without Hollins's conduct being disavowed. Crampton was instructed to read this letter to Marcy.[71]

Finally, in the President's message of December 4, 1854, a definite stand was taken by the American government. The message gave a detailed account of the bombardment and the events connected with it, but with such omissions [72] and misrepresentations [73] as

[70] Crampton to Clarendon, Sept. 18, 1854, *ibid.,* no. 229. The charges made against Jolly were promptly investigated by order of the British government, and Jolly was completely exonerated. Fanshawe to the Secretary of the Admiralty, Nov. 25, 1854, Ad. Sec. In-Letters, 5629, no. 204.

[71] F. O., Am., vol. 591, no. 198.

[72] For instance, the message failed to state that before the bombardment began arms and ammunition had been removed from Greytown and put aboard the *Cyane.*

[73] The message declared Greytown to be a " marauding establishment too dangerous to be disregarded and too guilty to pass unpunished, and yet incapable of being treated in any other way than as a piratical resort of outlaws or a camp of savages depredating on emigrant trains or caravans and the frontier settlements of civilized states ", which was only partly true. Richardson, *Messages and Papers,* V, 282. Further-

to leave an erroneous impression of the incident. In concluding his consideration of the matter, the President wrote: " It certainly would have been most satisfactory to me if the object of the *Cyane's* mission could have been consummated without any act of public force, but the arrogant contumacy of the offenders rendered it impossible to avoid the alternative either to break up their establishment or to leave them impressed with the idea that they might persevere with impunity in a career of insolence and plunder." [74]

Thus the American government tried to justify the act of its official, and, in view of the instructions sent to Hollins and Fabens, it is rather difficult to see what other course was possible. But the whole affair was unjustifiable. It is true that the insult to Borland and the depredations upon the property of the Transit Company demanded some action on the part of the United States government, but to bombard and then burn a town deserted by its inhabitants, and thus to destroy the property of the innocent with that of the guilty, was an act unworthy of a civilized nation. Furthermore, in considering the guilt of the Greytown people it should be remembered that there were mitigating circumstances. Because of Hollins's interference, their grievance of the preceding year against the Transit

---

more, the message stated that Hollins had appealed to Jolly " to interpose and persuade them (the people of Greytown) to take some course calculated to save the necessity of resorting to the extreme measures indicated in his proclamation." *Ibid.*, 283. Neither the report of Fabens nor that of Hollins justify such a statement. Moreover, nearly a month before the President's message appeared, Jolly distinctly stated in reply to a question from the Admiralty that Hollins " did at no time entreat or request him to exert his influence with the authorities at Greytown to act differently ". Inclosure in Fanshawe to the Secretary of the Admiralty, Nov. 25, 1854, Ad. Sec. In-Letters, 5629, no. 204.

[74] Richardson, *Messages and Papers,* V, 280-284.

Company still existed; and Borland had protected the murderer of one of their number, who had apparently been innocent of any offense.

The President's message was practically the last word between the two countries upon the general subject of the bombardment. The British government had asked for a disavowal of the act, and the President had replied by defending it. The British government did not press the matter further.[75] The protectorate over Mosquito, like the kingdom which it pretended to protect, was but a shadow when a strong nation was the aggressor.

It may be suggested that had not the British government been embarrassed by the Crimean War at the time, Hollins's proceedings might have had more serious results. It is possible that in such case the call for disavowal might have been worded less mildly, and the correspondence might have taken on a more belligerent tone, but it is unlikely that the affair would have gone beyond this. The protest and call for disavowal by the British government were merely made for the purpose of saving—or trying to save—British dignity. If a disavowal could be obtained, so much the better; if not, the matter would be dropped. The British government fully realized that a war over such a flimsy pretext as the Mosquito kingdom would not only receive the condemnation of the world at large, but, what was

[75] In conversation with Buchanan, Clarendon severely criticised the presidential message relative to the destruction of Greytown, which Buchanan in turn defended. Buchanan, *Works,* IX, 337.

The Nicaraguan government had also protested against Hollins's act, but it had not ventured to demand a disavowal of the act. Griffith to Hammond, Aug. 27, 1854, " Private ", F. O., Am., vol. 598.

more to the point, would also fail to receive either the approval or the support of the British people.[76]

In addition to a disavowal of the outrage, the British government had attempted to secure indemnity for property of British subjects which had been destroyed by Hollins. In accordance with instructions, Crampton informed Marcy that his government considered compensation due for these losses;[77] but the Secretary of State gave little reason to believe that such damages would be paid, and took the ground that as the inhabitants of the town formed a sort of *de facto* government, they had no claim to protection on countries of which they were natives.[78] However, Wheeler, a new minister to Central America, with Fabens, was instructed to investigate the claims for damages presented by various nations,[79] and for a time Marcy held out some hope that " innocent sojourners " at the place might be compensated;[80] but later he stated that so far as he had been able to examine the reports sent in no such persons existed.[81] He informed Crampton, however, that American citizens who claimed damages were treated just as the people of other countries.[82] Finally, after Cramp-

---

[76] The attitude of the British public regarding the subject was reflected in the press in the spring of 1853. The London *Globe* for March 3 remarked that if cause for war with the United States were wanted, the very positive grounds necessary for a quarrel with kinfolk " should not be mixed up with the assertion of anything quite so aboriginal as the ill-defined rights, titles, and dominions of the tawny,—and to confess the truth,—somewhat trumpery majesty of Mosquito." And the *News* for April 2 expressed the opinion that the sooner the British government gave up its interference in the paltry squabbles of the savages of Mosquitia, and the semi-savages of Honduras and Nicaragua, the better it would be for its reputation.

[77] Clarendon to Crampton, Aug. 31, 1854, F. O., Am., vol. 591, no. 191.

[78] Crampton to Clarendon, Sept. 18, 1854, *ibid.,* vol. 598, no. 229.

[79] Clarendon to Crampton, Feb. 16, 1855, *ibid.,* vol. 616, no. 32.

[80] Crampton to Clarendon, Mar. 12, 1855, *ibid.,* vol. 620, no. 60; Crampton to Clarendon, July 16, 1855, *ibid.,* vol. 622, no. 136.

[81] *Ibid.*   [82] *Ibid.*

ton had repeatedly called the attention of the American government to the subject of claims,[83] the Foreign Secretary consulted the law officers of the Crown with regard to it and was informed by them that as the United States government had adopted the acts of its naval officer, it could not, in accordance with the principles of international law, be called upon to make compensation to British subjects for the losses occasioned to them by those acts. In a confidential note Clarendon made known this opinion to Crampton, and added that it was of great importance that a maritime power like England should uphold the doctrines of international law thus laid down, since her fleets were likely often to be engaged in hostilities against seaport towns. Consequently, he wrote, the British government did not think it advisable that Crampton should officially press the Greytown claims.[84] With this the matter was dropped and no claims were ever paid by the United States for damages caused by the bombardment of Greytown.

Long before the correspondence arising from the bombardment ended, there had grown from the rumors of armed expeditions to be sent from the United States to Central America a reality which in time roused the old British suspicion of American designs on the isthmus, and struck terror to the hearts of the Central American republics. This was the filibustering movement. Early in 1854 reports were abroad that an American colonization society had secured certain lands

---

[83] Crampton to Clarendon, Mar. 12, 1855, F. O., Am., vol. 620, no. 60; Clarendon to Crampton, May 21, 1855, *ibid.*, vol. 616, no. 100; Crampton to Clarendon, July 16, 1855, F. O., Am., vol. 622, no. 136; Jan. 28, 1856, *ibid.*, vol. 640, no. 11.

[84] *Ibid.*, vol. 638, no. 45.

in the Mosquito territory.[85] These reports evidently had reference to an organization called the Central American Agricultural and Mining Association, formed by Colonel Kinney of Philadelphia.[86] The land in which the association was interested lay to the south of the San Juan, in territory claimed by Nicaragua, and was part of a grant made in 1839 to Peter and Samuel Shepherd of Georgia by the Mosquito king.[87] The organization professed that its object was the colonization of this territory and the development of its resources.[88]

When this report, somewhat exaggerated, was added to the rumors regarding aid to be sent Squier,[89] the British government took a further precautionary step. Though it felt that such expeditions would not be countenanced by the United States government, there still remained the danger that they might escape the vigilance of the American authorities. Consequently, on March 9, 1854, Clarendon instructed Wyke to give warning, confidentially, to the Central American republics to which his commission extended.[90]

But the recent American policy in Mexico had already roused these states to keen watchfulness of their northern neighbor. All except Honduras were now thoroughly frightened, and turned towards England for protection. The situation offers an interesting contrast to that which existed upon Squier's arrival in

[85] Bowen to Wyke, Feb. 25, 1854, F. O., Cen. Am., vol. 82, no. 3.
[86] Crampton to Clarendon, Dec. 11, 1854, F. O., Am., vol. 600, no. 89.
[87] Stout, *Nicaragua*, 171-172.
[88] *Ibid.*, 173.
[89] It seems likely that the rumors that Squier intended to drive the British from Mosquito and Ruatan had their origin in the preparations of the Kinney expedition. There is no evidence to prove that Squier ever contemplated such action.
[90] F. O., Cen. Am., vol. 82, no. 5.

1849, when three of the states turned eagerly towards the United States for protection against British encroachments. Though Guatemala had not forgotten her old claims on Belize territory, in the last part of 1853 the prime minister of the republic approached Wyke expressing a desire to settle the Belize boundaries by secret treaty with Great Britain, in order to protect his state from American designs,[91] his idea apparently being that the American government might use the boundary dispute as an excuse for intervention. But the British government prudently replied that this would not be conducive to the interest of Guatemala, as such a treaty would be more likely to produce than avert the dangers anticipated from American encroachments.[92] A little later Nicaragua revealed her fears by soliciting a treaty which would bring her into closer relations with the British government. She even promised to let her Mosquito claims lie dormant, in the hope that the Indians would later voluntarily unite themselves with her, and offered to acknowledge Greytown a free port under the protection of all nations.[93] The matter was presented by Wyke to his government, but Clarendon replied that if a treaty should be formed with Nicaragua it was expedient that some mention be made of the Mosquito territory.[94] Wyke believed that Spanish pride would prevent the Nicaraguans from acknowledging the independence of the Mosquitos, so it was thought best to let the matter rest for a while.[95]

[91] Savage to Webster, April 21, 1851, Dept. of State, Des., Guat., vol. 3, no. 6; Wyke to Clarendon, Nov. 27, 1853, F. O., Cen. Am., vol. 79, no. 37; Clarendon to Wyke, Jan. 19, 1854, F. O., Cen. Am., vol. 82, no. 3.
[92] Ibid.
[93] Wyke to Clarendon, Mar. 13, 1854, ibid., no. 9.
[94] Ibid., no. 7.
[95] Wyke to Clarendon, July 29, 1854, ibid., no. 22.

Meanwhile, however, the British government, though on the verge of the Crimean War, had not been indifferent on its own account to the reports of contemplated attacks on Central America by American citizens. The interference of the American government in Mexico and the filibustering expeditions of William Walker into that state doubtless quickened British attention. As early as February 2, 1854, Clarendon wrote to Crampton about the matter, stating that such projects, if carried out without the knowledge of the United States government, would amount to buccaneering acts; and that Great Britain could not believe that the United States would fail, on learning of such intentions, to put an immediate stop to them. Crampton was instructed to notify Marcy immediately of these views, and to inquire whether anything was known of the contemplated plans, and also whether means would be employed to prevent their execution.[96]

About a week later the Foreign Secretary again wrote, sending further information with reference to the proposed expeditions, and directed Crampton to communicate with Marcy regarding it. Should he fail to receive a satisfactory reply from the Secretary of State, he was to express the feelings of surprise and deep concern with which the knowledge of these manœuvres had been received by the British government, which hoped that they would not only be discountenanced, but prevented, by the United States; for it must be obvious that if attempts should be made to execute such schemes other governments might be forced to take measures for defeating them—a course which might lead to misunderstandings between Great

[96] F. O., Am., vol. 590, no. 20.

Britain and the United States.[97] The instructions were executed by Crampton, to whom Marcy declared himself ignorant of any such designs as were reported, but expressed the desire of the American government to keep on good terms with Great Britain.[98]

But Crampton had been preceded, in his representations to the American government, by Marcoleta, who persistently labored to prevent the departure of the Kinney expedition. Later in the year the Nicaraguan minister increased his efforts, for then the rumors took more definite shape and it was stated that the colonization association intended, if necessary, to use force in taking the land,[99] and that the expedition also planned to seize Greytown.[100] As many members of the colonization association were also affiliated with the Transit Company,[101] there seemed good foundation for the report. Consequently, Marcoleta again communicated with Marcy, declaring that the Mosquito king could not legally make land grants.[102] Marcy replied that the American government had no power to prevent its citizens from leaving the country when " engaged in business purposes ", and added that the question of the validity of the grant would have to be settled between the company and the Nicaraguan government.[103]

Though it was more difficult to enforce the neutrality laws of the United States against the filibusters than most foreign powers realized, yet it is quite evident that the American government did not use its best efforts to do so, and that local officials were at times guilty of

[97] F. O., Am., vol. 590, no. 31.

[98] Crampton to Clarendon, Mar. 6, 1854, *ibid.*, vol. 594, no. 53.

[99] Crampton to Clarendon, Dec. 11, 1854, *ibid.*, vol. 600, no. 89.

[100] *Ibid.*   [101] *Ibid.*   [102] *Harper's Magazine*, X, 542.

[103] Crampton to Clarendon, Dec. 11, 1854, F. O., Am., vol. 600, no. 89.

gross neglect of duty in the execution of orders. Part
of this neglect was undoubtedly due to the desire of the
South for the extension of slave territory, but there
seems good reason to believe that the failure of the
British government to withdraw from Central America,
as required by the Clayton-Bulwer treaty, also strongly
contributed to this indifference to international obligations.

Marcoleta's persistence, however, was not in vain.
Evidently as a direct consequence of his protests, a
correspondence took place between Marcy and Kinney
with reference to the proposed expedition. The latter
declared that his object was to improve and occupy the
land within the limits of his grant; everything was to
be done peacefully, without invading the rights of
either communities or states.[104]   Marcy replied that if
the expedition was merely a peaceful emigration, and
if those connected with it chose to abandon all claim
to protection from the United States and to submit
themselves to the jurisdiction of some other country,
the American government would not interfere with
it.[105]   He expressed the determination of the United
States government, however, to preserve the neutrality
laws of the nation,[106] which required that it prevent the
departure of any expedition intended to disturb the
peace of a friendly state.

This correspondence was published in the *Union* of
February 7, 1855,[107] and gave much satisfaction to those
concerned over the subject. A letter written by Crampton to Clarendon a few days later stated that Marcy's

[104] *Harper's Magazine*, X, 542.
[105] *Ibid.*; Crampton to Clarendon, Feb. 10, 1855, F. O., Am., vol. 619,
no. 33.   [106] *Ibid.*   [107] *Ibid.*

determination to enforce the neutrality laws was generally considered fatal to the expedition, for it did not seem likely that Kinney would persist in his enterprise in face of the risk which must now attach to it.[108]

But all hope that the undertaking had been abandoned soon vanished, for in a few weeks a letter describing the proposed undertaking was published in the newspapers. It promised six hundred and forty acres of land to all colonists engaging to serve in a military capacity for twelve months.[109] This seemed to prove that, as had been reported, the land was to be taken by force, if necessary. A letter written by Kinney in January, 1855, to a prospective colonist reflects the same idea. After describing the country to be settled and stating that the colonists should be armed, Kinney wrote: "We do not suppose there will be much necessity for fighting, but we believe that the establishment of such a colony in that part of the world will result in a few years in the entire control of all Central America by the American people." [110] The aim was obviously to conquer Central America by colonization.

When the first-mentioned letter appeared in the newspapers, Marcoleta again addressed Marcy, asking that the United States government prevent the "perfidious schemes" from being carried out.[111] This effort led to investigation by the American government, and,

[108] Crampton to Clarendon, Feb. 10, 1855, F. O., Am., vol. 619, no. 33.

[109] Marcoleta to Marcy, Mar. 14, 1855, Dept. of State, Notes to Dept., Cen. Am. Legat., Nic., vol. 2.

[110] Inclosure in Ross to Clarendon, Nov. 30, 1855, F. O., Cen. Am., vol. 87.

[111] Marcoleta to Marcy, Mar. 1855, Dept. of State, Notes to Dept., Cen. Am. Legat., Nic., vol. 2.

as a result, on April 27, Kinney, and Fabens, who was apparently his most important colleague, were indicted on the charge of preparing a military expedition against Nicaragua.[112] However, when the case came up for trial the two were acquitted for want of sufficient evidence.[113] But the latter was deprived of his consular office, because of the part which he had taken in the affair.[114] Nevertheless, Marcoleta continued his complaints,[115] and consequently the American government gave orders for the detention of any vessel which Kinney might attempt to use for the purpose of his expedition.[116] But in spite of these precautions, Kinney and several of his associates escaped to Jamaica, where they waited a favorable opportunity for the execution of their designs.[117]

But before Kinney made his escape the attention of foreign diplomats at Washington had been attracted to a more formidable foe to Central American independence. This was William Walker.[118] On July 10, 1855, Crampton informed Clarendon of the aid given

---

[112] *U. S. Docs.*, ser. no. 822, doc. 68, pp. 8-9.

[113] Stout, *Nicaragua*, 176.

[114] Lumley to Clarendon, May 14, 1855, F. O., Am., vol. 621, no. 10.

[115] Marcy to Marcoleta, May 15, 1855, Dept. of State, Notes from Dept., Cen. Am. Legat., vol. 1.

[116] *Ibid.*, pp. 80-81.

[117] Crampton to Clarendon, June 18, 1855, F. O., Am., vol. 621, no. 124. Kinney soon reached Greytown where he remained for a time. But he seemed to give up his plans for a colony and later wandered in different parts of Central America, where he occasionally aroused some uneasiness on the part of the British or Central Americans, but after June, 1855, his movements were no longer a subject of diplomatic correspondence. Seymour to Bell, June 17, 1857, and Seymour to Darling, Aug. 17, 1857, F. O., Hond., vol. 3.

[118] For an account of Walker's career in Central America, see general histories of Central America, and also the following: Walker, *War in Nicaragua*; Lucas, *Nicaragua: War of the Filibusters*; Wells, *Walker's Expedition to Nicaragua*.

by Walker to the Central American Liberals, and expressed the belief that should a government be established in Nicaragua by either of the contending parties through the aid of American auxiliaries, the independent existence of Nicaragua might be regarded as in a very precarious condition.[119] When news of the fall of Granada reached the United States shortly afterwards, the concern of Crampton and of the Central American agents at the capital was much increased, for they felt that Walker could not have succeeded without aid from the Transit Company.[120] This state of affairs, in the opinion of Crampton, showed flagrant violation of international duty on the part of the American government, as well as an aim on the part of American citizens to bring about the annexation of Nicaragua to the United States.[121]

But though Crampton faithfully sent in his reports of the filibustering movement,[122] after the first half of the year 1854 he seems to have received but few instructions from his government regarding the matter. This neglect, however, was probably not due to indifference, but to a realization that the expeditions had a definite diplomatic significance which was at first not suspected. The determined stand of the United States government with reference to the interpretation of the Clayton-Bulwer treaty, as well as the bombardment of Greytown and the defense of the act by President Pierce, had

[119] F. O., Am., vol. 621, no. 134.

[120] For a good account of the part played by the Transit Company, see Scroggs, " William Walker and the Steamship Corporation in Nicaragua ", in *Am. Hist. Rev.,* X, 792-812.

[121] Crampton to Clarendon, Nov. 13, 1855, F. O., Am., vol. 624, no. 242.

[122] Crampton to Clarendon, July 10, 1855, *ibid.,* vol. 621, no. 134; July 30, 1855, *ibid.,* vol. 622, no. 154; Nov. 13, 1855, *ibid.,* vol. 624, no. 242.

evidently convinced the British government that indifference to filibustering was part of American policy in dealing with the Central American question. In view of this, British protests might be even worse than useless.

Marcoleta, and Molina, however, and Irisarri, the newly-arrived representative of Salvador [123] and Guatemala, continued and increased the protests on behalf of Central America.[124] Perhaps partly in consequence of their efforts, the American government, near the close of 1855, displayed a stronger sense of international duty. Wheeler, Borland's successor, in spite of instructions, had recognized Walker's government, but his act was promptly disavowed by the United States and the assurance given that the American government had no intention of recognizing Walker.[125] The favorable impression made by this announcement was increased by the fact that almost simultaneously came the refusal of the Washington authorities to receive a representative sent by Walker.[126] But more effective still in allaying the suspicion that the American government was willing to connive at the proceedings of its citizens in Central America was the proclamation of President Pierce warning all Americans not to take part in any hostile operations in Nicaragua, carried on by Walker.[127]

[123] At about this time Salvador tried to form a treaty with England for protection against the filibusters. Wyke to Clarendon, Nov. 29, 1855, F. O., Cen. Am., vol. 85, no. 57.

[124] *U. S. Docs.*, ser. no. 822, doc. 68, pp. 21, 42-43, 46-47, 48-49.

[125] Dept. of State, Notes from Dept., Cen. Am. Legat., vol. 1, pp. 99-101.

[126] Crampton to Clarendon, Dec. 17, 1855, F. O., Am., vol. 624, no. 266; Wells, *Walker's Expedition to Nicaragua*, 100.

[127] *Ibid.*

CHAPTER VII.

THE CRISIS, 1855-1856; SIGNS OF BRITISH RETREAT.

More than a year passed after Buchanan presented his second statement of American views on the Central American question before any serious attempt was again made to reconcile the differences between the two governments. Various reasons produced this seeming unconcern. The Foreign Secretary was deeply engrossed in the Crimean War; besides, he probably felt after receiving Buchanan's second paper, that the position which the British government had assumed could better be maintained by evasion than by discussion.[1] Marcy, too, had other demands on his attention; the Kansas-Nebraska struggle was on. Moreover, since the North believed that the Democratic interest in Central America originated largely in the desire for extending slave territory, it would have been most unwise to insist upon settlement of the Central American question, and thus risk complications with England, when the nation was facing a domestic crisis produced by an effort to introduce slavery into Kansas.

During this period, therefore, Buchanan was left practically to his own resources regarding Central American negotiations. But the completion of the reciprocity treaty,[2] and later the resignation from the

---

[1] Clarendon promised Buchanan an answer to his second paper, and later said that he had prepared one, but it was never presented. Buchanan, *Works*, IX, 278; *U. S. Docs.*, ser. no. 840, doc. 1, p. 76.

[2] London *Morning Post*, Dec. 5, 1854.

premiership of Aberdeen, who was friendly to the United States, and the accession of Palmerston,[3] under whose direction Greytown had been seized in the name of the Mosquitos, caused Buchanan to lose all hope of an early settlement of the Central American dispute. Furthermore, such casual and desultory conversations as he obtained with Clarendon [4] were not conducive to a revival of the hope.

But in August, 1855, the discussion was reopened by the United States. The approaching session of Congress made it desirable that the question be placed on a more satisfactory basis; and the fact that both of the parties concerned were less occupied with other matters than in the preceding year made the prospect of settlement better than it had been. Moreover, the determined policy displayed by the United States government was evidently now expected to produce favorable results. Consequently, Marcy directed Buchanan to secure a definite and final statement from the British government as to the position it proposed to maintain on the subject, especially regarding the Bay Islands. If the British government meant to avoid the operation of the Clayton-Bulwer treaty in reference to the Bay Islands, there was little use in asking it to respect any other of the obligations imposed by that act. Marcy's letter showed the same attitude as the year before, and declared that a fulfillment of treaty stipulations required that Great Britain withdraw from the Mosquito coast, the Bay Islands, and the Belize territory lying between the Sibun and the Sarstoon.[5]

---

[3] Buchanan, *Works*, IX, 297, 299, 300, 320, 339-342.

[4] *Ibid.*, 298, 337-343.

[5] *U. S. Docs.*, ser. no. 840, doc. 1, pp. 69-72.

Buchanan accordingly reopened the question,[6] but with small hopes of a satisfactory result.[7] Clarendon's response showed a determination consistently to maintain the former extreme position. The British government, he stated, adhered to the opinion which it had " uniformly held, that the convention of April 19, 1850, was merely prospective in its operation, and did not in any way interfere with the state of things existing at the time of its conclusion. If it had been intended to do so, . . . it would have contained, in specific terms, a renunciation, on the part of Great Britain, of the possessions and rights which, up to the conclusion of the convention, she had claimed to maintain, and such renunciation would not have been left as a mere matter of inference." [8]

In an unofficial reply to Buchanan's report of the result of his efforts, Marcy gave what may be considered the frank views of the United States government regarding the conduct of Great Britain. He wrote:

Notwithstanding the intimation before given by the British Govt., I was not prepared to believe that when pressed to a definite decision, it would dare to take the ground that the provisions of the Clayton and Bulwer treaty were only prospective in their operation . . . Her position in that respect raises a very serious question. The United States will never acquiesce in that interpretation of the Convention and Great Britain cannot, it seems to me, believe that this government will do so. That she is wrong, no reasonable, calm-judging man can doubt, and the judgment of this country, and, I should think, the reflecting portion of the English people, will look upon it as something more and worse than an error. . . . From the present course of the British government on the Central American controversy, . . . I am inclined to conclude that it

[6] Buchanan, *Works*, IX, 403-405.
[7] *Ibid.*, 394-395.
[8] *U. S. Docs.*, ser. no. 840, doc. 1, pp. 76-77.

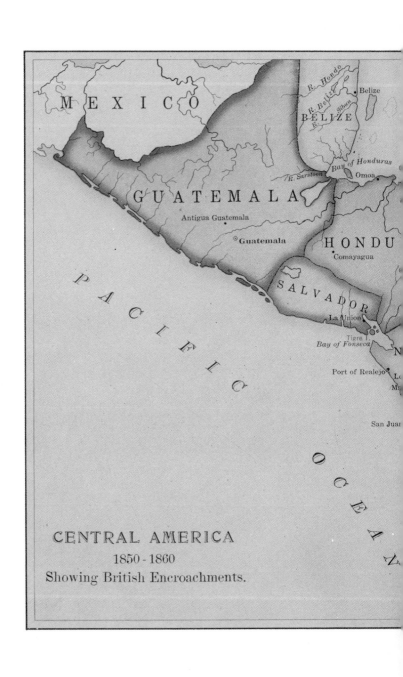

CENTRAL AMERICA
1850 - 1860
Showing British Encroachments.

BAY ISLANDS

ATAN   BONACCA

Port Royal

athouse

Honduras
Truxillo

Cape Cameron

R. Roman

R. Black

ATLANTIC OCEAN

Cape Gracias á Dios

AS

gucigalpa

MOSQUITO

Segovia or Wanks

R. Hueson

SHORE

CARAGUA

L. Mandgua

R. Bluefields

gua

nada

Lake
Nicaragua

el Sur

R. Rama

Bluefields

Ft San Carlos

R. San Juan

Machuca
Rapids

Greytown (San Juan del Norte)
Pt. Arenas
R. Colorado

COSTA

San Jose

RICA

NEW GRANADA

THE M.-N. WORKS, BUFFALO, N.Y.

cares very little about maintaining cordial relations with the United States. I can discover nothing in the present condition of Great Britain or her future prospects to justify her in holding her head so high. . . . With her, as with all others, this country desires to maintain the relations of friendship, but from her and them it claims a respect for our sovereign rights, and good faith in international compacts; and neither will be sacrificed for the sake of peace. The prospect, to my prevision, looks a little cloudy; but, as our old friend Mr. Ritchie was wont to say " *nous verrons* ".[9]

The determination of Great Britain to maintain her unreasonable interpretation of the Clayton-Bulwer treaty caused a change in the United States towards that agreement. The members of the government took the attitude that the treaty obligations were in a way suspended;[10] and a portion of the press declared that Clarendon's reply to Buchanan amounted to an abrogation of the arrangement.[11] Had not the North condemned filibustering as a slavery extension measure, it is probable that, in consequence of the British stand, the American government would have at this time come out more strongly in favor of Walker. As it was, and especially in view of the feeling roused by the Kansas-Nebraska question, such a result was impossible. Indeed, as has already been noted, in the autumn of 1855[12] the American government displayed more vigor in its efforts to prevent aid from being sent to Walker. The reason for this, however, was most probably a desire to place the United States in a more advantageous position in the discussion rising from the discovery of Crampton's share in the British attempt

---

[9] Dept. of State, Inst., Gt. Brit., vol. 16, pp. 396-397.
[10] Napier to Clarendon, Oct. 22, 1857, F. O., Am., vol. 674, no. 220.
[11] *Daily Alta California,* Dec. 5, 1855; Wells, *Walker's Expedition to Nicaragua,* 135.
[12] See above, p. 195.

to recruit soldiers in the United States for the Crimean War.[13]

The appearance of the recruitment difficulty coincident with the more menacing attitude of the Central American question placed British-American relations in a much more serious light. Though it is evident that the irritation caused by the unreasonable British interpretation of the Clayton-Bulwer treaty produced much of the American indignation over the subject of British enlistment and determined the attitude of the government regarding the latter subject,[14] yet considerable ill-feeling was caused by the recruiting question itself; and the one difficulty so reacted upon the other as soon to put the relations of the two countries in a critical state.

Naturally, most of the sensitiveness and suspicion was found on the American side; and it was quickened by the belief that France and England meant to make use of the alliance which they had formed during the Crimean War for the purpose of interfering in American affairs.[15] This belief appeared well founded when, in the last part of October, the *Times* and other leading British newspapers announced that the government had sent several war vessels to reinforce its West Indian squadron.[16] This had been done, the *Times* stated, for the purpose of repressing the movements then in progress in various American cities for the invasion of countries with which the United States was at peace. Great Britain was determined to supply the ability

[13] Crampton to Clarendon, Dec. 31, 1855, F. O., Am., vol. 624, no. 281.
[14] Hansard, *Parl. Debates,* 3d ser., CXLII, 1511-1512; *Blackwood's Magazine,* LXXX, 122; *Daily Alta California,* Dec. 16, 1855.
[15] Buchanan, *Works,* IX, 434, 462-463.
[16] *Ibid.,* 433-436; *Harper's Magazine,* XII, 253.

which the American government lacked, to enforce its own laws.[17]

Such representations by journals believed to enjoy the confidence and reflect the views of the British ministry were certain to create excitement in America. Therefore, Buchanan, who described the outlook as " squally ",[18] changed his plans for returning home and determined to await the arrival of his successor. As soon as possible [19] after reading the *Times* article, he secured an interview with Clarendon and asked the purpose of increasing the British naval armament so near to American coasts, giving as his reason the desire to prevent, if possible, the irritation in the United States which the appearance of such a fleet would naturally produce.[20] The Foreign Secretary emphatically condemned the statement of the press [21] and declared that the fleet had not been sent with the least unfriendly intention towards the United States. Its despatch, he said, had resulted from information secured by the British government that several privateers for Russian service were being built at New York.[22]

Buchanan was not convinced by this explanation,[23] but his anxiety was somewhat relieved by the attitude taken by the British people. Recent events had attracted the attention of the British public to the dispute, and had created a desire to learn the real facts of the controversy. Buchanan felt that this new alertness of the British public mind was a strong indication that Palmerston would not be sustained in raising difficulties with the United States.[24]

[17] *Harper's Magazine*, XII, 253.
[18] Buchanan, *Works*, IX, 436.
[19] *Ibid.*, 433-434.   [20] *Ibid.*, 438.   [21] *Ibid.*, 439-440.
[22] *Ibid.*, 438.   [23] *Ibid.*, 438-439.   [24] *Ibid.*, 446.

Later, after it had been proved that the report regarding the building of privateers in New York was false,[25] Buchanan called Clarendon's attention to the mistaken nature of the report and desired the withdrawal of the fleet.[26] The President's message, he stated, would undoubtedly present the unsatisfactory condition of the Central American question and as the news of the sending of the fleet would reach the United States but a short time before the message was issued, the two would be connected in public opinion, thus rendering the question more complicated.[27] Clarendon again declared that the despatch of the fleet was not intended as a menace to the United States, and promised to consider recalling the vessels.[28] Buchanan tried to emphasize the expediency of doing so. He showed how a withdrawal could allay public indignation in the United States, and pointed out the disastrous character of a possible war between the two nations.[29]

As time passed, Buchanan counted more and more on British public opinion to keep the peace; but he realized that an unfriendly press might bring the people to a willingness to fight America, especially if they could be induced to believe that national honor required war.[30] Therefore he was anxious that the whole Central American question be brought before them clearly and in a firm but temperate manner, for he believed that this would force Palmerston to adopt a more friendly policy, or to retire.[31] He counted on the President's message to effect this, and consequently looked forward

---

[25] Buchanan, *Works,* IX, 450.
[26] *Ibid.*   [27] *Ibid.,* 451.   [28] *Ibid.*
[29] *Ibid.,* 452-453.   [30] *Ibid.,* 456, 461.   [31] *Ibid.,* 461, 479-480.

eagerly to the early appearance of that document.[32] However, the political confusion of the period delayed for some time the organization of the House of Representatives, and thus deferred the message, until, on December 31—probably in consequence of the urgings of Buchanan,[33] as well as of the general unsatisfactory relations with England [34]—it was finally sent to Congress even though the speaker of the House still remained unchosen.[35]

The message contained a detailed consideration of British relations. On the whole the language was temperate, but a hostile note was discernible and a determination not to yield on either the recruiting difficulty or the dispute over Central America.[36]

The President's stand was supported by the Senate. The speeches which followed the receipt of the message offer an interesting contrast to those produced three years before by Palmerston's declaration regarding Belize. Then there was distinct division on party lines ; now there was a complete acceptance of the view represented in the President's message, and a practically unanimous denunciation of Great Britain. Though a few advocated abrogation of the treaty, as a whole the Senate favored requiring Great Britain to fulfill her treaty obligations, even though such insistence result in war. Still, there was a strong feeling that there would be no war ; but that England, when she saw that the United States was firm, would yield, for war over such questions as those in dispute would find little favor

[32] *Ibid.,* 479-480.
[33] *Ibid.*
[34] Rhodes, *History of the United States,* II, 120-121.
[35] Schouler, *History of the United States,* V, 339.
[36] Richardson, *Messages and Papers,* V, 328-331.

with the British nation.[37] The Senate in its attitude upon the question evidently reflected the feelings of the nation as a whole.[38]

The President's message had been accompanied by the Central American correspondence, and had been quickly followed by a definite stand on the part of the American Senate. All of this expression of opinion, as well as the exposition of the matter in controversy, had, as was expected, a marked influence in England. Expressions friendly to the United States appeared in the London *Times* and the *News,* which, Buchanan reported, seemed to indicate the general public opinion that the United States was right. He felt that now the Central American question might easily be settled with any other premier than Palmerston.[39]

Parliament met on January 31 and it soon became evident that British public opinion had wrought a change in British governmental attitude. In the speeches in answer to the Queen's address Lord Derby criticised the British policy regarding America. There was no other nation on earth, he declared, with which war would be so mutually suicidal as with the United States. Clarendon, in reply to the attack, stated that as regarded the Central American question the only difference of opinion which could take place was as to the legal interpretation of the treaty; therefore, believing that when differences of this kind arose between two governments correspondence was generally useless as a means of settlement, he had lost no time in making

[37] *Cong. Globe,* 34 Cong., 1 sess., pt. 1, pp. 107-111, 283-286, 323, 468-471, *passim; ibid.,* Appendix, 70-84, 87, *passim.*

[38] *Harper's Magazine,* XII, 255; New York *Times.* Jan. 3, 19, 1856, Feb. 1, 23, 1856.

[39] Buchanan, *Works,* X, 21, 27.

the offer to the United States government to refer the whole question in dispute to any third power that might be willing to undertake the reference, both parties agreeing to be bound by the decision. This offer, he regretted to say, had not been accepted by that government; but he had since renewed it, and he thought it was so plain that this was the fairest and most rational mode of settling the difference that he earnestly hoped that the offer would be in the end accepted.[40]

The intention of Clarendon's remarks was obviously to disarm public criticism and parliamentary opposition by making it appear that the non-settlement of the long-standing and dangerous Central American question was due solely to the unreasonableness of the American government. But, notwithstanding the efforts of the ministry, Cobden in the House of Commons called almost immediately for the correspondence respecting American relations.[41] This call was made just at the time when it was expected that any mail would bring word that the refusal of the British ministry to recall Crampton had been answered by his prompt dismissal by the United States;[42] and it was evidently the aim of Cobden and his associates to forestall any retaliatory measures on the part of their government, should the dismissal take place.

Palmerston tried to avoid producing the correspondence by stating that it was not complete; but Cobden was insistent. He wished the correspondence laid before the House in order that it might discuss the Central American dispute: the causes of the quarrel should be made known and the question met fearlessly

[40] Hansard, *Parl. Debates,* 3d ser., CXL, 39-40.
[41] *Ibid.,* 462.
[42] Buchanan, *Works,* X, 30.

and honestly.[43] The subject of American relations, he declared, would be safer in the hands of the House than in the hands of the government or of the press. A hostile collision with the United States would be a most horrible calamity, and would find no favor with the British people. Yet the policy of the government was producing a deadlock which would make it impossible to escape war.[44]

Palmerston responded by emphasizing the view of the British government that the Clayton-Bulwer treaty was intended to be prospective in its operation,[45] and stated, as Clarendon had done, that the government had offered to submit the question to arbitration, but had received no reply from the United States.[46] He then admitted that, though the correspondence on the enlistment question was not yet complete, that regarding Central America, though perhaps not technically closed, was ready to be presented and would be laid on the table at once.[47] In conclusion he agreed with Cobden that a war with the United States would be most lamentable, and expressed his determination to do all possible to end the dispute peacefully.[48]

A week later the same subject was introduced in the House by Roebuck, who asked for Crampton's instructions. He denounced the action of the government on the recruiting question, declaring that the facts of the case had been so misrepresented as to make it appear that the British were in the right and had done all that honor demanded, while the Americans were in the wrong.[49] Roebuck's desire, like Cobden's, was to pro-

[43] Hansard, *Parl. Debates.* 3d ser., CXL, 467.
[44] *Ibid.*, 466-467. [45] *Ibid.*, 467-468. [46] *Ibid.*, 469.
[47] *Ibid.* [48] *Ibid.*, 471-472. [49] *Ibid.*, 837-844.

mote a discussion which would show the friendly feelings of the British nation towards America. Palmerston's reply to Roebuck was similar to that made to
Cobden; while defending the action of the government
and declaring that the recruiting correspondence was
not yet closed, he expressed the strong desire of the
British nation to remain at peace with their American
kindred.[50]

The announcement that an offer of arbitration on the
Central American dispute had been made by Great
Britain came as a complete surprise to Buchanan. In
various conversations the Foreign Secretary had suggested referring the matter to a third power, but
Buchanan had regarded such suggestions merely as
informal and as originating entirely with Clarendon.
Consequently, though he had carefully reported the
conversations to Marcy, he had not taken them seriously and had simply expressed the opinion that there
was nothing in the question to arbitrate, and that,
besides, it would be difficult to find an impartial arbi-
trator.[51]

Upon learning of Clarendon's remarks in the House,
however, Buchanan promptly called upon Clarendon
and inquired whether the suggestions made to him had
constituted the offers referred to. Clarendon replied
in the affirmative, stating that the offer had been made
in a most formal manner by direction of the Cabinet.
The offer had been made thus orally as a preliminary to
more formal consideration of it. On November 10,
1855, Clarendon added, he had reported the last offer

[50] *Ibid.*, 844-850.
[51] *Parl. Papers,* 1856, *Coms.,* LX, "Correspondence with the United
States respecting Central America ", 297-298; Buchanan, *Works,* IX, 456.

of arbitration made to Buchanan in a letter to Crampton, instructing him to communicate the contents of the letter to the American secretary of state.[52]

Immediately after this interview Buchanan wrote to Marcy reporting the matter,[53] and Clarendon also communicated it to Crampton,[54] and it soon appeared that there had been a general misapprehension of the Foreign Secretary's meaning. Not only had Buchanan, and, consequently, Marcy, gained a wrong impression of Clarendon's intention, but Crampton, believing that Buchanan was to have full charge of the Central American question, had simply considered what Clarendon had told him with reference to the offer of arbitration as for his own private information; consequently he had not read the letter carefully, and had entirely overlooked the instruction to communicate the offer to Marcy.[55] As soon, however, as the misunderstanding was cleared up, Crampton acquainted various members of the American government with the fact that arbitration had been offered by Great Britain.[56] Though some criticism followed because of what was called Crampton's negligence,[57] the information undoubtedly had a beneficial effect on American public feeling, especially as it was preceded by a conciliatory tone in the parliamentary debates and in the British press.

Still, an offer of arbitration was not a settlement of the question; and it appealed to the nation as a whole as little as it had appealed to Buchanan. Moreover,

[52] *Parl. Papers*, 1856, *Coms.*, LX, " Correspondence with the United States respecting Central America ", 297.

[53] *Ibid.*; Buchanan, *Works*, X, 35.

[54] *Parl. Papers*, 1856, *Coms.*, LX, " Correspondence with the United States respecting Central America ", 297-298.

[55] *Ibid.*, 298-299. [56] *Ibid.*, 299. [57] *Ibid.*

the horizon was again darkened by the persistently
unsatisfactory attitude of the British government
towards the enlistment dispute. On February 25 the
Senate called for the correspondence on the subject,[58]
and President Pierce promptly transmitted it.[59] The
following day the President sent a message to both
houses of Congress recommending to their favorable
consideration a request from the secretary of war for
a special appropriation of three million dollars for military equipment.[60] In the debates which followed, the
question of war with Great Britain was freely discussed, and at this time, as earlier in the year, a determination was shown to insist upon the fulfillment of
treaty terms even at the price of war; but there was
also the conviction that if the American government
stood firm Great Britain would avoid war by retreating
from her position.[61]

For some weeks after this, the two matters in dispute
remained in practically a state of deadlock. With
regard to the Central American question, it was no easy
matter to determine upon a course of action. Though
throughout the country there were some who favored
arbitration and others who advocated annulling the
Clayton-Bulwer treaty, still there were strong objections to both. The other alternative was to force the
British to fulfill treaty obligations, even at the risk of
war, a course for which the majority of the nation
seemed ready, but one which was not to be chosen
lightly.[62] The enlistment question was in a graver state;

[58] *U. S. Docs.*, ser. no. 819, doc. 35, p. 1.
[59] *Ibid.*
[60] Richardson, *Messages and Papers*, V, 362.
[61] *Cong. Globe,* 34 Cong., 1 sess., pt. 1, pp. 618-627, Appendix, 175-177, 234-242, 300-306, 435-442.
[62] Dept. of State, Inst., Gt. Brit., vol. 16, pp. 468-469.

the published correspondence had made it evident that the demand for Crampton's recall was justifiable, yet the order of recall had not been given, and no other adequate amends had been offered by Great Britain.[63]

During the month of May the situation became more tense. The dismissal of Crampton seemed certain and imminent, and it was felt by many that this step on the part of the American government would be the signal for an outbreak of hostilities between the two nations. Different causes had also increased feeling on the Central American question. Though Crampton had continued to call attention to the evil which the filibusters wrought in Central America, and though Marcy had denounced Walker and his methods,[64] still, by one means or another large numbers of American citizens with filibustering aims were able to leave the United States; and recently Marcy had tried to avoid discussion of the subject with foreign diplomats, and had displayed impatience and ill-humor when approached regarding it.[65] Moreover, Walker, by his high-handed proceedings, not only constantly endangered the lives and property of British subjects in Nicaragua,[66] but

[63] *Harper's Magazine*, XII, 689.

[64] Clarendon to Crampton, Jan. 17, and Feb. 19, 1856, F. O., Am., vol. 638, nos. 21, 46; Crampton to Clarendon, Mar. 31, 1856, *ibid.*, vol. 642, no. 75.

[65] Crampton to Clarendon, Mar. 4, 1856, *ibid.*, vol. 641, no. 53; April 29, 1856, *ibid.*, vol. 643, no. 11. Marcy's ill-humor was probably increased by the fact that he had consistently been opposed to Walker's schemes from the first, but had not been supported by the President. Marcy to Dallas, June 16, 1856, " Unofficial ", Dept. of State, Inst., Gt. Brit., vol. 16, Walker, *War in Nicaragua*, 267.

[66] Clarendon to Crampton, Jan. 10, and Feb. 19, 1856, F. O., Am., vol. 638, nos. 14, 46; Wyke to Clarendon, June 24, 1856, F. O., Cen. Am., vol. 89, no. 37.

even levied exactions upon the British as well as upon other foreigners in the region.[67]

The seeming connivance on the part of the American government at a violation of the spirit of the Clayton-Bulwer treaty, while assuming an air of righteous indignation towards Great Britain for an alleged infraction of its letter, naturally produced a feeling of distrust and resentment in England. Moreover, the similarity between Crampton's offense, for which the American government indignantly demanded amends, and the shortcomings of local American officials—evidently winked at by the Washington authorities—which made possible the establishment and maintenance of Walker's government, did not escape British notice.[68] Consequently, when Costa Rica determined to open war upon Walker, the British government, while refusing all of her appeals for direct protection,[69] consented to sell Costa Rica two thousand muskets to aid her in the war against the filibuster.[70] Knowledge of this soon reached the United States through the Nicaraguan seizure, on the San Juan, of the mail for Costa Rica which contained the correspondence upon the subject which had passed between the Costa Rican minister and the British foreign secretary.[71] The usual charges of treaty violation were made against Great Britain, and

[67] Crampton to Clarendon, Mar. 3, 1856, F. O., Am., vol. 641, no. 52.
[68] Lumley to Clarendon, June 19, 1856, F. O., Am., vol. 643, no. 4; San Francisco *Evening Bulletin,* Aug. 1, 1856.
[69] Hansard, *Parl. Debates,* 3d ser., CXLII, 310-311.
[70] *Parl. Papers,* 1856, *Coms.,* LX, " Correspondence with Wallerstein ", 11-12, 15-17. The Costa Rican agent decided not to accept the terms of the British government, so the arms were never delivered. Hansard, *Parl. Debates,* 3d ser., CXLII, 311.
[71] Wells, *Walker's Expedition to Nicaragua,* 149.

much excitement was created.[72] Largely as a result of this act of Great Britain the President determined to receive Padre Vijil, a new representative from Walker's government.[73] American resentment was further increased by the news that Captain Tarleton of the British vessel *Eurydice* had boarded the American packet *Orizaba* for the purpose of examining the ship's papers in an effort to prevent recruits from reaching Walker.[74] So serious did the situation become that both nations found it desirable to increase their naval forces in the Gulf of Mexico.[75]

These hostile acts reported against Great Britain led Dallas, who had recently succeeded Buchanan, to take a very gloomy view of the future as well as of the situation in general. Recent British action in connection with Central America, he believed, showed the intention to dispose of the Clayton-Bulwer treaty and to bring the isthmus under British control, thus disjointing the American Union.[76] He felt that British disregard for American friendship would also appear in connection with the recruitment dispute, and expected that news of

[72] Crampton to Clarendon, May 5, 1856, F. O., Am., vol. 643, no. 113; *Cong. Globe,* 34 Cong., 1 sess., pt. 2, pp. 1069-1072.

[73] Dept. of State, Inst., Gt. Brit., vol. 16, p. 529. The presidential message announcing the reception of Vijil, stated that the establishment of diplomatic relations with Nicaragua was imperative because of the interruption of interoceanic communication across both Nicaragua and Panama. Richardson, *Messages and Papers,* V, 373-374.

[74] Crampton to Clarendon, May 12, 1856, F. O., Am., vol. 643, no. 118. Captain Tarleton's act was taken up by Dallas with the British government, but it soon became evident that no insult had been intended against the American flag; consequently the matter was dropped. Dallas to Marcy, July 11, 1856, Dept. of State, Des., Eng., vol. 69, no. 19; *cf.* Wells, *Walker's Expedition to Nicaragua,* 203-224.

[75] Keasbey, *Nicaragua Canal,* 236; Hansard, *Parl. Debates,* 3d ser., CXLII, 1508.

[76] Dept. of State, Des., Eng., vol. 69, no. 11. Most of the despatch is printed in *U. S. Docs.,* ser. no. 3853, doc. 161, p. 28.

Crampton's dismissal would be followed by the notice that his own passports were at his disposal.[77]

A letter of June 16, 1856, from Marcy to Dallas shows that Dallas's belief in British bad faith was shared by his government. The President, Marcy wrote, had recognized Walker's government because of the aid furnished Costa Rica by Great Britain. The intercepted documents, he stated, had satisfied the American people that Great Britain was aiding Costa Rica and other Central American governments to " crush out " the only existing authority in Nicaragua ; and the object of her policy was not considered questionable. " This government could not remain entirely inactive and see Great Britain obtain complete ascendancy in all the states of Central America." [78] The unreasonable interpretation which the British government had placed upon the Clayton-Bulwer treaty, as well as its colonization of the Bay Islands, certainly gave strong support to the conviction of British perfidy.

On May 28, 1856, the American government discontinued diplomatic relations with Crampton in consequence of his having aided in violating American neutrality laws by recruiting soldiers for the Crimean War within the territory of the United States.[79] But before the fact of Crampton's dismissal was known in England, it became very evident that Dallas and his government were mistaken in their analysis of the situation, and in their predictions regarding the future. The news that Walker's agent had been received at

[77] Dept. of State, Des., Eng., vol. 69, no. 13.

[78] Dept. of State, Inst., Gt. Brit., vol. 16, p. 529. *Cf.* Wells, *Walker's Expedition to Nicaragua,* 226-236.

[79] *Dic. Nat. Biog.,* XII, 6-7.

Washington [80] reached London a few days before the report of Crampton's dismissal.[81] It was this American recognition of the filibuster government which caused the British nation to reveal its real feelings and intentions. The *Times,* which, earlier in the year, had blustered and threatened, in the face of the real crisis quickly assumed a conciliatory tone. After remarking about the low state of political morality in America which made Vijil's reception possible, it added:

But it is no case of war, it is not even necessarily a ground of diplomatic complaint. The Clayton-Bulwer treaty has not been in terms violated, and it may probably be expedient in the present critical state of the relations between the two countries, rather to pass this matter by in silence than to incur the risk of introducing fresh difficulties into a discussion already sufficiently perilous, or give an excuse to those who are even now only too ready to seek an occasion of quarrel. If war does come we must meet it as we may. Let us, at any rate, have the satisfaction of reflecting that this greatest of human calamities has not been precipitated by any undue sensitiveness or any avoidable interference on our part.[82]

The *Times* now also advocated a policy of peace in reference to the recruiting question. Though the dismissal of Dallas must immediately succeed the receipt of notice that Crampton had been dismissed, such an act, the *Times* declared, by no means implied a state of war. " We may be at peace with America ", it added, " though without any diplomatic representative; and,

[80] *U. S. Docs.,* ser. no. 3853, doc. 161, p. 30. Disgusted at the studied coldness of the diplomatic body at Washington, Vijil soon returned to Nicaragua. Lumley to Clarendon, June 30, 1856, F. O., Am., vol. 644, no. 26; *Dublin Review,* XL, 376-377. His successor was not received by the American government. Marcy to Wheeler, Sept. 18, 1856, Dept. of State, Inst., Am. States, vol. 15, p. 279.

[81] Crampton to Clarendon, May 28, 1856, F. O., Am., vol. 643, no. 134.

[82] London *Times,* June 2, 1856, quoted in *Littell's Living Age,* 2nd ser., XIV, 113-114.

perhaps, at the point at which matters have arrived, the absence of an Ambassador may in some degree diminish the apprehension of danger." [83]

The other leading newspapers took a similar attitude. The *Examiner* [84] and the *Press* [85] were even more strongly for peace than the *Times*. The *News* expressed the hope that the British cabinet might think twice before sending away Dallas; [86] while the *Telegraph,* less friendly to the government, seized the occasion to denounce its policy while pointing out the folly of war with America. A war with the United States, because of the American navy, would be a much more serious contest than the Crimean War. " Surely ", it said, " the war just terminated by a disgraceful peace, which we were obliged to accept, ought to be a lesson to curb the overweening pride of our countrymen." [87]

That the attitude of the country thus reflected in the press was quite in harmony with the views of the British government Dallas learned in an interview with the foreign secretary early in June. At this time he read to Clarendon two letters from Marcy upon the subjects in dispute. In the letter on recruiting, which was written in a conciliatory tone, Marcy stated that the American government gladly accepted the assurance of Great Britain that no violation of the law had been authorized

---

[83] London *Times,* June 3, 1856, quoted in *Littell's Living Age,* 2nd ser., XIV, 114.

[84] London *Examiner,* June 7, 1856, quoted in *Littell's Living Age,* 2nd ser., XIV, 242.

[85] London *Press,* June 2, 1856, quoted in *Littell's Living Age,* 2nd ser., XIV, 122.

[86] London *News,* June 4, 1856, quoted in *Littell's Living Age,* 2nd ser., XIV, 118.

[87] London *Telegraph,* June 2, 1856, quoted in *Littell's Living Age,* 2nd ser., XIV, 118-119.

or countenanced, and explained that the withdrawal of Crampton had been requested because of his personal acts; however, the United States was anxious to continue diplomatic relations with Great Britain.[88]

The second letter, written May 24, reviewed in a temperate manner the history of the Central American question, and added that, while the United States government could not consent to arbitration on the *meaning* of the Clayton-Bulwer treaty, which seemed to it beyond doubt, yet it would not object to the submission of some of the *questions of fact* connected with it to arbitration, such as the question of the sovereignty over the Bay Islands, and of the boundaries of Belize and Mosquito territory. But Dallas was instructed first to communicate with the foreign secretary in order to determine whether the differences could not be promptly terminated by direct negotiation; and if they could not, to discuss the conditions to govern the arbitration of the points of difference.[89]

Dallas reported to Marcy that Clarendon had shown himself much gratified at the tone and import of the communication regarding Central America, and had remarked that " it would be disreputable to both governments, if, upon a platform written with so much clearness, and in a spirit so candid and conciliatory, they failed to reach an adjustment of the whole difficulty." The United States, Clarendon declared emphatically, did not seem to realize the immense change which had taken place in British public opinion and policy regardng colonial establishments; " while Great Britain could not submit to be pushed out of a place

[88] *Brit. and For. State Papers*, XLVIII, 256-270.
[89] *U. S. Docs.*, ser. no. 3853, doc. 161, pp. 2-10.

she actually occupied, he would not give three coppers
to retain any post on the Central American territory or
coast from which she could honorably retire ".[90]

Dallas was much encouraged by the interview, and
informed Marcy that he felt that there now existed in
Great Britain a real disposition to close all difficulty
over the Central American question. " Indeed, I was
agreeably surprised," he wrote, " though I forebore to
manifest it, at the apparent warmth of welcome given
to your paper, and augur beneficial results." [91]

The same conciliatory attitude was displayed three
days later in the House of Commons when Lord Russell
tried to forestall any governmental retaliation upon
Dallas in consequence of Crampton's dismissal.[92] It
seemed particularly desirable, he said, that Dallas be
retained, since a discussion of the Central American
question had been reopened by him in such a manner
as to give hopes of a settlement.[93] Russell also called
attention to the danger of a collision between the British and American naval forces on the coast of America
in consequence of Crampton's dismissal, and inquired
whether suitable precautions had been taken to prevent
it, dwelling strongly upon the misfortunes which would
result from war between the two countries.[94] In reply
Palmerston gave the assurance that Dallas would not be
dismissed, and expressed a readiness on the part of the
government to enter into communication with him for
a settlement of the Central American question.[95] " It
would be lamentable in the extreme ", he stated, " if

[90] Dallas to Marcy, June 13, 1856, Dept. of State, Des., Eng., vol. 69,
no. 15. Extracts from the despatch are given in *U. S. Docs.*, ser. no.
3853, no. 161, pp. 33-35.

[91] *U. S. Docs.*, ser. no. 3853, no. 161, p. 35.

[92] Hansard, *Parl. Debates*, 3d ser., CXLII, 1502-1503.

[93] *Ibid.*, 1503.   [94] *Ibid.*, 1504-1505.   [95] *Ibid.*, 1508.

two countries which have so many interests in common should, through the perverseness of any man, be brought into a state of hostility with each other." [96]

The attitude here displayed by Palmerston put an end to the recruiting dispute [97] and really opened a new and more friendly era in the relations between the two countries. It gave Dallas high hopes of an agreement on the Central American question.[98] In the opinion of Dallas and of the English public, the favorable turn in the relations between the two governments was due exclusively to the " equally able, firm, and conciliatory despatches last sent to be laid before Lord Clarendon ".[99] That the increased friendliness of the American government, probably produced in part by the unexpected close of the Crimean War, gave the British government an opportunity to adopt a more moderate attitude without loss of dignity, and that it also made possible a reopening of the Central American negotiations under more favorable conditions, is quite obvious; but this increased friendliness did not avert any real danger of war, for in the questions in dispute no such danger had existed. During this whole period war could have been produced only by some rash act on the part of the Americans which would have forced the British to fight in order to vindicate their honor; and in such a case it would have been necessary that the grievance against the United States be a very real one.

[96] Hansard, *Parl. Debates,* 3d ser., CXLII, 1509.

[97] The only display of resentment on the part of the British government in consequence of Crampton's dismissal was several months' delay in appointing his successor.

[98] Dept. of State, Des., Eng., vol. 69, no. 16. Part of the despatch is given in *U. S. Docs.,* ser. no. 3853, doc. 161, pp. 35-37.

[99] *U. S. Docs.,* ser. no. 3853, doc. 161, p. 36.

Reasons various and of varying importance determined the British attitude. The enlistment question needs scarcely to be considered here, since the feeling produced in connection with it was largely due to irritation over British conduct regarding the Clayton-Bulwer treaty and Central America.[100] Besides, soon after the facts came to light, the conviction seems to have become general in England that the fault lay largely with the British. The two matters which caused practically all of the feeling in the Central American dispute were the retention of the Mosquito protectorate and the colonization of the Bay Islands. Though consistency led the American government to demand the withdrawal of British settlers from the territory between the Sibun and the Sarstoon, that government realized that a compliance with the demand was not likely to result, and that it was, under the circumstances, rather too much to expect.[101]

Of the other two matters, the simpler was that of the protectorate. It has been shown that the British government was sincere in its desire to rid itself of this, and had only been prevented from so doing by a false sense of honor, and by the political confusion in Central America. Moreover, war between Great Britain and the United States could not have been produced by the Mosquito question in itself. Since the British government considered the Mosquito kingdom a farce and a joke, it had no intention of making the nation ridiculous in the eyes of the world by going to war to defend such a make-believe. Besides, no support could have

[100] See above, pp. 199-200.
[101] *Parl. Papers*, 1860, *Coms.*, LXVIII, " Correspondence respecting Central America ", 99.

been secured from the British people for the pursuit of such a war.

With the Bay Islands the case was somewhat different; the British government had seized these to prevent their occupation by any other power, and had organized them into a colony to protect British subjects settled there. Like the assertion of the British protectorate, the colonization of the Bay Islands had not met with popular favor; furthermore, it was a clear violation of the Clayton-Bulwer treaty. The British government had realized this for some time, and the British public had also come to question the action of the government.[102]

In June, 1854, while searching for data with which to refute the statements of the American government,[103] the foreign secretary had learned, through evidence from the Colonial Office, that in the period between 1830 and 1840 the British government had more than once acknowledged the sovereignty of Central America over Ruatan.[104] This fact might have been kept concealed from the United States; but there was evidence still more damaging to the position taken by the British government. This was in the form of a letter written in 1836 by the Colonial Office itself to one S. Coxe, who had inquired in behalf of a colonization company regarding the boundaries claimed by the British government for Belize. The reply from the Colonial Office, after naming the boundaries on the north, south, and west, added, " The British Crown claims also the

[102] London Daily *News*, Jan. 31, 1853; London *Economist*, XIV, 560; Wodehouse to Labouchere, Mar. 28, 1857, F. O., Hond., vol. 3.
[103] Hammond to Merivale, May 30, 1854, C. O., Hond., vol. 89.
[104] Merivale to Hammond, June 12, 1854, C. O., Hond., vol. 89.

waters, islands, and cays lying between the coast defined and the meridian of the easternmost point of Lighthouse Reef." [105] Unfortunately for the claims of the British government—that the Bay Islands were dependencies of Belize—these islands were situated sixty miles to the *east* of the meridian described.[106] More unfortunately still, from the British point of view, a copy of the letter had fallen into the hands of a member of Kinney's colonization association who had recently made a public statement as to its contents.[107]

In view of these facts, the British government had no resort but to retreat as gracefully as possible. The stubborn policy of the Pierce administration, shown as clearly by the defense of Hollins's destruction of Greytown and the indifference to filibustering, as in the correspondence over the meaning of the Clayton-Bulwer treaty, undoubtedly emphasized the necessity for a prompt and definite concession.[108]

But, all question of justice of British claims aside, the British government and people, for commercial reasons, were strongly averse to war with the United

[105] *Parl. Papers,* 1856, *Coms.,* XLIV, " Belize ", 1. What appears to be the original draft of this letter, found in the Public Record Office, gives the boundaries as above, states that claim is made to the islands along the coast, and then adds, " as well as any other islands and keys in the Bay of Honduras which G. Britain may have heretofore occupied or been entitled to occupy ", but the lines quoted were struck out. Glenelg to Coxe, Nov. 23, 1836, C. O., Hond., vol. 49. The idea of making known the British claim to the Bay Islands was, apparently, after more careful consideration, abandoned.

[106] *De Bow's Review,* XXVII, 558.

[107] Hansard, *Parl. Debates,* 3d ser., CXLIII, 645.

[108] The bombardment of Greytown was declared by the British government to be an obstacle in the way of settling the Central American dispute, but the actions of the government indicate that this was merely an excuse offered in the vain hope of delaying the retreat insisted upon by the United States. Buchanan, *Works,* IX, 250, 298, 300.

States; though willing to evade and, if possible, to delay the issue to save their pride, they intended cautiously to avoid having war thrust upon them. During the preceding few years, trade with America, especially in cotton and cotton products, had increased tremendously. Consequently, when the Central American dispute began to look serious the members of Parliament from the manufacturing districts became concerned [109] and promptly after the meeting of Parliament began to bring pressure to bear upon the government. [110] Later, at the time of Crampton's dismissal, the British press in general took alarm and emphatically called attention to the disaster to British trade which would result from war with America. [111] But the same consideration had secured the attention of the British government; [112] and, as is shown by a Foreign Office " departmental

[109] Buchanan, *Works,* IX, 365.

[110] Cobden represented Manchester, and Roebuck, Sheffield.

[111] The London *Examiner* for June 7, 1856 called attention to the tremendous amount of trade carried on between the two countries. In 1854, it stated, the total value of imports from the United States was £29,795,590, and of this the value of the raw cotton alone amounted to £17,274,677. In the same year the value of British exports to the United States was £21,410,369. Such were the British commercial interests in time of peace. Great would be the scandal to humanity if two countries which so served to enrich each other should turn their powers to injuring each other. Quoted in *Littell's Living Age,* 2nd ser., XIV, 242.

The London *Telegraph* for June 2, 1856, pointed out that a war with the United States would be a guerilla war on the ocean, which would end in the destruction of British commerce. The mills in the north would stop and hundreds of thousands of people would be thrown out of work. Quoted in *Littell's Living Age,* 2nd ser., XIV, 119.

[112] The fact that great damage to American commerce would result in consequence of war with England was early realized in the United States, but the Americans, who had the grievance on their side, were willing to risk war and face its consequences. Besides, there was the strong probability that if the American government put on a bold front the British would concede the points in dispute. New York *Times,* Mar. 6, 1856; Philadelphia *Evening Journal,* June 25, 1856, quoted in the London *Times,* July 15, 1856; *Cong. Globe,* 34 Cong., 1 sess., 79-80, 84, 241.

minute " of 1856, that government decided that the trade in cotton with the United States was of far more value than any interests possessed in Central America ; consequently, it could not afford to risk war by further offending the United States. This decision shaped the whole British policy towards America during the years immediately preceding the Civil War.[113]

[113] See below, p. 230, note 25.

CHAPTER VIII.

ADJUSTMENT IN ACCORDANCE WITH AMERICAN VIEW, 1856-1860.

The war cloud past, conditions were more favorable than ever before to a final and satisfactory settlement of the dispute. For the first time in the history of the Central American question, the differences of opinion which produced it had been thoroughly discussed by the British and American governments and were so well known that little chance remained for misunderstanding or evasion. Moreover, England was willing to meet any reasonable demands of the United States. Consequently much might have been expected from the last attempt at direct settlement between the two governments, made in 1856 and 1857.

On June 26, 1856, Clarendon wrote Dallas a reply to Marcy's instruction communicated to him on June 11. The Foreign Secretary's letter was cordial in tone, and, while still maintaining that the Clayton-Bulwer treaty was prospective in intention, it declared the British government to be as anxious as the President to preserve the friendly relations between the two countries, and expressed a readiness to resume negotiations with a sincere desire to bring them to a speedy and satisfactory conclusion. Attention was again called to the wish of the British government to retire from the Mosquito protectorate. As to Belize, Clarendon added, the only question to be settled regarding it, which concerned Central America, was that of boundaries be-

tween the two; and no insurmountable difficulties need
be expected in this regard.   Since the United States
government held that under any interpretation of the
treaty the Bay Islands were no part of British
dominions previous to 1852, this question might be
arbitrated, should it not respond to direct negotiation.[1]

With the elements of the problem thus laid before
them, Dallas and Clarendon began discussion.   An
interview held on June 30 made it clear that the Mosquito protectorate would give but little trouble; Belize
and the Bay Islands were the subjects over which difficulties were likely to arise.   But Dallas expressed the
hope that the British government would let the islands
return to Honduras; and Clarendon, on the other hand,
was anxious that the United States would not even in
appearance " be ingenious to make difficulties " regarding Belize.[2]   Thus was indicated the general basis on
which a settlement would be possible, and from the
first the negotiators seem to have tacitly adopted it.

During the preliminary discussion, however, little
was said about the Bay Islands, for Herran, an agent
from Honduras, had arrived in London to negotiate
for their restoration.[3]   Since the British press, including even the *Times,* regarded the return of the islands
as required by justice as well as consistent with British
honor,[4] Dallas had little doubt of Herran's success;
but he anxiously watched the negotiations between
Clarendon and Herran and cautioned the latter not to
yield to the British desire to make Ruatan a free port
but to insist upon its unconditional surrender.[5]   After

[1] *Parl. Papers,* 1856, *Coms.,* LX, " Further correspondence with the
United States respecting Central America ", 7-9.
[2] *U. S. Docs.,* ser. no. 3853, doc. 161, pp. 40-43.
[3] *Ibid.,* p. 46.   [4] *Ibid.*   [5] *Ibid.,* p. 51.

the Bay Islands treaty was complete, Dallas learned that it made the islands a free state under the sovereignty of Honduras.[6] This arrangement was obviously intended as a protection to the British subjects settled on the islands. While feeling that the terms of Great Britain were not very magnanimous, Dallas believed that if Honduras was willing there was no cause for oppposition from the United States;[7] consequently, he raised no objection, and the treaty was transmitted to the Honduran government for ratification.

When the arrangement between England and Honduras seeemed on a fair way to satisfactory conclusion, the negotiations between Dallas and Clarendon progressed more rapidly. The draft of a treaty was drawn up, and after certain changes in detail by the United States government, it was signed by the negotiators on October 17.[8] This document, like the Webster-Crampton project, was a set of proposals for adjustment to be offered Nicaragua and Costa Rica, but it was first to be ratified by the British and American governments.[9] Like that project also, the new arrangement established boundary limits for the Mosquito Indians, within which they were to be permitted to govern themselves. By voluntary compact, however, they might become incorporated with the republic of Nicaragua. All of the Mosquito territory south of the Wanx River, not included within the reservation, should, without prejudice to the rights of the republic of Honduras or to any question of boundary of the

[6] *U. S. Docs.,* ser. no. 3853, doc. 161, p. 55.
[7] *Ibid.*
[8] *Parl. Papers,* 1860, *Coms.,* LXVIII, " Correspondence respecting Central America ", 24-29.
[9] *Ibid.,* 27.

latter and Nicaragua, be regarded as within the limits
and under the sovereignty of Nicaragua. Greytown
also came under this last stipulation, but as a free city
with a free port. In return for its privileges, the town
should pay an indemnity to the Mosquitos for a limited
period. The treaty gave Costa Rica free use of San
Juan harbor and certain rights of navigation on the
river. Her boundary dispute with Nicaragua was to
be arbitrated by the British and American governments.[10]

The questions concerning Belize and the Bay Islands
were adjusted by separate articles. These called for
definition of the Belize boundary limits as they existed
April 19, 1850, by treaty between Great Britain and
Guatemala; and stated that, in consideration of the
agreement negotiated by Herran and Clarendon, the
two contracting parties engaged to recognize the free
territory of the Bay Islands as part of the republic of
Honduras.[11]

President Pierce approved the treaty and mentioned
it favorably in his annual message of December, 1856.[12]
That such a compromise arrangement should have been
satisfactory to the President is a matter of some surprise, in view of his former demand that Great Britain
completely withdraw from Central America; and it
leads to the conclusion that Pierce's early aggressiveness was assumed partially for political purposes.
After he had failed of renomination by the Democratic convention, his demands on the British became
much more modest. But the Dallas-Clarendon treaty
did not receive congressional attention until Pierce

[10] *Ibid.*, 24-28.   [11] *Ibid.*, 28-29.
[12] Richardson, *Messages and Papers*, V, 410-411.

went out of office; and when it did come up for consideration it met with little favor from Buchanan, the new President, or from the Senate. Particular objection was made to the article relating to the Bay Islands. As the islands were considered Honduran territory, there was strong feeling against any mention, in an agreement made with England, of the treaty for their restoration.[13] Furthermore, though the Senate had not yet seen a copy of the Herran-Clarendon treaty, it had learned that that treaty contained a clause prohibiting the introduction of slavery into the Bay Islands.[14] Such a stipulation was offensive to southern members.[15]

Finally, after various changes the Dallas-Clarendon arrangement was ratified on March 12, 1857,[16] by a majority of but one vote.[17] The chief change in the treaty was in connection with the article regarding the Bay Islands. This was struck out and replaced by a simple engagement on the part of the contracting parties to recognize and respect those islands, as under the sovereignty and as part of the republic of Honduras.[18]

The treaty thus modified was returned to Dallas by Cass, Buchanan's secretary of state, accompanied by a note explaining that the amendments had made the pact more acceptable to the President than before, but not entirely satisfactory. However, in order to remove the

---

[13] *Parl. Papers*, 1860, *Coms.*, LXVIII, " Correspondence respecting Central America ", 40-41.

[14] *Ibid.*, 23.

[15] *Ibid.*, 39-40, 41. London *Morning Post*, Dec. 22, 1857; Napier to Clarendon, May 3, 1857, F. O., Am., vol. 671, no. 64.

[16] *Parl. Papers*, 1860, *Coms.*, LXVIII, " Correspondence respecting Central America ", 31-32.

[17] *Ibid.*, 40.

[18] *Ibid.*, 31-32. *Cf.* above, p. 227.

only remaining cause for misunderstanding, he had thought it best to ratify the agreement.[19]

As soon as the British cabinet had examined the amended treaty, Clarendon reported that since the treaty with Honduras was not yet ratified, the change in the article relating to the Bay Islands had raised an insurmountable difficulty. The adoption by the British government of the Senate amendment would tempt Honduras to reject the arrangement negotiated by Herran, and thus the Bay Islands would be resigned without satisfactory guarantees for protecting the British settlers.[20] But as he was very loath to see the negotiations again fail,[21] Clarendon immediately revised the treaty amended by the Senate, adding to the article by which the contracting parties recognized the Bay Islands as under the sovereignty of Honduras, the clause: " whenever and so soon as the Republic of Honduras shall have concluded and ratified a treaty with Great Britain by which Great Britain shall have ceded and the Republic of Honduras shall have accepted, the said islands, subject to the provisions and conditions contained in such Treaty." [22]

Thus modified, the treaty was again returned to the United States and presented to Cass by Napier, the

[19] *Ibid.*, 32-33.

[20] In a letter to Cass of April 16, 1857, Dallas stated that the Senate amendment would not have constituted an impediment to ratification had it not been for Palmerston's remarkable success in the recent elections. Dept. of State, Des., Eng., vol. 70, no. 49.

[21] The opposition earlier shown by Buchanan to the Sarstoon as the southern boundary of Belize had caused the British government to fear that, as president, he would refuse his consent to any such arrangement. In appreciation of his concession on this point, the British government was anxious to save the treaty. Foreign office memorandum, April 8, 1857, F. O., Cen. Am., vol. 94.

[22] *Parl. Papers,* 1860, *Coms.,* LXVIII, " Correspondence respecting Central America ", 39.

recently-appointed British minister.[23] After it had been examined by the President, Napier was promptly notified that the proposition, though changed in form, was the same in substance as that recently rejected by the Senate; therefore it could not be considered. Believing as he did that the Bay Islands belonged to Honduras, the President could not possibly sanction any arrangement by which their restoration should be made dependent upon conditions either already prescribed or left to be prescribed. Moreover, there was another obstacle to American acceptance of the arrangement. Napier had supplied Cass with a copy of the Herran-Clarendon treaty, the conditions of which the American government found highly unsatisfactory. Should Honduras ratify this treaty, Cass declared, she would ratify the establishment of an independent state within her own limits—a state at all times liable to foreign influence and control. On the other hand, should this treaty or a similar one be rejected by Honduras, Great Britain would retain possession of the islands with the implied concurrence of the United States, and these islands might eventually become a permanent portion of the British empire. The American government could not become a party to such an arrangement.[24] But before Cass's letter was received by Napier, a despatch from Wyke had reached Clarendon, reporting the failure of the Honduran assembly to ratify the treaty negotiated by Herran.[25] Consequently, the many months of negotiation had again brought no result.

[23] *Parl. Papers,* 1860, *Coms.,* LXVIII, " Correspondence respecting Central America ", 42-43.

[24] *Ibid.,* 44-46.

[25] *Ibid.,* 40. The other Central American states were influential in securing the rejection of the treaty. They feared that under the terms of surrender Honduras would be unable to protect the islands from

Following this last failure, the American government revealed a strong inclination towards the abrogations of the Clayton-Bulwer treaty. In conversation with Napier, Cass clearly intimated that this would be the best solution of the difficulty,[26] and Buchanan showed the same attitude.[27] Senator Douglas, of Illinois, Cass informed Napier, had contemplated nullifying the treaty by a vote of the Senate declaring it not to be binding; if the motion were made. he declared, it would be based on the alleged violation or non-execution of the treaty by Great Britain. Upon inquiry from Napier whether the American constitution contained any provision for such action, Cass replied that such a course had been taken before—about 1798—and it might be again.[28] This attitude on the part of the President and Secretary of State convinced Napier that unless the discussion was closed before the next meeting of Congress, an attempt would be made to set aside the treaty.[29] Therefore, on June 7, he wrote to Clarendon reporting the unsatisfactory state of affairs. The Clayton-Bulwer treaty, he said, could not long be maintained on the British interpretation of it. If the British government wished to stand upon the treaty, it would be necessary to reconcile it to the views of the United

filibusters. Wyke to Clarendon, April 16, 1857, F. O., Guat., vol. 95, no. 32. On July 28, 1857, Wyke wrote to Hammond with reference to the fears of the Guatemala government, " they are now inclined to believe that for the sake of our Cotton market we would sacrifice them on the shrine of American Ambition and allow these countries to be over-run and conquered by American Adventurers sooner than risk a quarrel with the Northern Union." F. O., Guat., vol. 95.

[26] Napier to Clarendon, May 3, 1857, F. O., Am., vol. 671, no. 64; June 7, 1857, *ibid.,* vol. 672, no. 90; June 7, 1857, *ibid.,* vol. 673, no. 96.
[27] *Ibid.*
[28] Napier to Clarendon, May 3, 1857, *ibid.,* vol., 671, no. 64. The reference was evidently to the treaty of alliance with France, made in 1778.
[29] *Ibid.*

States by concessions to Central America. This perhaps could not be accomplished before Congress met, but if the intentions of the British government were of a liberal and conciliatory character, and were frankly made known to the American government, the danger of a violent explosion in Congress might be averted. Hence, in order to expedite matters, Napier suggested that an able commissioner be sent to Central America for the purpose of settling the Belize boundaries, and the Mosquito question, and for arranging the surrender of the Bay Islands on fair terms. It would be well, he believed, for the commissioner to make a preliminary visit to Washington as a public mark of friendly feelings as well as for invoking the unofficial aid of the United States in the matter. Though the arrangement would be a virtual execution of the American interpretation of the treaty, it would be attained by an independent and benevolent course of action on the part of the British government. Moreover, this plan would avoid direct negotiation at Washington, and the consequent intervention of the Senate.[30]

Two weeks later Napier again wrote, expressing greater certainty that Congress would attempt to abrogate the Clayton-Bulwer treaty. Even if the President did not recommend abrogation in his message, he would be likely to use language such as would arouse bad feeling between the two countries. Therefore, Napier stated, he was convinced that the best way to secure the Clayton-Bulwer treaty would be by promptly and frankly conforming the British position to the American construction of it; accordingly he once more urged

[30] F. O., Am., vol. 672, no. 90.

that a commissioner be sent to Central America to make suitable arrangements.[31]

Recent events connected with the Panama Railroad, an American line opened in 1855,[32] increased British fears for the Clayton-Bulwer treaty. In April, 1856, the train on this route was attacked by Panamanian outlaws, who killed several of the passengers and stole a large quantity of goods.[33] In consequence, American newspapers reported that the United States intended to obtain a strip of territory across Panama in order to secure the safety of the route.[34] This immediately aroused British suspicion,[35] which was increased by the fact that the President's message, appearing shortly after these reports, had referred to the neutralization features of the Clayton-Bulwer treaty as applicable to any transit line across the isthmus of Panama, " within the limits of Central America ".[36] An article from the Panama *Herald,* copied in the *Union,* seemed to put an ominous interpretation upon this part of the message. Panama was not in Central America, it declared, and, as the eighth article of the Clayton-Bulwer treaty was merely provisional,[37] it was a mistake to suppose that Great Britain had promised or guaranteed any protection to the Panama Railroad.[38]

In consequence of these suspicions, and of reports of proposals made by American commissioners to the

[31] *Ibid.,* no. 109.

[32] Edwards, *Panama,* 426.

[33] *U. S. Docs.,* ser. no. 3853, doc. 237, p. 26.

[34] Lumley to Clarendon, Nov. 19, 1856, " Confidential ", F. O., Am., vol. 647, no. 110.

[35] Foreign Office to Lumley, Nov. 19, 1856, *ibid.,* vol. 639, no. 32.

[36] Richardson, *Messages and Papers,* V, 411.

[37] See above, p. 98.

[38] Lumley to Clarendon, Dec. 9, 1856, " Confidential ", F. O., Am., vol. 647, no. 122.

New Granada government,[39] Clarendon had instructed Napier to observe to Cass that the British government did not doubt that the United States would admit that for either of the two powers to exercise exclusive control over the Panama route would be contrary to the spirit and intention of the eighth article of the Clayton-Bulwer treaty.[40]

In reply to Napier's representations, Cass denied any intention on the part of the United States to occupy or acquire any part of New Granada or to obtain possession of the railroad route.[41] Cass's letter, however, was not entirely reassuring, for the Secretary of State failed to commit himself to any acknowledgment that the eighth article of the Clayton-Bulwer treaty contemplated a joint protection by the United States and Great Britain over the Panama Railroad.[42] This omission attracted Napier's attention, and led him to fear that if the pending claims for damages against New Granada were not settled before Congress met, hostile measures might be passed by the American government causing New Granada to forfeit to the United States her right to Panama, or, at least, her rights over the railway.[43] These views were also communicated by Napier to his government,[44] and they most probably had weight in aiding it to reach a decision regarding his suggestions for settling the Central American dispute.

[39] These commissioners were empowered to form a treaty with New Granada for transferring the control of the Panama Railroad to the United States and for securing to the United States in full sovereignty five islands in the harbor of Panama. *U. S. Docs.,* ser. no. 3853, doc. 237, pp. 25-34. The treaty was not ratified.

[40] Clarendon to Napier, April 10, 1857, F. O., Am., vol. 667, no. 50.

[41] The commissioners had been appointed by the Pierce administration.

[42] Napier to Clarendon, April 28, 1857, F. O., Am., vol. 670, no. 55.

[43] Napier to Clarendon, June 24, 1857, *ibid.,* vol. 672, no. 114.

[44] *Ibid.*

The situation in Central America made Napier's plan for settlement by a special mission seem particularly feasible at this time. The experience of the Central American states with the filibusters, as well as the greater friendliness of the British government and its agents towards Central America, had produced a confidence which augured well for the success of direct negotiation. Therefore, the British government decided to carry out Napier's suggestions to the letter. Sir William Gore Ouseley, who had filled various diplomatic offices [45] and was intimately known to Buchanan,[46] was selected as special commissioner.

As the time for the opening of Congress approached, however, the American government had grown more impatient over the delay in the settlement of the Central American question.[47] Napier realized this, and on October 19, as soon as he learned that his suggestions had been adopted, he obtained an interview with Buchanan and informed him of the intentions of his government. The decision had been made some time past, he explained, but delay had been occasioned by the difficulty of selecting a competent person for the mission and also by recent reports from India, which had absorbed the attention of the British government. Though he could not say what would be the exact nature of Ouseley's instructions, Napier stated that he believed the British government intended to execute the Clayton-Bulwer treaty according to the general tenor of the interpretation put upon it by the United States, but to do so by separate negotiation with the Central American republics.[48]

[45] *Dic. Nat. Biog.*, XLII, 364.
[46] *U. S. Docs.*, ser. no. 3853, doc. 194, p. 114.
[47] *Ibid.*, pp. 112-114.   [48] *Ibid.*, p. 115.

The British minister later referred to the contingency which he aimed to prevent, remarking that if, in consequence of the language in the President's message, a resolution should be proposed in Congress for abrogating the Clayton-Bulwer treaty such a step would not only frustrate the purposes of the special mission but " would have a calamitous influence on the future relations of England and America ". It would therefore be very gratifying to him, he stated, to be able to inform his government that, pending Ouseley's negotiations, no proposal to annul the treaty would be sanctioned or encouraged by the President or the members of his government.[49]

Buchanan replied that he intended to give an account of the Dallas-Clarendon negotiations in his message, and admitted that this part of the message was already prepared; yet, notwithstanding this, he asserted, if the British government really intended to execute the Clayton-Bulwer treaty according to the American interpretation and would, before Congress met, make some communication to him in that sense, such as he could use, he would cancel what he had written and insert another passage referring to the special mission to be sent by the British. Moreover, under the circumstances, no attempt in Congress against the Clayton-Bulwer treaty would receive any support from him.[50]

Subsequent conversations with Buchanan, however, revealed the fact that he expected the unequivocal restoration of the Bay Islands, the abandonment of the Mosquito protectorate, and the restriction of Belize to its boundaries of 1786.[51] Napier felt that his govern-

[49] *U. S. Docs.*, ser. no. 3853, doc. 194, p. 116.
[50] *Ibid.*, pp. 116-117.
[51] *Parl. Papers*, 1860, *Coms.*, LXVIII, " Correspondence respecting Central America ", 60-62.

ment would not yield to the last demand; hence he seriously questioned whether such a statement as the British government would be willing to make with reference to Ouseley's mission would be sufficient to restrain Buchanan from inserting in his message language such as would cause difficulties between the two governments.[52] Consequently, he suggested to Clarendon that the formal proposal to arbitrate the question be renewed. Such a proposal, connected with the mission of Ouseley, would, he believed, place the policy of the British government in a very favorable light.[53]

Though Clarendon instructed Napier to renew the offer of arbitration,[54] his suspicions as to Buchanan's intentions were roused, and he doubted the efficacy of the measures suggested to save the Clayton-Bulwer treaty from a hostile attack. Therefore, after Ouseley's departure for the United States, he wrote him that in consequence of the probability that the Clayton-Bulwer treaty would be abrogated by the American Congress, it was necessary to proceed with great caution; that he must not commit the British government in any way as regarded the Bay Islands until the intentions of the American Congress with reference to the Clayton-Bulwer treaty were fully ascertained.[55]

Clarendon's distrust of the American government had probably been increased not only by what Napier had told him of Buchanan's expectations in connection with the Ouseley mission, but also by further developments in reference to Panama. Though Napier's fears of difficulty in connection with the American collection of damages against New Granada had evidently been averted by the appointment of a joint American and

[52] *Ibid.*, 63.   [53] *Ibid.*   [54] *Ibid.*   [55] *Ibid.*, 64.

New Granadian commission for the adjustment of the claims,[56] the British government was still uneasy over the matter. Consequently it had proposed a tripartite guarantee of the Panama route on the part of Great Britain, France, and the United States. The United States, however, had promptly refused, on the ground that she had already made such an agreement with New Granada in the treaty of 1846; moreover, it was against the policy of the United States to enter into such engagements as that suggested.[57] Somewhat later still, a report reached England of a movement in Panama to separate that state from New Granada and secure annexation to the United States.[58] As a result, Clarendon instructed Napier to inquire unofficially what course the American government would pursue in case such annexation should be offered.[59] There seems to be no record that such inquiry was made by Napier; but Clarendon's letter contains the last indication of suspicion against the United States during this period, in connection with Panama.

On November 18, Ouseley arrived in Washington, and two days later was presented to Cass, by Napier, who stated that he would in a few days make a written

[56] Napier to Clarendon, Aug. 3, 1857, F. O., Am., vol. 673, no. 155.

[57] Clarendon to Napier, Oct. 15, 1857, *ibid.*, vol. 669, no. 278.

[58] Clarendon to Napier, Nov. 27, 1857, *ibid.*, no. 322. It was evidently upon the suspicions of the British government and the proposals of the American commissioners (see above, pp. 225-226) that Barral-Montferrat, *De Monroë à Roosevelt*, 81-82, based his statement that President Buchanan, through Marcy, proposed to the British government that the two nations divide their influence on the American isthmus, England carrying out her own plans in Nicaragua and Honduras, and the United States doing the same in Panama. This statement is both confused and erroneous. Cass, and not Marcy, was Buchanan's secretary of state. Moreover, while neither the British nor American archives contain any evidence that such proposal was made by the American government, the data found and given above clearly disprove it.

[59] Clarendon to Napier, Nov. 27, 1857, F. O., Am., vol. 669, no. 322.

communication to the American government respecting the special mission. This communication was made on November 30. The specific objects of the mission, Napier wrote, would be the cession of the Bay Islands to Honduras, the localization of the Mosquito Indians under Nicaraguan sovereignty, and the definition of the boundaries of British Honduras. The transfer of the islands would not be unconditional, but it would be unambiguous; the government of Honduras would obtain not only a titular, but a virtual and useful possession under provisions necessary for the security of the settlers and favorable to the expansion of commerce. In arranging for the settlement of the Mosquito question, Ouseley would be guided by the provisions of the Dallas-Clarendon treaty. Modifications might be made in the boundaries mentioned in that document, but they would not be less favorable to Nicaragua and Honduras; nor would they trespass on the territory applicable to transit purposes. In arranging details the aim would be to grant an indulgent consideration to the wishes and necessities of the Central American governments, when they were compatible with the safety and welfare of the Indians. The boundary limits of Belize would be arranged by negotiation with Guatemala. The British government trusted to obtain a recognition of limits for Belize, which, judging from previous communications on the subject, might be accepted in a spirit of conciliation, if not with absolute approval by the President. Though the proposed arrangement, Ouseley concluded, might not strictly coincide with the interpretation of the Clayton-Bulwer treaty adopted by the United States, it nevertheless involved no slight relaxation of the sense in which the engagements of 1850 were contracted by Great Britain. Consequently, it was hoped that the concessions of the British government would be met in a similar temper by the United States, and that, if successfully accomplished, its results would be regarded as an honorable compromise of contending opinions, and as a definite settlement of the Central American dispute.[60]

No formal expression of opinion upon this communication seems to have been made by the American government before the appearance of the President's message—which made mention of it—on December 8. The message first called attention to the Dallas-Clarendon negotiations and to the objectionable treaty made by Great Britain with Honduras, and then continued:

> The fact is that when two nations like Great Britain and the United States, mutually desirous, as they are, and I trust ever may be, of maintaining the most friendly relations with each other, have unfortunately concluded a treaty which they understand in senses directly opposite, the wisest course is to abrogate such a treaty by mutual consent and to commence anew. . . . Whilst entertaining these sentiments, I shall, nevertheless, not refuse to contribute to any reasonable adjustment of the Central American questions which is not practically inconsistent with the American interpretation of the treaty. Overtures for this purpose have been recently made by the British government in a friendly spirit, which I cordially reciprocate, but whether this renewed effort will result in success I am not yet prepared to express an opinion. A brief period will determine.[61]

The message was hardly as conciliatory as might have been expected from the assurances given Napier by Buchanan, but in view of the President's deep dislike for the Clayton-Bulwer treaty, the language is not

[60] *Parl. Papers,* 1860, *Coms.,* LXVIII, " Correspondence respecting Central America ", 70-72.
[61] Richardson, *Messages and Papers,* V, 442-445.

to be wondered at. Moreover, it was undoubtedly influenced by a conviction, gained since Napier's first communication regarding the special mission, that, in negotiating wth Central Amerca, Great Britain did not intend to follow the American interpretation of the treaty as closely as was at first expected.

Though Napier felt that the language of the President might afford some cause for exception on the part of the British government, he reported to Clarendon on the day the message appeared, that in the United States it would be considered conciliatory.[62]

A few days later, Napier again wrote to Clarendon in reference to the message, stating that it now remained for the British government to decide whether to arrange for the abrogation of the treaty by mutual consent, which Buchanan had favored, or to pursue the earlier plan to send a commissioner to Central America. Should the cabinet decide on either course, he suggested that its decision be made known to the United States and be carried out immediately.[63]

The British government, however, had been disappointed in the lack of American cordiality shown towards its overtures for the settlement of the dispute,[64] and by the equivocal character of the President's message. It felt that it had gone far enough in the display of a conciliatory spirit. Consequently, Clarendon replied that the government was decidedly of opinion that it would neither be consistent with British dignity nor interest to make any proposal to the United States government until it had received a formal answer to the

---

[62] F. O., Am., vol. 675, no. 277.

[63] *Parl. Papers,* 1860, *Coms.,* LXVIII, " Correspondence respecting Central America ", 75.

[64] *Ibid.,* 73; Clarendon to Napier, Nov. 20, 1857, F. O., Am., vol. 669, no. 314.

offer of arbitration,[65] which had been made by Napier on November 30.[66]

This decision of Great Britain produced a triple deadlock which lasted for several weeks. The American government had agreed not to make any move towards abrogating the treaty until it could be seen what interpretation of its provisions would result from Ouseley's mission. Moreover, as appeared later, Cass was waiting for further details regarding Ouseley's instructions, which Napier had intimated that he would receive;[67] Ouseley could not proceed until instructed to do so; and, finally, Napier was prohibited from taking any action until the American government made reply to the formal offer of arbitration.

The existing situation, however, seemed particularly favorable to a settlement of the Central American dispute. Presumably in consequence of Walker's announcement that he intended to maintain Nicaragua as an independent sovereignty,[68] as well as because of the more reasonable attitude shown by Great Britain towards the matter in dispute, the American government had for some time displayed unusual energy against the filibuster, and Nicaragua was at least temporarily freed from Walker.[69] Furthermore, a good

[65] *Parl. Papers*, 1860, *Coms.*, LXVIII, " Correspondence respecting Central America ", 78.

[66] *Ibid.*, 74.   [67] *Ibid.*, 78, 79, 89, 90.

[68] Walker, *War in Nicaragua*, 265-269; *Blackwood's Magazine*, LXXXI, 552; Napier to Clarendon, June 1, 1857, F. O., Am., vol. 672, no. 87; *Cong. Globe*, 35 Cong., 1 sess., pt. 1, p. 295.

[69] *Parl. Papers*, 1860, *Coms.*, LXVIII, " Correspondence respecting Central America ", 78, 80. In the autumn of 1857 Napier reported to Clarendon that he believed both Buchanan and Cass now to be honestly opposed to the filibustering attempts against Nicaragua; but that this attitude was not shared by other members of the American cabinet. Napier to Clarendon, Sept. 22, 1857, " Private and unofficial ", F. O., Am., vol. 673; Napier to Clarendon, Nov. 16, 1857, *ibid.*, vol. 674, no. 248.

understanding existed between the United States and Great Britain regarding a transit treaty negotiated by the former with Nicaragua, to take the place of the Squier treaty, which had never been ratified by the American Senate. This later arrangement, the Cass-Yrissari treaty, provided for an open and neutral transit through Nicaragua, and granted to the United States the power to land troops, if necessary, to protect the route.[70] Such an arrangement was hardly in strict conformity with the letter of the Clayton-Bulwer treaty; but the British government learned indirectly that should it oppose this measure as a treaty violation, a movement would be initiated for the purpose of annulling the Clayton-Bulwer agreement by act of Congress.[71] Probably in consequence of this, the British government had made no objection, and finally Napier had frankly announced to Cass that none would be made.[72]

Napier was anxious that advantage be taken of these favorable conditions for the adjustment of difficulties.[73] Consequently, on February 17, 1858, he addressed Cass, informing him that the British government wished to know the decision of the United States upon the offer of arbitration, and remarking that should the United States be opposed to this mode of settlement his government would give a friendly consideration to any observations which Cass might choose to make on the objects of the special mission.[74]

[70] *Ibid.*, 69-70. The obstruction of the route by the conflict in Nicaragua made this stipulation seem necessary.

[71] Napier to Clarendon, Nov. 30, 1857, *ibid.*, vol. 675, no. 266.

[72] *Parl. Papers,* 1860, *Coms.,* LXVIII, "Correspondence respecting Central America ", 78.

[73] *Ibid.*, 78, 80.

[74] *Ibid.*, 80-81.

But since the Kansas question was again absorbing the attention of the American government, there was further delay.[75] Meanwhile, desultory conversations upon the Clayton-Bulwer treaty took place between Napier and Cass. Napier, upon Clarendon's authorization,[76] unofficially notified Cass that the British government would not object to abrogation of the treaty by mutual consent,[77] and suggested that, should the United States favor such action, a proposal to that effect be inserted in the reply to the offer of arbiration. The treaty of abrogation, Napier thought, should contain a self-denying engagement with refei˯ ˓ce to the interoceanic route, and he mentioned this to Cass, adding that the abrogation of the treaty would throw Central America open to territorial acquisition by the United States. The British government, however, would retain British Honduras and the Bay Islands.[78] Later, Napier was instructed by Malmesbury, who had succeeded Clarendon in February, 1858, to inform Cass that the British government was willing to consent to unconditional abrogation. Such stipulation as Napier had suggested regarding the canal, the Foreign Secretary feared, might perpetuate the entanglement with the United States. Should the British government be so fortunate as to extricate itself from the difficulties resulting from the treaty, it wished to guard itself against any similar difficulties in the future. Napier,

[75] *Parl. Papers*, 1860, *Coms.*, LXVIII, " Correspondence respecting Central America ", 86-87.

[76] *Ibid.*, 83.

[77] On January 22, 1858, Clarendon wrote to Napier: " The more I consider the matter, the more I incline to the belief that throwing over the C.-B. Treaty will be our best way out." F. O., Am., vol. 695.

[78] *Parl. Papers*, 1860, *Coms.*, LXVIII, " Correspondence respecting Central America ", 83-84.

however, was to show no eagerness for settlement by either abrogation or arbitration.[79]

The statement of the British government regarding the conditions under which it would consent to abrogation undoubtedly influenced the United States to make a definite choice of the three alternatives offered by the British for settling the dispute. Its views were expressed in a letter written by Cass to Napier on April 6. After reviewing the recent history of the question, Cass complained of not receiving the further details promised regarding Ouseley's mission. Since the President was asked to co-operate in the arrangements, it was necessary that he know the nature of these arrangements. This information was the more important in consequence of the idea which seemed to prevail that the American interpretation of the Clayton-Bulwer treaty was found in the provisions of the Dallas-Clarendon treaty, for such an idea was entirely erroneous. Yet the President trusted that the more complete information which he hoped to receive concerning the mission of Ouseley might justify him in anticipating from it a substantial execution of the Clayton-Bulwer treaty according to the general tenor of the American interpretation. In that event he would be happy to give his cordial co-operation, and to direct the ministers of the United States in Central America to render any assistance in their power towards promoting its success.[80]

[79] *Ibid.,* 85-86. In conversation with Dallas upon the subject, Malmesbury said, " we do not offer to abrogate the Clayton-Bulwer Treaty, but if such be the disposition of the President, we shall make no difficulty whatever." Dallas to Cass, April 13, 1858, Dept. of State, Des., Eng., vol. 71, no. 99.

[80] *Parl. Papers,* 1860, *Coms.,* LXVIII, " Correspondence respecting Central America ", 87-90.

The prosecution of the plan to adjust the difficulty by special mission, Cass continued, must naturally exclude the adoption of any other alternative. Therefore he had been much surprised upon receiving an offer of arbitration, after the President had been notified of the mission of Ouseley and had expressed his concurrence in it; and he had regarded the offer as sufficiently answered by the President's express agreement to the mode of adjustment contemplated by the mission, even if it had not been twice rejected before. But, Cass added, in order to avoid misunderstanding, he was instructed to state that the same reasons which caused the rejection of the first offer of arbitration still existed, and for these reasons it was still declined.[81]

Should Ouseley's mission prove successful, there would, of course, be no need to consider the question of abrogation; but it appeared that, should the treaty be abrogated, the British government would relinquish none of its pretensions in Central America, and that the Bay Islands in particular " would remain attached to the British Crown ". Since it was well known that the views of the United States were wholly inconsistent with these pretensions and that it, therefore, could never willingly acquiesce in their maintenance by Great Britain, Napier must readily perceive what serious consequences might follow a dissolution of the treaty, if no provisions should be made at the same time for adjusting the questions which led to it. If, therefore, the President did not hasten to consider the alternative of repealing the treaty of 1850, it was because he did not wish prematurely to anticipate the failure of Ouseley's mission, and was disposed to give a new

[81] *Parl. Papers*, 1860, *Coms.*, LXVIII, " Correspondence respecting Central America ", 90-91.

proof to the British government of his sincere wish to preserve the amicable relations which now subsisted between the two governments.[82]

This decision of the United States in favor of arranging the dispute through the proposed Ouseley mission would seem on first appearance to have been a diplomatic victory for Great Britain; but the victory was more apparent than real, as soon became evident. American dislike for the Clayton-Bulwer treaty was still as intense as ever. In May a joint resolution for its abrogation was reported from the Committee on Foreign Relations;[83] and though neither Cass nor Buchanan encouraged congressional action, abrogation had evidently been the course which they favored for disposing of the dispute,[84] until it became clear that in such case the British government would retain the Bay Islands. The aim of both men was evidently to dispose of the Clayton-Bulwer treaty, which was opposed to the expansionist policy of the administration, and also to drive the British out of Central America. The latter consummation was the most immediately desired; hence after it became clear that the British would retain the Bay Islands if the treaty were set aside, choice was made of the plan to settle the dispute by a special commissioner.

Yet, after this decision had been imparted to the British government, Cass, with surprising frankness, expressed to Napier a desire for the dissolution of the treaty after the arrangements contemplated by the

[82] *Ibid.,* 91.
[83] *Cong. Globe,* 35 Cong., 1 sess., pt. 2, pp. 1944-1945.
[84] Napier to Clarendon, May 3, 1857, F. O., Am., vol. 671, no. 64; June 7, 1857, *ibid.,* vol. 672, no. 90; Ouseley to Malmesbury, July 6, 1858, F. O., Guat., vol. 98, no. 55.

Ouseley mission should have been made. The treaty, he said, was obnoxious to the American people, and an impediment to cordial understanding between the two countries.[85] Napier, however, pointed out tnat the concessions committed to the Ouseley mission " were based on the supposition that the stipulations of the Clayton-Bulwer Treaty were to remain, and be the future rule of the relations of the two countries in Central America." If the British government gave up its possessions, he said, it would keep the treaty ; it could not be expected that both possessions and treaty would be abandoned.[86]

Since the American government had made known its choice as to methods of settling the dispute, it was decided by the British government that Ouseley should proceed at once to Central America. On July 15 Malmesbury notified him of this decision, but stated that his business would be confined to making treaties with Nicaragua and Honduras with reference to the Mosquitos, and with Guatemala defining the Belize boundaries. He was to have no commission to negotiate regarding the Bay Islands.[87] This deviation from the instructions of the previous administration was evidently due to suspicion, roused by Cass's remarks to Napier, that the United States still had secret designs against the Clayton-Bulwer treaty. The Bay Islands, the possession which the government was most reluctant to give up, were not to be relinquished until it was certain that the American government meant to abide by the treaty. Before Ouseley's definite powers were sent, the British plan was further changed and the com-

---

[85] *Parl. Papers*, 1860, *Coms.*, LXVIII, " Correspondence respecting Central America ", 99-100.
[86] *Ibid.*   [87] *Ibid.*, 99.

missioner was simply instructed to form commercial treaties with Nicaragua and Costa Rica and an additional treaty with the former with reference to the Mosquitos.[88] No authority was given for the settlement of the Belize boundaries.

On August 18 Malmesbury replied to Cass's letter of April 6. A tone of resentment at the attitude of the American government is discernible in the reply. Napier was instructed to inform the American secretary of state that the British government had nothing further to add to the explanations already given with reference to Ouseley's mission. Offers of arbitration and abrogation had been refused by the United States; therefore Great Britain appeared completely to have exhausted the means of arrangement at her disposal. Consequently there was no alternative but to leave it to the American government to originate any further overtures for an adjustment of the controversies.[89]

A little later Napier was instructed with reference to his relations with the United States government. At a convenient season he should inform that government of the intentions and objects of the British cabinet relating to Ouseley's errand, but in doing so he must not ask either advice or assistance from the United States; such requests would be, under existing circumstances, derogatory to the dignity of the Crown. The United States government had successively refused every solution of the controversies which had been offered; hence Great Britain and Nicaragua were now about to treat as independent states, and the United States government was to be informed of this merely as an act of friendship and courtesy.[90]

[88] *Ibid.*, 100-120.   [89] *Ibid.*, 123-124.   [90] *Ibid.*, 124.

The perversity of the United States, however, had by no means made Great Britain indifferent to American friendship. The situation was a delicate one. Though the British government was willing to abrogate the Clayton-Bulwer treaty if the first move for the purpose were made by the American government,[91] British honor could not endure its abolition by the American Congress. Such action must require a reckoning between the two governments, and this would be certain to produce strained relations, disastrous to commerce, if not even war itself. Both results were to be avoided, if possible, and the latter was not to be thought of at this time, as there was possibility of war with France.[92] Hence, it was highly desirable to preserve the treaty against congressional action; and efforts were made to keep in close touch with the American government and to convince it of British good intentions.

Malmesbury now showed considerable anxiety lest nothing be accomplished towards settlement of the Central American dispute before the meeting of Congress, and he urged Ouseley to execute his instructions as quickly as possible and arrange to have the negotiations terminated not later than the last of November. Any delay in commencing the negotiations, he said, would frustrate the objects which the government had in view and render the continuance of his mission unnecessary.[93]

For some weeks after Ouseley's departure, the American government remained silent upon the general

[91] Clarendon to Napier, Jan. 22, 1858, F. O., Am., vol. 695.

[92] Napier to Malmesbury, April 12, 1858, *ibid.,* vol. 691, no. 85; Napier to Malmesbury, April 13, 1858, *ibid.,* nos. 89 and 90.

[93] *Parl. Papers,* 1860, *Coms.,* LXVIII, " Correspondence respecting Central America ", 125, 134.

subject of his mission, but on November 8 Cass wrote
Napier a reply to Malmesbury's communication of
August 18. Though Cass's letter displayed a slight
tone of resentment at some of the statements made by
Malmesbury, it was, on the whole, frankly conciliatory.
The American government had evidently come fully to
realize that in trying to grasp all it might lose all—
that if the British were to be driven from Central
America, the Clayton-Bulwer treaty, which also barred
the isthmus to the Americans, must be preserved.
Hence the change in tone. In his letter Cass considered
the elements of the dispute and called attention to the
fact that there was no apparent disagreement except as
to the conditions governing the surrender of the Bay
Islands, and as to the limits to be set for Belize. Was it
possible that these differences, if approached in a spirit
of conciliation and good feeling, could not be adjusted
in a friendly manner? To believe this would be to
underestimate the importance of the adjustment and the
intelligent appreciation of this importance, which must
be entertained by both nations. What the United States
wanted in Central America, next to the happiness of
its people, was the security and neutrality of the interoceanic routes leading through it. This was equally the
desire of the whole commercial world. Such an object
would be accomplished if the principles and policy of
the Clayton-Bulwer treaty were carried into effect. An
adjustment of the Central American question according to the general tenor of the American interpretation
of the Clayton-Bulwer treaty was all that the President
had ever desired, and instead of having rejected the
proposal for such a settlement he had expressed his
cordial acceptance of it, so far as he understood it, and

had anticipated from it the most gratifying consequences. Nothing now remained but to inquire whether the good results expected in the beginning from Ouseley's mission might not yet be happily accomplished.[94]

Malmesbury quickly responded to the cordial tone in this letter, and in his reply to Napier expressed his " lively satisfaction " with it. The friendly character of the letter and the high appreciation it displayed of the importance of ending the irritating discussion, he believed, could not but tend to bring the dispute to a speedy and permanent conclusion. The existing administration, Malmesbury informed Napier, considered itself morally obliged to carry out the political views of its successors, as embodied in Napier's note to Cass of November 30, 1857, in respect to the Bay Islands. Consequently, it was the intention of the British government, as soon as Ouseley should have settled the question of the Mosquito territory, to instruct him to enter immediately into negotiations with Honduras regarding the Bay Islands. As soon as Ouseley's present task should be accomplished, the details of this second mission would be made known to the American government. The British government, Malmesbury concluded, interpreted Cass's note of the 8th of November as meaning that if the principles of the Mosquito territory were arranged, the Bay Islands ceded to Honduras, and the boundaries of British Honduras established, the Clayton-Bulwer treaty would remain as the acceptable and practical rule for the relations of England and the United States in Central America and would thereafter

[94] *Parl. Papers,* 1860, *Coms.,* LXVIII, " Correspondence respecting Central America ", 147-154.

be recognized and respected as such by the United States. It was the wish of the British government as it was also the wish of the United States that the good results expected in the beginning from the Ouseley mission might yet be effected.[95] A copy of this letter, furnished by Napier and read at a meeting of the President's cabinet, gave much satisfaction.[96] But before Malmesbury's letter was received the American government had fully settled upon a conciliatory course. Though no report of progress had come from Ouseley, on December 6, the President's message appeared containing a clause in reference to British relations quite in harmony with the friendly tone of Cass's letter written a month before. An earnest desire was expressed in the message for the settlement of every misunderstanding with Great Britain, as any serious interruption of the commerce between the two countries would be equally injurious to both. In fact, no two nations had ever existed which could do each other so much good or so much harm as these two. Though gratified that he could announce that the controversy over visitation and search had been settled, the President was truly sorry not to be able to say the same for the controversy over the Clayton-Bulwer treaty. As the purposed negotiations mentioned in the last message were still pending, their present conditions could not be reported. A final settlement of the question was greatly to be desired, as it would wipe out the last subject of dispute between the two countries.[97]

The increase in cordiality on the part of the United States produced a greater briskness in the British gov-

[95] *Ibid.*, 155-157.   [96] *Ibid.*, 165.
[97] Richardson, *Messages and Papers*, V, 507-508.

ernment with reference to the Central American negotiations. Ouseley had not made as much progress as had been hoped for, hence, in order to avoid unnecessary delay, on December 16 Malmesbury authorized Wyke to resume and complete the negotiations, should Ouseley be incapacitated by illness.[98] On the same date Malmesbury notified Ouseley that he could not exert himself too much to conclude the treaties for the negotion of which he had been empowered.[99]

Yet in spite of the Foreign Secretary's efforts, the Central American negotiations failed to make satisfactory progress. This was partly caused by new difficulties which had arisen in Central America, but more through the inefficiency of Ouseley himself. The new difficulties were largely due to the intrusion of Félix Belly, the agent of a French company desirous of constructing an isthmian canal. The Cass-Yrissari treaty had not been ratified by the Nicaraguan government when Belly arrived, and he at once proceeded to work against its ratification in order to secure for his own company exclusive control of the route.[100] The American government, he declared, supported the filibusters, and should the treaty go into effect the whole of Central America would be dominated by the United States.[101] Nicaragua, as a result of Belly's efforts, set aside the Cass-Yrissari treaty, and settled her boundary dispute

[98] *Parl. Papers*, 1860, *Coms.*, LXVIII, "Correspondence respecting Central America", 160-161.

[99] *Ibid.*, 161. British interest in the removal of all obstacles to the formation of a neutral transisthmian highway had probably been stimulated by the recent organization of British Columbia, a colony resulting from the discovery of gold on Fraser River. Dallas to Cass, Nov. 26. 1858, Dept. of State, Des., Eng., vol. 72, no. 138.

[100] Scroggs, "William Walker and the Steamship Corporation in Nicaragua ", in *Am. Hist. Rev.*, X, 810.

[101] *Ibid.*, Lamar to Cass, June 26, 1858, Dept. of State, Des., Nic. and Costa Rica, vol. 3.

with Costa Rica,[102] after which the two states granted Belly a joint canal concession.[103] It had been the aim of the British government to introduce into the commercial treaty with Nicaragua terms for the neutralization of the transit similar to those contained in the Cass-Yrissari treaty; Belly's manipulation made the Nicaraguans unreasonable in their demands, and caused delay.[104]

Belly's representations regarding American support of filibustering movements also proved a handicap to Ouseley, for they increased Central American fears of attack from Walker, who was at this time in the United States preparing a new expedition. There was little danger of trouble from the filibusters, however, for the British government had ordered an extra war vessel to the Central American coast to protect it pending negotiations. The commander was instructed to prevent any descent upon Greytown or Mosquito, but if the filibusters attempted to go up the San Juan he was not to act except in conjunction with the forces of Nicaragua and Costa Rica, and then only upon written request from the commanders.[105] As France was plan-

[102] In consideration of aid in case of the return of the filibusters, Nicaragua made a large cession of territory to Costa Rica, Scroggs, *op. cit.*

In the summer of 1857 the American government had sent Carey Jones as special agent to Central America to investigate the quarrel between Costa Rica and Nicaragua, with a view to effecting a settlement; but Jones was inefficient and his efforts vain. Napier to Clarendon, July 6, 1857, F. O., Am., vol. 672, no. 133; Oct. 31, 1857, *ibid.*, vol. 674, no. 228.

[103] Scroggs, *op. cit.*; Johnson, *Four Centuries of the Panama Canal*, 65. The efforts of Belly came to nothing as far as forming an open route in Nicaragua was concerned. American attempts in this direction also resulted in failure, and interest was diverted to the Panama railway.

[104] Lamar to Cass, April 28, 1859, Dept. of State, Des., Nic. and Costa Rica, vol. 4, no. 50.

[105] The American government objected to these instructions and declared that the landing of troops to protect Ouseley's negotiations would

ning to negotiate a commercial treaty with Nicaragua, by friendly understanding the same instructions were given the French naval commanders.[106]

The most serious obstacle, however, to a prompt and satisfactory settlement of the Central American difficulty, was Ouseley's lack of ability for his task, which was quickly shown. At the very outset he made a blunder by first negotiating the commercial treaty for which Nicaragua was very anxious, and which was little likely to cause difficulty, and neglecting the Mosquito arrangement, the terms of which might have been expected to give trouble.[107] He was rebuked by his government for this lack of judgment and again told that the Mosquito treaty was the important one. No general commercial treaty with Nicaragua would be approved by the British government, Malmesbury informed him, until the convention for the adjustment of the Mosquito question

---

be a direct violation of the Clayton-Bulwer treaty. The British government replied that such an act would be the same in principle as the landing of American troops to protect the transit route, as contemplated by the Cass-Yrissari treaty, and insisted that it intended to protect the negotiations. No occasion for landing British troops arose, however, and with the accession of Russell to the Foreign Office the instructions were changed and permission withdrawn from the British naval commanders for operations against the filibusters on Central American soil. *Parl. Papers,* 1860, *Coms.,* LXVIII, " Correspondence respecting Central America ", 137-138, 139-141, 280.

[106] *Ibid.,* 159, 161, 231. The American government had refused to co-operate with the British naval forces in protecting Central America. Napier to Clarendon, Oct. 22, 1857, F. O., Am., vol. 674, no. 220.

[107] *Parl. Papers,* 1860, *Coms.,* LXVIII, " Correspondence respecting Central America ", 170-171, 185. The British government attributed Ouseley's inefficiency to his constant illness while in Central America. Dallas to Cass, May 2, 1859, Dept. of State, Des., Eng., vol. 73, no. 181. He was also handicapped by conflicting instructions. Before leaving England he was told that the cession of Mosquito to Nicaragua should be treated as a concession for which Central America was to thank England's moderation and good will. It was to be his duty to try to save the dignity and honor of Great Britain even at the expense of material interests, and he was not to show anxiety for a settlement. Ouseley to Malmesbury, Mar. 31, 1859, F. O., Guat., vol. 103, no. 40.

had been signed. The aim was to settle the latter point and thus to obviate any further discussion with the United States regarding it.[108]

But the difficulty of communicating with him prevented the interruption of Ouseley's mistaken course,[109] and, consequently, the commercial treaty was signed and awaiting the ratification of the Nicaragua assembly [110] before any headway could be made on the other treaty. Moreover, when the draft of the former was received by the British government it was disclosed that, in violation of instructions,[111] Ouseley had introduced important alterations in the original which had been furnished him.[112]

Ouseley's unsatisfactory progress decided the British government to entrust to Wyke the settlement of the Belize boundary. Accordingly, on February 16, 1859, Malmesbury sent him instructions, enclosing a draft of a convention. The proposed line of boundary at the south was to be the Sarstoon River; but in view of the claim of the United States that the territory between the Sibun and the Sarstoon belonged to Central America, the instructions stated that it was necessary that the line to be established by the proposed convention should be described therein, " not as involving any cession or new acquisition from the Republic of Guatemala, but as it is in fact, simply as the definition of a boundary long existing, but not hitherto ascertained." [113] Consequently, the first paragraph of the convention read:

It is agreed between Her Britannic Majesty and the Republic of Guatemala, that the boundary between the British

---

[108] *Parl. Papers*, 1860, *Coms.*, LXVIII, " Correspondence respecting Central America ", 170-171.

[109] Ouseley to Malmesbury, Mar. 30, 1859, F. O., Guat., vol. 103, no. 38,

[110] *Parl. Papers*, 1860, *Coms.*, LXVIII, " Correspondence respecting Central America ", 186.

[111] *Ibid.*, 120, 197.   [112] *Ibid.*, 186-195.   [113] *Ibid.*, 172

Settlement and Possessions in the Bay of Honduras, as they existed previous to and on the 1st day of January, 1850, and have continued to exist up to the present time, was, and is as follows.[114]

Two years before, a basis had been laid for the contemplated treaty by the superintendent of Belize.[115] This, with the fact that Wyke was well acquainted with the Central American character and also possessed considerable diplomatic ability, prompted a quick and easy accomplishment of the task assigned. As soon as he received his full powers, Wyke set to work. At first he found the Guatemalan government opposed to the terms stipulated by the draft,[116] but he devised a plan which, while it made the arrangement satisfactory to the Guatemalans, would tend to aid the British commercially.[117] Owing to better communications between Guatemala and the Port of San José on the Pacific and to the competition of the United States, for the past few years the commerce of Guatemala with Belize, as well as the British carrying trade with Guatemala, had been on the decline. Hence a route of transport to some point on the Atlantic was very desirable.[118] By an additional article to the treaty, Wyke pledged the British government to aid Guatemala in establishing such a line of transport,[119] and thereby induced the republic to accept the remainder of the draft just as it stood.[120] The convention was signed by the negotiators and ratified by the Guatemalan assembly on April 30.[121] The arrangement received the approval of the British government, and ratifications were exchanged in the early part of September.[122] Thus one element of contention

---

[114] *Parl. Papers*, 1860, *Coms.*, LXVIII, " Correspondence respecting Central America ", 172, 174.

[115] *Ibid.*, 171.   [116] *Ibid.*, 250.   [117] *Ibid.*, 251.   [118] *Ibid.*

[119] *Ibid.*, 254.   [120] *Ibid.*, 251-255.   [121] *Ibid.*, 251.   [122] *Ibid.*, 300.

between the British and American governments appeared to be removed.

Notwithstanding the slow progress of the Central American negotiations, the cordial relations which had been established between Great Britain and the United States remained, on the whole, uninterrupted during the remainder of the period considered in this chapter. Though Cass did not fail to call Napier's attention to the delay in the Mosquito negotiations and to the unsatisfactory quality of the commercial treaty formed by Ouseley with Nicaragua,[123] by a policy of perfect frankness the British government retained the confidence of the United States.[124] However, as the year advanced and it became known that the Belize boundary question, regarding which Great Britain had had her wishes, was settled, but that the other matters in dispute, which it was expected would be arranged according to American views, were not,[125] the American press began to show some impatience and irritation.[126] This state of affairs roused Cass to remind Lyons, who had succeeded Napier, that it would be necessary for the President to treat the Central American question in his message. If, at the opening of Congress, Great Britain should still be in possession of Mosquito and the Bay Islands, a strong effort would most probably be made by certain

[123] *Ibid.*, 214, 215-217, 224-225, 234. Ouseley had admitted into the commercial treaty a clause regarding the landing of armed expeditions, indirectly aimed at American filibusters. *Ibid.*, 193-194, 224-225.

[124] *Ibid.*, 213, 216-217, 224-225, 239-246, 247, 250. On May 31, 1859, Ouseley himself wrote to Buchanan explaining and excusing his delay in making the settlement regarding Mosquito. Buchanan, *Works*, X, 322-323.

[125] *Parl. Papers*, 1860, *Coms.*, LXVIII, " Correspondence respecting Central America ", 267.

[126] *Ibid.*, 234.

young and ardent politicians of the " manifest destiny " school, to abrogate the Clayton-Bulwer treaty. He had no doubt, Cass assured Lyons, but that the British government would execute with the most scrupulous good faith the arrangements regarding which the two governments had come to an understanding; but the essential point was to do this in time. It was impossible, he declared, to overrate the importance of enabling the President to announce the conclusion of the whole affair in his message in December; he therefore begged Lyons to omit no effort to impress this fact upon the British government.[127]

About a month later, on August 11, the President himself spoke in the same strain, but with more emphasis, and complained that the Belize boundary question only, of the whole dispute, had been settled. Should things be in the existing condition when Congress met, he warned Lyons, there would be an outburst of feeling in the country with which it might be impossible to contend. " It would indeed be lamentable ", he added, " if two countries whose interests were more deeply involved in a mutual good understanding than those of any other two nations in the world, should be kept asunder by questions which might be settled so easily." [128]

But before the American government began to complain, the fact that Ouseley had been in Central America for several months without having accomplished anything towards settling the dispute, as well as the conviction of his inefficiency, had determined the British

[127] *Parl. Papers,* 1860, *Coms.,* LXVIII, " Correspondence respecting Central America ", 264-266.

[128] *Ibid.,* 287-288. To allay the existing irritation the government published articles in the Washington *Union,* explaining the purpose of Ouseley's mission. Napier to Malmesbury, April 4, 1859, F. O., Am., vol. 712, no. 108.

government to place the negotiations for the transfer of the Bay Islands in other hands. But, unfortunately, Wyke, who had demonstrated his fitness for the task, had been forced by ill health to return to England.[129] However, he was soon able to resume his duties, and, on August 15, Russell, who had succeeded Malmesbury in June, instructed Ouseley to return home, as his mission had been conducted in an unsatisfactory manner,[130] and commissioned Wyke to complete the negotiations,[131] as well as to treat for the disposal of the Bay Islands.[132] Since the latter was the most pressing point in dispute, this was to be settled first. In connection with it, arrangement was to be made for the transfer to Honduras of the part of Mosquito territory which lay within the Honduras frontier.[133] These arrangements being accomplished, Wyke should proceed to Nicaragua and complete the commercial and Mosquito treaties, if

[129] *Parl. Papers*, 1860, *Coms.*, LXVIII, " Correspondence respecting Central America ", 255-256.

[130] *Ibid.*, 281-282. The Nicaraguans according to Ouseley, were afraid that the filibusters might snatch Mosquito from them as soon as the British protectorate was abandoned, so in their perplexity, they seemed to wish to delay the transfer of the territory. Believing that this would seriously affect the negotiations of the treaty regarding the Mosquitos, Ouseley dropped the Mosquito negotiations and went to Costa Rica where he negotiated a commercial treaty. After his return to Nicaragua no further progress was made; hence, when Ouseley finally received notice of his recall a year after his arrival in Central America, the Mosquito question was as far from settlement as it had been when he came, though much discussion had taken place. *Ibid.*, 205, 206-207, 225-233, 238-239, 241-248, 256, 259-263, 283-286, 294, 297-298.

[131] *Ibid.*, 268.

[132] On August 2, 1858, Russell had written: " I believe our occupation of the Bay Islands to be a violation of the Clayton-Bulwer Treaty and the sooner we settle that matter the better." Note on draft of treaty with Nicaragua, F. O., Supplement, Guat., vol. 91.

[133] *Parl. Papers*, 1860, *Coms.*, LXVIII, " Correspondence respecting Central America ", 269-272.

Ouseley had not already done so before he arrived.[134] Drafts for all of the treaties were enclosed.[135]

Meanwhile Lyons, at the direction of Russell,[136] expressed to Cass regret at the unfortunate delays which had prevented the settlement of the dispute. The British government, he said, could make no promise that the matter would be settled before the President's message was issued, but it would use its utmost efforts to accomplish that object, and if it failed it would be made clear that such failure was not due to any fault of the British government. A fresh mission was about to be sent to Central America with a view to finishing the negotiations.[137] Both the President and the Secretary of State, Lyons reported to Russell, expressed their pleasure and satisfaction at the announcement.[138]

This continued display of British frankness and good faith now finally produced in the American government a willingness to aid actively in facilitating the proposed arrangements.[139] Accordingly, Dimitry, the newly-appointed minister to Nicaragua and Costa Rica, was instructed to use every effort to form the most frank and friendly relations with the British negotiator, and to co-operate with him in any manner which he might

---

[134] *Parl. Papers,* 1860, *Coms.,* LXVIII, "Correspondence respecting Central America", 269, 272-275. Later, in order to insure the prompt success of the negotiations, instructions were sent Wyke to permit certain modifications calculated to make the treaties more satisfactory to the Central American governments concerned. Russell to Wyke, Aug. 16, 1859, "Confidential", F. O., Guat., vol. 102, no. 9; Nov. 29, 1859, *ibid.,* no. 15.

[135] *Parl. Papers,* 1860, *Coms.,* LXVIII, "Correspondence respecting Central America", 270-272, 275-280.

[136] *Ibid.,* 266.   [137] *Ibid.,* 289.   [138] *Ibid.*

[139] On Ouseley's departure for Central America, the American government had, after reflection, refused even to notify its agent in Central America that the government had no desire to impede the negotiations. Napier to Malmesbury, Oct. 25, 1858, F. O., Am., vol. 694, no. 245; Nov. 8, 1858, *ibid.,* no. 251; Nov. 9, 1858, *ibid.,* no. 257.

desire. Dimitry was also to urge the Nicaraguan government to come to an agreement with Great Britain
regarding the Mosquito protectorate without further
delay.[140] Clarke, the United States minister at Guatemala, was directed to go to Honduras for the purpose
of forwarding to the best of his ability the success of
Wyke's mission.[141]

But the presence of the two American agents proved
a hindrance instead of a help to Wyke; for Clarke
failed to learn of the altered policy of his government
in time,[142] and Dimitry did not interpret his instructions with sufficient broadness;[143] consequently, during
practically the remainder of the negotiations the two
followed the policy of their predecessors and tried to
hinder British action.[144]

Notwithstanding the demonstrations of friendship
on the part of the United States, the British government anxiously watched lest something rise to provoke
a note of hostility in the President's message on the
Central American question. But the good feeling remained undisturbed, and before the message was issued
its substance on the matter in dispute was made known,
in a spirit of friendliness, to Lyons, who found it of an
entirely satisfactory nature.[145] It merely stated that as
a result of unexpected obstacles the British govern-

[140] *U. S. Docs.,* ser. no. 3853, doc. 237, pp. 164-166.
[141] Lyons to Russell, Sept. 19, 1859, F. O., Am., vol. 715, no. 196.
[142] Wyke to Russell, Nov. 29, 1859, F. O., Guat., vol. 102, no. 8; Jan.
10, 1860, *ibid.,* vol. 108, no. 1; Inclosure in Lyons to Russell, Feb. 28,
1860, F. O., Am., vol. 735, no. 75.
[143] Wyke to Russell, Jan. 28, 1860, F. O., Guat., vol. 108, no. 2.
[144] Hall to Russell, Feb. 29, 1860, *ibid.,* vol. 109; Hall to Russell, April
30, 1860, *ibid.,* no. 25.
[145] Inclosure in Lyons to Russell, Nov. 30, 1859, F. O., Am., vol. 716,
no. 275; Lyons to Russell, Dec. 1, 1859, *ibid.,* no. 276; Jan. 17, 1860, *ibid.,*
vol. 734, no. 23.

ment had not been able to complete treaty arrangements with Honduras and Nicaragua; consequently the President could not announce, as he had earlier believed that he would be able to, that the Central American question had been satisfactorily settled; but it was confidently expected that the final adjustment of the difficulty would soon be effected.[146]

The confidence of the American government in British good faith prevented support in Congress for movements against the treaty. Both a joint resolution for abrogation [147] and a call for the correspondence upon the subject [148] failed to endanger the agreement.

Meanwhile, negotiations in Central America were progressing rapidly and in an entirely satisfactory manner. On November 28, Wyke signed a treaty with the Honduras government regarding the Bay Islands and the Mosquito Indians. The opening paragraph of the first article of this treaty was so worded as to save British pride while it satisfied Honduras.[149] It read:

Taking into consideration the peculiar geographical position of Honduras, and in order to secure the neutrality of the islands adjacent thereto, with reference to any railway or other line of interoceanic communication which may be constructed across the territory of Honduras on the mainland, Her Britannic Majesty agrees to recognize the Islands of Ruatan, Guanaca, Elena, Utile, Barbarete, and Morat, known as the Bay Islands, and situated in the Bay of Honduras, as a part of the Republic of Honduras.[150]

The terms governing the restoration were simple and reasonable; the Honduras government engaged

---

[146] Richardson, *Messages and Papers,* V, 561.

[147] *Cong. Globe,* 35 Cong., 2 sess., pt. 1, pp. 9, 104-106.

[148] *Ibid.,* pp. 45-47.

[149] *Cf. Parl. Papers,* 1860, *Coms.,* LXVIII, " Correspondence respecting Central America ", 22.

[150] *Ibid.,* 308.

not to transfer the islands to any other state, and to permit the British inhabitants freedom of religion and the right to property previously held, as well as the right to emigrate from the islands.[151] The treaty further recognized the Mosquito territory lying within the frontier of Honduras as part of the republic, and the Indians residing thereon as under Honduran sovereignty.[152] A new clause, added by Wyke [153] to the original draft, pledged the government of Honduras to pay to the Indians semi-annually for ten years the sum of two thousand, five hundred dollars.[154]

After six weeks of work, Wyke was equally successful in his negotiations with Nicaragua, and signed a treaty with that government on January 28, 1860. By this Great Britain agreed to recognize as under the sovereignty of Nicaragua the part of Mosquito territory lying within Nicaraguan frontiers. The British protectorate over the Indians should cease three months after the ratification of the treaty. A definitely bounded reservation was to be set aside for the Mosquitos, within which they should be permitted to govern themselves under any regulations which they might adopt not inconsistent with the sovereign rights of Nicaragua; but nothing in the treaty should be construed to prevent the Mosquitos from later incorporating themselves into the Nicaraguan republic. All *bona fide* land grants made by the Indians subsequent to January 1, 1848, lying within the territorial reserve, with certain exceptions, should be confirmed. Like Honduras, Nicaragua agreed to pay to the Indians two thousand, five hundred dollars semi-annually for ten years. Greytown, under Nicaraguan sovereignty, was to be a free port.[155]

[151] *Ibid.*   [152] *Ibid.*, 309.   [153] *Ibid.*, 307, 309.
[154] *Ibid.*   [155] *Ibid.*, 315-318.

Wyke's manner of executing his instructions received the hearty approval of his government.[156] After some slight changes both treaties were ratified and in due time carried into effect.[157] On August 4, Russell transmitted copies of the treaties to Lyons, with instructions to communicate them to Cass. " These Treaties ", Russell wrote, " as you will perceive, provide for the relinquishment of the Protectorate of the Mosquito Indians by Great Britain, and for the cession of the Bay Islands to Honduras; and thus, it may be hoped, finally set at rest the questions respecting the interpretation of the Clayton-Bulwer Treaty which have been the subject of so much controversy between this country and the United States." [158]

The belief that this long-desired consummation had been effected was voiced in President Buchanan's message of December, 1860. With reference to the Central American controversy he wrote:

Our relations with Great Britain are of the most friendly character . . . The discordant constructions of the Clayton and Bulwer treaty between the two Governments, which at different periods of the discussion bore a threatening aspect, have resulted in a final settlement entirely satisfactory to this government.[159]

[156] *Cf. Parl. Papers,* 1860, *Coms.,* LXVIII, " Correspondence respecting Central America ", 311, 324.

[157] Fear of Walker caused Honduras to request that the transfer of the Bay Islands be postponed for a time. This request was granted by the British government, and the delay was acquiesced in by the United States. Russell to Lyons, Sept. 22, 1860, F. O., Am., vol. 733, no. 213; Irwine to Russell, Oct. 9, 1860, *ibid.,* vol. 739, no. 44.

[158] *Parl. Papers,* 1860, *Coms.,* LXVIII, " Correspondence respecting Central America ", 329.

[159] Richardson, *Messages and Papers,* V, 639-640. In a letter to Russell, Lyons, the British minister at Washington, stated that this passage probably contained the most cordial mention of Great Britain which had appeared in any presidential message. F. O., Am., vol. 740, no. 311.

Lyons had been fearful that the part played by a British man-of-war in Walker's defeat and death might cause an outcry against Great

Through the negotiations of Wyke, the Clayton-Bulwer treaty was restored to its original authority as the rule governing future British and American relations in Central America; and by the President's message it was virtually recognized by the United States government as being so restored. This rehabilitation of the treaty was brought about not through a complete victory of one government over the other, but through a compromise, though an unequal one, for Great Britain conceded the more. In 1853 Great Britain maintained that the Clayton-Bulwer treaty applied only to the future, and that her existing possessions in Central America were untouched by it; the United States, on the contrary, held that the treaty was retrospective as well as prospective, and that, consequently, the British were bound by it to withdraw from the whole of Central America. By Wyke's treaties the British gave up their occupation of Mosquito and relinquished the Bay Islands, but, contrary to the earlier demands of the United States, retained the Belize territory south of the Sibun. The arrangement corresponded almost exactly with the Dallas-Clarendon treaty as amended by the American Senate; the concession which the British government could not make directly to American demands in 1857, was accomplished indirectly two years later by the negotiation of a new treaty with Honduras.

In the decade since the negotiation of the Clayton-Bulwer treaty, however, the attitude of the contracting

Britain; but no such demonstration took place. Its non-appearance was perhaps partly due to the fact that the news of Walker's end arrived during the Prince of Wales' tour. Lyons to Russell, Nov. 6, 1860, *ibid.,* vol. 739, no. 278. However, Walker's selfishness and cruelty had before this turned the majority of Americans against him.

parties had changed very materially towards Central America, and the shifting of viewpoints was not without its influence in promoting a settlement of the dispute. Though in 1850 Great Britain had not the interest in territorial expansion on the isthmus of which the United States suspected her, yet for commercial reasons she was not indifferent to it, and was keenly jealous of the United States; on the other hand, the American government, under a Whig administration, was little inclined to territorial acquisition for itself, in Central America, but was much opposed to British control there. During the three or four years preceding Wyke's negotiations British interests in the region had decreased while American interests had increased; Great Britain, as it were, resigned in favor of the United States. British interests in the region had become almost wholly commercial, and were directed not so much towards the establishment of an interoceanic transit route as to the development of the resources of Central America itself. The British government had become convinced that that region, exploited by American enterprise, protected by a stable Anglo-Saxon government, would contribute much more to British commercial wealth than would be possible in a state of political independence attended by confusion and unrest which paralyzed all industrial development. With this new viewpoint died all British jealousy of the United States in connection with Central America, and England began to hope as well as to expect that the Central American states would eventually become a part of the American Union.[160]

[160] Hansard, *Parl. Debates,* 3d ser., CXLII, 1511-1512; London *Times,* Dec. 4, 1856, Dec. 20, 1858; *Blackwood's Magazine,* LXXIX, 742; *Littell's*

In the United States, meanwhile, attention to Central America for transit purposes was somewhat subordinated to interest in the territory itself—partly with the view to increasing slave soil, and a strong belief had developed that in spite of opposition, even in spite of treaties, sooner or later Central America would be Americanized and absorbed into the Union.[161] Had Democratic control of the government continued a few years longer, and with it the demand for extension of slavery, it seems more than likely that such expectations would have been realized; but with a Republican victory came the War for Secession, one great reason for territorial expansion was swept aside, and American interests and energies were diverted into other channels.

Living Age, 2nd ser., XIV, 312; San Francisco *Evening Bulletin,* July 18, 1856, Aug. 14, 1856; Buchanan, *Works,* X, 114-116.

On July 31, 1858, Napier wrote confidentially to Malmesbury suggesting that it be made known to the United States government that the mission of the United States in the regeneration of the Spanish colonies was recognized by the British government, which would view with satisfaction the extension of United States authority southward in a peaceful and legitimate manner, in so far as the rights of others were not intrenched upon. F. O., Am., vol. 693, no. 193.

A few weeks before, these sentiments had been expressed by Malmesbury to Dallas, with the request that the latter make them known to his government. Malmesbury said, Dallas reported to Cass, " that he was one of that class of statesmen who believed that all the Southern part of North America must ultimately come under the government of the United States: that he had no objection to what seemed the inevitable course of things: that on the contrary, he thought it would be beneficial as well to the population occupying the countries referred to as to the United States, and the rest of the world." Dept. of State, Des., Eng., vol. 71, no. 99.

[161] Lumley to Clarendon, Sept. 9, 1856, F. O., Am., vol. 646, no. 69; *U. S. Docs.,* ser. no. 964, doc. 74, p. 7; Schouler, *History of the United States,* V, 416; *Cong. Globe,* 34 Cong., 1 sess., pt. 1, p. 395, Appendix, pp. 87, 306; *Daily Alta California,* Jan. 22, 1857.

CHAPTER IX.

Development of American Opposition to the
Clayton-Bulwer Treaty, 1860-1895; End of
Mosquito Reserve, 1894.

For many years subsequent to 1860 the United States
paid little attention to Central America. This was
partly due to preoccupation with the Civil War and
the problems to which it gave rise, but other changes
had also taken place which had decreased American
interest in the isthmus: with the abolition of slavery
was removed the chief demand for territorial expansion; and the building of the Panama Railroad and the
completion of the transcontinental line to the Pacific
for a time diverted attention from Central America as
the solution for interoceanic transportation problems.
Consequently for some time nothing arose clearly to
reveal how the nation as a whole regarded the settlements made by the Wyke treaties, or to show whether
it was satisfied to consider the Clayton-Bulwer treaty
the future rule of conduct for the British and American
governments in reference to Central America. Yet,
in the first two decades of the period now under consideration, a few occasions arose which led first the
United States government, and later the American
people, to reveal their attitude towards the treaty and
gradually to disclose and emphasize a new interpretation of it.

In 1866 Seward wrote to Adams, the American
minister to London, regarding the need of the United

States for a coaling station between Panama and San Francisco. Tigre Island, he said, would be very desirable for the purpose, but the Clayton-Bulwer treaty stood in the way of its acquisition. Therefore Adams was instructed to " sound " Clarendon upon the subject, but to use only general terms and not let it be known that the American government particularly coveted Tigre. In this connection the Secretary of State remarked that, should the canal never be begun it was a question whether the renunciatory clauses of the Clayton-Bulwer treaty were to have perpetual operation. Technically speaking, he thought, the question might be decided in the negative; still, as long as it remained a question it would not be consistent with good faith for either of the nations to do anything contrary to even the spirit of the treaty.[1] These reflections of Seward contain the first definite hint of the view later emphatically stated by the American government.

A month after this Adams took occasion to approach the British foreign secretary on the subject, but avoided stating definitely to what territory on the Central American coast he had reference, on the ground that the terms of the Clayton-Bulwer treaty were not clear in his mind; and Clarendon also stated that his remembrance of the treaty was vague but suggested that both look into its stipulations.[2] Whether or not this was done, and the question again broached, is not evident, but Tigre remained a Honduran possession.

A little later the American government gave further evidence of its attitude towards the Clayton-Bulwer treaty. In 1862 Great Britain had taken advantage of

[1] *U. S. Docs.*, ser. no. 3853, doc. 194, pp. 155-157.
[2] *Ibid.*, doc. 237, p. 20.

America's embarrassment by the Civil War to place the Belize settlement on full footing as a British colony.[3] Though, technically, the colonization of the territory between the Sibun and the Sarstoon was a violation of the Clayton-Bulwer treaty, the American government paid no attention to the action. However, in 1872 the minister from Guatemala complained to the Washington authorities that the British in Belize were encroaching upon the territory south of the Sarstoon. Consequently, in April of the following year Fish, the American secretary of state, communicated with Schenck, the American minister to England, stating that if authorized or countenanced by the British government, such encroachments would be tantamount to a breach of the engagement not to occupy any part of Central America. Schenck was instructed to ascertain the correctness of the representations made to the American government, and should they prove to be correct, he was to remonstrate formally to the British foreign secretary against any trespass by British subjects with the connivance of their government, upon the territory of Guatemala, as an infringement of the Clayton-Bulwer treaty which would be very unacceptable to the United States.[4] The result of Schenck's execution of these instructions does

---

[3] Lucas, *Historical Geography*, II, 309; Gibbs, *British Honduras*, 134; Trendell, *Her Majesty's Colonies*, 349. In 1856 when the relations between the British and American governments were critical, there was a renewed attempt on the part of the Belize settlers to have the settlement declared a colony. Bell to Labouchere, Aug. 8, 1856, C. O., Hond., vol. 93. For a time Clarendon thought of securing the view of the American government on the matter, in order to avoid misunderstanding, but finally it was thought inexpedient to do anything at that time in regard to it. Clarendon to Hammond, Oct. 28, 1856, F. O., Cen. Am., vol. 94; Merivale to Hammond, June 8, 1856, *ibid.*, vol. 93; Clarendon to the Admiralty Office, June 10, 1856, *ibid.*

[4] *U. S. Docs.*, ser. no. 3853, doc. 194, pp. 162-164.

not appear, but Fish's letter shows the American view that the first article of the treaty was still binding—at least as regarded the British government.

The attitude of Fish was consistently maintained seven years later by Evarts, when it was rumored that Great Britain was about to acquire the Bay Islands. Evarts wrote to Logan, American minister to Central America, that the Clayton-Bulwer treaty seemed unquestionably to preclude British acquisition of that territory. Therefore, the report of British intentions might well be discredited, though it should awaken the attention and excite the vigilance of the American government.[5]

From the first, however, there was a tendency on the part of the United States, acquiesced in or unnoticed by Great Britain, to ignore the eighth article of the Clayton-Bulwer treaty by which the contracting parties agreed " to extend their protection by treaty stipulations to any other practicable communications, whether by canal or railway, across the isthmus which connects North and South America ", and provided that such canals or railways be open on equal terms to the subjects and citizens of Great Britain and the United States.[6] No such joint protection was extended to the Panama Railway, completed before 1860. Moreover, the American government negotiated two new canal treaties with Colombia which completely ignored the eighth article of the Clayton-Bulwer treaty. The first of these, negotiated in 1869, stipulated by its sixth article that: " As fast as the canal and its appendages and appurtenances shall be constructed, the control,

[5] Wharton, *Digest of International Law,* II, 209.
[6] *Parl. Papers,* 1856, *Coms.,* LX, " Correspondence with the United States respecting Central America ", 52.

possession, direction, and government of the same shall belong to, and be exercised by, the United States of America." [7] The other, made the following year, contained the same stipulation. [8] Neither of the treaties was ratified, but they show a distinct tendency on the part of the American government away from the policy of internationalism in the control of a transisthmian canal, and towards an American canal controlled by Americans.

The formal opening of the Suez Canal in 1869 undoubtedly had a very strong ir^uence in causing the negotiation of the treaties just mentioned. The successful completion of this first interoceanic canal roused great enthusiasm, and naturally inspired American desire to undertake a similar labor in the New World. This feeling was voiced in a report of the secretary of the navy on December 1, 1869, which emphasized the importance of constructing a ship-canal across Darien. Now that the Suez Canal had been opened, the report said, the United States was undoubtedly stimulated to such efforts as would lead to the success of its own great enterprise: " It would be a matter of lasting regret, if the people and government of the United States were anticipated in this great work." Investigations should be at once commenced for determining the most feasible route. [9]

Various surveys of the isthmus followed, [10] but nothing definite was accomplished before de Lesseps, in 1878, secured a concession from Colombia for building a canal across Panama. The news of such an

[7] *U. S. Docs.*, ser. no. 1885, doc. 112, pp. 34-38.
[8] *Ibid.*, pp. 38-46; *cf.* Arias, *Panama Canal*, 20.
[9] *U. S. Docs.*, ser. no. 1411, doc. 1, p. 24.
[10] Coolidge, *The United States as a World Power*, 272-273.

undertaking, by the successful builder of the Suez route, filled the American people with jealousy and alarm. Resolutions were introduced into both houses of Congress declaring that control over any trans-isthmian canal must be in the hands of the United States.[11] This opinion was shared by President Hayes and expressed by him in a special message to Congress, March 8, 1880:

> The policy of this country is a canal under American control. The United States cannot consent to the surrender of this control to any European power or to any combination of European powers. If existing treaties between the United States and other nations or if the rights of sovereignty or property of other nations stand in the way of this policy—a contingency which is not apprehended—suitable steps should be taken by just and liberal negotiations to promote and establish the American policy on this subject consistently with the rights of the nations to be affected by it.
>
> The capital invested by corporations or citizens of other countries in such an enterprise must in a great degree look for protection to one or more of the great powers of the world. No European power can intervene for such protection without adopting measures on this continent which the United States would deem wholly inadmissable. If the protection of the United States is relied upon, the United States must exercise such control as will enable this country to protect its national interests and maintain the rights of those whose private capital is embarked in the work.[12]

The President's allusion to existing treaties which might stand in the way of the American canal policy evidently called attention to the Clayton-Bulwer treaty, for a strong movement promptly set in against that agreement. On March 22 a joint resolution was intro-

[11] *Cong. Record,* IX, 2312; X, 1392; XI, 107, 1568.
[12] Richardson, *Messages and Papers,* VII, 585-586.

duced into the House of Representatives requesting the President to notify the British government of the abrogation of the treaty.[13] This resolution was referred to the Committee on Foreign Relations, which, on April 16, returned a report[14] requesting that the President take immediate steps towards abrogating the treaty.[15] In connection with the demonstrations against the treaty[16] plans were discussed by Congress for defeating the aims of the French company.[17]

On June 24, 1881, Blaine took definite action for the execution of this newly-voiced policy. An excellent opportunity for this was offered by the report that Colombia desired to terminate the treaty made with the United States in 1846 and to secure from the powers of Europe a joint guarantee of the neutrality of the proposed Panama Canal.[18] Accordingly, the Secretary of State sent identical letters to the American diplomatic agents at the various European courts,[19] instructing them, that should the rumors take tangible shape, they were to call attention to the provisions of the treaty of 1846, and to intimate to the governments to which they were accredited that any attempt to supplement the guarantee contained in that treaty would necessarily be regarded by the American government as " an uncalled-for intrusion into a field where the local and general interests of the United States of America must be considered before those of any other power save those of the United States of Colombia alone." This position, the American ministers were reminded, was not the development of a new policy ; it was simply

[13] *Cong. Record*, X, 1775.
[14] *U. S. Docs.*, ser. no. 1937, doc. 1121.   [15] *Ibid.*, p. 7.
[16] *Ibid.*, ser. no. 1982, doc. 224.   [17] *Ibid.*, pp. 1-40.
[18] *Ibid.*, ser. no. 3853, doc. 194, p. 174.   [19] *Ibid.*, 177.

the pronounced adherence to principles long since enunciated and firmly established as a part of the national policy, and should be so represented to the foreign governments.[20]   It is noteworthy that Blaine's letter contained no hint of the existence of the Clayton-Bulwer treaty; that agreement was utterly unnoticed, and the declarations were directly contrary to its terms.

In his reply to Blaine's letter, Granville, the British foreign secretary, merely called attention to the fact that the position of the two nations, as regarded the canal, was determined by the Clayton-Bulwer treaty. The British government, he added, relied with confidence upon the American observance of all of the engagements of that treaty.[21]

But before Granville's communication was received, Blaine again wrote, this time with reference to the Clayton-Bulwer treaty.[22]   That arrangement, he stated, had been made more than thirty years before, under temporary conditions which had long ago ceased to exist and could never be reproduced. The President believed that some changes in the treaty were necessary, and as the British interests in the question were slight as compared with those of the United States, it was hoped that a readjustment of the treaty terms might be reached in a spirit of amity and concord. Reasons for the desired modifications followed. Great Britain had a large navy and the United States had not; the treaty bound the United States not to use its military force for the defense of the interoceanic route, while it left the naval power of Great Britain unrestrained, ready at

[20] *Ibid.*, pp. 174-177.   [21] *Ibid.*, 178.

[22] It would seem from this that Blaine's failure to mention the treaty in his first letter was due to forgetfulness or ignorance of its terms, and not to a determination, later abandoned, to ignore it.

any moment to seize both ends of the canal, thus rendering its military occupation entirely within the discretion of Great Britain. Furthermore, the United States government would not consent to perpetuate any treaty which impeached the right of the nation to priority on the American continent. Should the Pacific coast be attacked, the United States would be handicapped in an attempt to protect it, for no discrimination was made by the treaty in favor of American vessels going through the canal to defend United States territory, as compared with vessels bent on a hostile errand. For purposes of self-protection the United States claimed the right to control the isthmian transit, and offered by such control the absolute neutralization of the canal as respected European powers, which could in no other way be attained and perpetuated. The fact that since the Clayton-Bulwer treaty had been completed, commercial powers, other than the contracting parties, had developed, required a modification of the treaty ; otherwise these powers might interfere with the transit. If the non-intervention enjoined upon the United States by the treaty should be applied to the canal projected by the French, it would prevent the American government from asserting the rights and privileges acquired from Colombia before the Clayton-Bulwer treaty was formed. Consequently, the United States wished the treaty so modified as to enable it to treat with all other nations seeking a foothold on the isthmus on the basis of impartial justice and independence. It was desired that the terms of the treaty be so changed as to give the United States a right to protect and control the canal, in conjunction with the country in which it was located. With the exception of the acquisition of sites necessary for military and naval stations, no territory would be acquired in Central America by the United States. Finally, since the eighth article which was designed to extend the terms of the treaty to other practicable lines of communication between the two oceans had never beeen put into effect, the American government wished to consider it obsolete.[23]

Ten days later Blaine again wrote, replying to Granville's letter received a few days before. He denounced the Clayton-Bulwer treaty as a source of former misunderstanding and controversy, and declared that the eighth article did not stretch the guarantees of article one over the Panama route. That article was simply an agreement to extend, by treaty stipulations, the protection of both countries to that or any other practicable transisthmian waterway or railway outside of Central America. The obligations entered into by the United States with Colombia in 1846 required that the United States be freed from the unequal and unequitable obligations to Great Britain " under the vague and, as yet, unperfected compact of 1850 ".[24]

On January 7, 1882, Granville replied to Blaine's letter of November 19, defending the Clayton-Bulwer treaty. The principles upon which the Secretary of State's arguments were formed were, he thought, novel in international law. The British government could not believe that the changes in the treaty suggested by the American government would promote the object intended, or be beneficial in themselves. The principles which guided the negotiators of the treaty were sound, and still applicable to the present state of affairs. The

[23] *U. S. Docs.*, ser. no. 3853, doc. 194, pp. 178-184.
[24] *Ibid.*, pp. 184-190.

wish of the British government was that these principles be put into effect; and that other states be invited by the contracting parties to enter into similar stipulations with them. Great Britain would be glad to see the United States take the initiative in extending the invitation to other powers, and was ready to join or support and indorse it.[25]

A little later a reply came to Blaine's attack on the Clayton-Bulwer treaty. The differences which had formerly arisen between the two governments regarding it, the Foreign Secretary pointed out, did not relate to the general principles to be observed in reference to interoceanic routes, but to the acquisition of territory. During the controversy the United States had indicated no desire to fortify the canal or to exercise political control over it; on the contrary, she had disclaimed any wish for exclusive or preferential control. During the dispute Great Britain had contemplated the abrogation of the treaty, but only on condition of reversion to the *status quo,* a solution which was then possible though dangerous to the cordiality between the two nations, but which subsequent events had rendered impossible. However, a better and more conciliatory settlement had been made by the independent and voluntary action of the British government. The points in dispute were practically conceded by Great Britain and the controversy terminated in a manner declared to be " entirely satisfactory " by the President of the United States.[26]

Frelinghuysen, who became secretary of state on the accession of President Arthur, undertook to answer Granville by a new line of argument. Blaine had repre-

[25] *U. S. Docs.,* ser. no. 3853, doc. 194, pp. 191-194.
[26] *Ibid.,* pp. 194-203.

sented that a wholly new situation had risen since the conclusion of the Clayton-Bulwer treaty, and had urged that Great Britain recognize the changes wrought by thirty years and consent to alterations in the treaty. Blaine's efforts proving vain, his successor turned to technical argument, with the idea of justifying independent American action. In 1859, he wrote, Great Britain had formed a treaty with Guatemala, in which what had been called the *settlement* at Honduras, in the declaration made on the exchange of ratifications of the Clayton-Bulwer treaty, was styled " Her Britannic Majesty's settlement and possessions." The United States had never given its consent to the conversion of this settlement into a British possession with British sovereignty. This step on the part of the British government, Frelinghuysen intimated, was a violation of the Clayton-Bulwer treaty. Moreover, it was understood that the British had spread beyond the boundaries made with Guatemala. If Great Britain had violated the Clayton-Bulwer treaty and continued to violate it, that agreement was, of course, voidable at the pleasure of the United States. When President Buchanan spoke of an amicable and honorable settlement of the dispute as having been made, he had referred not to the colonization of Belize, but to the adjustment of the Mosquito controversy.[27]

As to the provision in article eight of the Clayton-Bulwer treaty, no such " treaty stipulation " as was therein proposed had been made or suggested by Great Britain for the purpose of joining the United States in the protection of the canal or railway by the Panama route. After thirty years of independent protection of

[27] *Ibid.,* pp. 9-16.

the Panama railway, the American government was convinced that such joint protection was not needed. Moreover, the Clayton-Bulwer treaty was subject to the provisions of the treaty of 1846 with New Granada, while the latter treaty bound the United States to the sole protectorate of any transit by the Panama route. Furthermore, as the persons who had the concession for the canal—which the United States understood to be accepted by the two governments, under the provisions of the treaty—had not carried out the proposed enterprise, the United States felt justified in refusing to afford its joint protection to any other persons or company; and it felt free to protect any interoceanic communication in which it or its citizens might become interested, in such a way as treaties with the local sovereign powers might warrant and their interests might require. The American government could not take part in extending an invitation to other powers to participate in an agreement based on the convention of 1850, and it would look with disfavor upon an attempt at concerted political action by other powers in that direction. There was no provision in the Clayton-Bulwer treaty to invite, or obliging the United States to accept, the aid of other nations to protect or guarantee the neutrality of the Panama route.[23]

This letter brought a reply from Granville, showing that by the eighth article of the Clayton-Bulwer treaty the contracting parties had intended to establish a " general principle " applicable to " *all* interoceanic communications, and not to any one particular scheme or schemes ". The correctness of this view, he declared, was proved by the character of the treaties made by

[23] *U. S. Docs.,* ser. no. 3853, doc. 194, pp. 16-25.

Great Britain with Honduras in 1856, and with Nicaragua in 1860, and by treaties made by the United States with Honduras in 1864 and with Nicaragua in 1867. Moreover, in its treaty with Nicaragua the American government had not only agreed to extend its protection " to all such routes of communication (between the Atlantic and Pacific oceans), and to guarantee the neutrality and innocent use of the same ", but did further agree to employ its influence with other nations to induce them to guarantee such neutrality and protection. The government of the United States having, therefore, since the conclusion of the treaty of 1846 with New Granada, entered into treaties of a more recent date with Great Britain and other powers, carrying out the " general principle " established by the Clayton-Bulwer treaty, it could hardly now appeal, without inconsistency, to its treaty with New Granada as giving it exclusive rights of protection over the projected canal across the Isthmus of Panama. Besides, there was nothing in the treaty with New Granada which conferred on the United States any exclusive right of protection, or which was inconsistent with the joint protection of Great Britain and the United States.[29]

Granville next turned to the American allegation that such acts had been committed by Great Britain in British Honduras in violation of the Clayton-Bulwer treaty as would entitle the United States to denounce the agreement. The United States was not justified in any claim to abrogate the treaty on such grounds, for the treaty was not intended to apply to British Honduras. That territory had become British by conquest, and was possessed by Great Britain long prior to the conclusion

[29] *Ibid.*, doc. 237, pp. 411-413.

of the Clayton-Bulwer treaty; and, furthermore, by a postal convention made between Great Britain and the United States in 1860 the latter had recognized British Honduras as being a British " colony ". Consequently, the contention of the American secretary of state was not sound.[20]

Some further correspondence took place upon the subject in the following year, 1883,[31] which, however, added little to the arguments already given, and the discussion was brought to a close by Granville, who felt that a prolongation of it would be useless.[32]

An examination of the arguments presented shows clearly that Great Britain had decidedly the best of the controversy, for by incontrovertible evidence she had shown that the treaty by its eighth article established a general principle applicable to all transisthmian routes, and, therefore, to Panama. The defense offered by Granville in regard to Belize was obviously defective in part; but the charges made by Frelinghuysen were scarcely less so. Though Belize was not British by conquest, a long, unchallenged occupation of the territory gave Great Britain a strong title to it. Moreover, the United States by acquiescing in the Sarstoon boundary made by Wyke had virtually agreed to a British occupation of the territory between the Sibun and the Sarstoon, and, consequently, was scarcely entitled to object to its formal establishment as a colony. Finally, though the colonization had taken place twenty years before, until 1882 the American government had not thought fit to criticise the step.

The determined effort made by the American government from 1880 to 1883 to secure the right to protect

---

[20] *U. S. Docs.,* ser. no. 3853, doc. 237, pp. 413-417.
[31] *Ibid.,* pp. 417-425.   [32] *Ibid.,* p. 423.

all transisthmian lines of communication, and the attack on the Clayton-Bulwer treaty, which obstructed this exclusive policy, raises a question as to the cause of the American attitude. The question is practically answered by the fact that since the completion of the Clayton-Bulwer treaty thirty years of growth and progress had taken place in the United States. Shortly previous to 1850 the nation had annexed the Oregon Country and the Southwest. During thirty years this vast region had been settled and its resources were being rapidly developed. The population of the country as a whole had doubled, and there had been a tremendous increase in wealth and prosperity. These changes made inevitable a new feeling of dignity and a greater degree of self-confidence in the nation. Moreover, the conduct of most of the European powers during the Civil War inclined the United States more fully to realize that these nations were not to be trusted in matters involving American welfare.

These facts in themselves are sufficient to explain the American policy, but it seems desirable to consider others in connection with them. In the first place, it should be remembered that long-established British influence in Central America was what produced the treaty of 1850, which admitted Great Britain to a partnership with the American government in the regulation of transisthmian communication. The settlement of the dispute by such a treaty was encouraged by the lack of sufficient American capital to build the canal.[33] But the treaty from the first was unpopular because it compromised with the Monroe doctrine. Even as early as 1856 the United States was averse to extending the

[33] *Ibid.*, pp. 229-230.

provisions of the eighth article to the Panama route.[34] The stand of Blaine and Frelinghuysen was, consequently, a definite voicing of an attitude long held in silence rather than the presentation of a new interpretation of the treaty.

The great interest roused by the opening of the Suez Canal has been mentioned, and the consequent desire of the American nation to be the leader in a similar undertaking in the New World. Closely following this stimulation of interest, came news of de Lesseps's contract with Colombia. Though hitherto various foreign nations had directed attention to projects for routes across the Central American isthmus, never before, since growth in prosperity had made possible the construction of a canal by American capital, had a dangerous rival appeared. De Lesseps's success at Suez seemed to guarantee success at Panama. Such a situation was bound to reveal a bold and exclusive policy on the part of the United States.

Although worsted in argument, the United States gave little sign of acquiescing in the British view; and in 1884 she proceeded again to ignore the Clayton-Bulwer treaty by negotiating with Nicaragua a treaty for a canal to be entirely under American control, built by the United States and jointly owned by herself and Nicaragua.[35] This treaty was still before the Senate for ratification upon the accession of Cleveland, who withdrew it and reverted to the policy of a neutralized canal under international guarantee.[36] But Cleveland's action only caused a temporary check to an

---

[34] See above, pp. 233-234.
[35] Sparks, *National Development,* 225-226.
[36] Richardson, *Messages and Papers,* VIII, 327.

irresistible national movement; with the Harrison administration the former policy was resumed. The growing likelihood that de Lesseps's undertaking would prove a failure, however, somewhat abated American enthusiasm, and also again turned attention to the Nicaragua route.[37] The Maritime Canal Company, in 1887, obtained a concession for the construction of a canal on this line. Work was begun two years later,[38] but as the company's funds soon began to fail it appealed to the United States government for help. The subject was taken up by the Senate in 1890, and in the following year a bill was reported, amending the company's charter. The amendments provided for the guarantee of the company's bonds by the American government, secured the government against loss, and gave it a controlling voice in the management of the canal.[39] Accompanying the bill was a statement from the committee that as the Clayton-Bulwer treaty was obsolete it could not be an obstacle to the passage of the measure.[40]

The matter frequently came up for debate in the next four years and the treaty was vigorously denounced, but that the country was unwilling to assume responsibility for its abrogation, independent of England, was evident from the fact that several joint resolutions for that purpose failed to pass. However, in January, 1895, the canal bill passed by a good majority, showing the increasing determination of the country to have a canal under American control.[41]

The action of the Senate did not escape the notice of Great Britain. In July, 1894,[42] and again in February,

[37] Coolidge, *The United States as a World Power*, 274.
[38] Travis, *Clayton-Bulwer Treaty*, 240-241.
[39] Dewey, *National Problems*, 118-121.
[40] Travis, *Clayton-Bulwer Treaty*, 241-242.   [41] *Ibid.*, 242.
[42] *Parl. Debates*, 4th ser., XXVII, 15.

1895,[43] attention was called to it in the House of Commons, but the reply of Grey, the under secretary of state for foreign affairs, was that there was no reason to believe that the American government did not intend to keep its treaty engagements.[44] This confidence in American integrity was justified by the stand taken in 1896 by Secretary of State Olney. In a memorandum upon the Clayton-Bulwer treaty he declared Frelinghuysen's contention—that the treaty referred to a particular canal—to be "ingenious rather than sound", and held that the treaty was still in force. "If", he wrote, "changed conditions now make stipulations, which were once deemed advantageous, either inapplicable or injurious, the true remedy is not in ingenious attempts to deny the existence of the treaty or to explain away its provisions, but in a direct and straightforward application to Great Britain for a reconsideration of the whole matter." [45] This stand of Olney was substantially a return to the attitude of Blaine.

A second element of the old Central American dispute attracting attention during the period now under consideration was the relations between the English and the Mosquitos. The treaty of Managua, negotiated by Wyke in 1860, failed to banish British influence as completely as had been expected. Many foreigners, particularly English, continued to reside in the old Mosquito territory, and were the controlling power, advancing their own interests with little regard to the welfare of the Nicaraguans or Indians. This foreign element produced discord between the Mosquitos and

[43] *Parl. Debates*, 4th ser., XXX, 745-746.
[44] *Ibid.*, XXVII, 16; XXX, 746.
[45] Moore, *Digest of International Law*, III, 208-209.

the Nicaraguan government, and quarrels were frequent. The dissensions led to appeals to England, and the consequent interference of the British government. A dispute soon developed regarding the meaning of the treaty of Managua.[46]

Nicaragua was finally persuaded by the British government to submit the dispute to the arbitration of the Emperor of Austria. His award, given in 1880, favored the British interpretation of the treaty; it made Nicaraguan sovereignty over the reserve merely nominal, and practically established the right of the British to interfere in behalf of the Mosquitos.[47] However, there is no reason to believe that either previous or subsequent to the award the interference of the British was such as to constitute a violation of the Clayton-Bulwer treaty. If it had been, it is pretty certain that this lack of good faith would have attracted American attention.[48]

There is no available evidence that the American government took any notice of British relations with the Mosquitos from 1860 until 1888; and the interest finally then roused was largely due to the renewed popularity of the Nicaragua route, and to the project of the Maritime Canal Company.[49] In October, 1888, the Nicaraguan minister at Washington presented to Secretary of State Bayard a letter from the British

[46] *Brit. and For. State Papers*, LXXXI, 752.
[47] *Ibid.*, LXXII, 1212-1213.
[48] Travis, *Clayton-Bulwer Treaty*, 208-210, gives the British interference in Mosquito as one of the causes for the American attack on the Clayton-Bulwer treaty in 1880; but this view scarcely seems sound, for had such interference attracted the attention of the United States, a point would undoubtedly have been made of it by Blaine or Frelinghuysen in their correspondence of 1880-1883.
[49] *U. S. Docs.*, ser. no. 3275, doc. 20, pp. 69-70, 96.

minister in Central America to the Nicaraguan government, complaining that the Nicaraguans had infringed upon the boundaries of the Mosquito reserve and had also established a post office at Bluefields,[50] " thus interfering with the domestic affairs of the Reserve ". The establishment of forts, arsenals, post offices, etc., in the reserve by the Nicaraguans, was, in the opinion of the British government, inconsistent with the treaty of Managua as interpreted by the award.[51]

In consequence of this communication, Bayard wrote to Phelps, the American minister to England. Had the United States anticipated, he said, that under cover of the treaty of Managua the British government would continue to attempt any interference with the affairs of the Indians, it would not have hailed that treaty as a solution and termination of disputes concerning the British protectorate over the Mosquitos, but would have regarded the arrangement as a serious obstacle to any such settlement. However, he declared, nothing in the treaty of Managua or in the Austrian award was incompatible with the right of Nicaragua to establish post offices in the reserve or military posts for the common defense. Such a right was an essential incident of paramount sovereignty, and could be properly exercised only by Nicaragua. It was important to the United States as to all other powers that Nicaraguan sovereignty exist in fact over the Mosquito reserve, for with the sovereign alone could diplomatic relations be maintained, and to it alone could the powers look for redress of possible wrongs to their citizens.[52]

[50] Bluefields was the residence of the Mosquito government.
[51] *Brit. and For. State Papers*, LXXXI, 758-759.
[52] *Ibid.*, 746-754.

But more important than the question of Nicaraguan authority in the reserve, was the general question of the right of the British government to interfere in disputes between Nicaragua and the Mosquitos. The President could not but regard the continued exercise of the claim on the part of Great Britain to interfere on behalf of these Indians as the assertion of a British protectorate in another form; more especially when this effort was directed to preventing Nicaragua from exercising military jurisdiction in the immediate neighborhood of the Atlantic mouth of the projected canal. The United States could never see with indifference the reestablishment of such a protectorate. It would not only be contrary to the Monroe doctrine, but also to the terms of the Clayton-Bulwer treaty, the binding force of which Great Britain had hitherto so emphatically asserted. The history of the former controversy with regard to the same subject should admonish the British and American governments to spare no effort to avoid misunderstandings and to promote cordial co-operation and good intelligence between the two countries. With this purpose in view the American government desired that its attitude be made known to Great Britain.[53]

Salisbury, the British foreign secretary, replied in a reasonable and conciliatory manner. Because of complaints from the Mosquito chief, he explained, the British agent in Central America had been instructed to make friendly remonstrance to the Nicaraguan government and to draw its attention to the wording of the treaty of Managua and to the interpretation given it by the Austrian award. If Mosquito rights were infringed upon by Nicaragua, by whom could remon-

[53] *Ibid.*, 754-758.

strance be made if not by Great Britain, with whom Nicaragua concluded the convention defining these rights? However, the British government did not claim the right to intervene in every dispute between the Mosquitos and their sovereign; the extent of the intervention was indicated in the report annexed to the award. Moreover, the British government had no desire to assert a protectorate, or anything in the nature of a protectorate over the Mosquitos, and it would give that government the greatest possible satisfaction if Nicaragua and the Indians would come to an amicable arrangement for the incorporation of the latter into the Nicaraguan republic, thus relieving Great Britain from any further responsibility.[54] This explanation was evidently satisfactory to the United States, for with it the correspondence ended.[55]

The Austrian award practically established Mosquito independence of Nicaragua, and after it was given foreign influence increased. Extensive banana plantations were established by American immigrants, and a thriving commerce developed, particularly with the United States.[56] The peaceful prosperity of the territory roused the jealousy of the disorganized, poverty-stricken remainder of Nicaragua, and led the Nicaraguan government to determine to extend its influence over the reserve.[57] Consequently, in 1893, a Nicaraguan

[54] *Brit. and Foreign State Papers*, LXXXI, 754-758.

[55] Four years later Lincoln, the American minister to London, addressed a letter to the British foreign secretary, reopening the discussion, but no reply was given him. *U. S. Docs.*, ser. no. 3275, doc. 20, p. 28.

[56] Keely, " Nicaragua and the Mosquito Coast ", in *Pop. Sci. Mo.*, XLV, 164-165. In 1894 it was reported that ninety-four per cent. of the wealth, enterprise, and commerce of the reserve was American. Bluefields was " American to the core ". *U. S. Docs.*, ser. no. 3275, doc. 20, pp. 70, 87.

[57] *Ibid.*, p. 37.

commissioner, General Lacayo, was appointed,[58] with instructions to assert the sovereignty of the republic over the reserve and to use his influence to secure its incorporation into Nicaragua.[59] Lacayo's efforts, however, were vain.[60]

This was the situation in 1893 when war broke out between Honduras and Nicaragua.[61] As a result of rumors of a Honduran invasion of the reserve, the Nicaraguan government sent troops there who established martial law.[62] Immediately great excitement prevailed and the Americans in the reserve petitioned their government for protection by a war vessel.[63] The Nicaraguan commissioner meanwhile had meddled with Mosquito affairs in various ways, and had placed a duty on bananas sent out of the reserve.[64] In February, 1894, Bingham, the British consul, warned him that should he persist in his course, the British war vessel in the harbor would interfere.[65] Finally, however, because of the danger to life and property in the reservation, the commissioner himself and the foreign consuls requested protection from the British vessel *Cleopatra*;[66] and, on March 5, marines who were landed from the ship compelled the Nicaraguans to raise the siege laid upon

[58] *Ibid.*, pp. 37-38, 84. The appointment of a Nicaraguan commissioner was permitted by the treaty of Managua. *Brit. and For. State Papers,* LXXII, 1212.

[59] *U. S. Docs.,* ser. no. 3275, doc. 20, p. 84.

[60] *Ibid.*, pp. 11-12, 84-85.

[61] *Ibid.*, pp. 10-11. A clear and interesting account of the Mosquito coast in 1893 may be found in *Pop. Sci. Mo.,* XLV, 160-175.

[62] *U. S. Docs.,* ser. no. 3275, doc. 20, pp. 19, 20-23.

[63] *Ibid.*, pp. 12-13. The *Kearsarge* which was sent was lost on the way. When the loss became known the *San Francisco* was ordered from Brazil to Bluefields. *Ibid.*, p. 68.

[64] *Ibid.*, p. 38. This was a violation of the Austrian award. *Brit. and For. State Papers,* LXXII, 1213.

[65] *U. S. Docs.,* ser. no. 3275, doc. 20, p. 14.

[66] *Ibid.*, p. 36.

Bluefields.[67] Following this, a provisional government was formed for the reservation by Captain Howe of the *Cleopatra,* the British consul, Lacayo, and the commander of the Nicaraguan troops. The American citizens and Braida, the American consul, refused to have any part in the arrangement.[68] The Americans were strongly opposed to the provisional government for they felt it to be a step towards Nicaraguan rule in Mosquito, which they believed would be fatal to industry and commerce.[69] What they desired was local self-government based on the lines laid down in the treaty of Managua.[70] Thus it appeared that the interests of American citizens in Mosquito were at variance with the contention of the American government as to the rightful control of the territory.

An account of the occcurrence at Bluefields was promptly telegraphed, and later written, to the American government by Baker, the American minister at Managua;[71] and immediately upon receiving the telegram, Gresham, the American secretary of state, telegraphed to Bayard, then minister to England, instructing him to investigate and report the cause for Captain Howe's action.[72]

A telegram from Bayard, dated March 15, stated that the British government had given no instructions for the landing of the troops, and was waiting for further information regarding the matter. As soon as additional intelligence should be received, it would be promptly communicated to the United States. Kimber-

---

[67] *U. S. Docs.,* ser. no. 3275, doc. 20, pp. 15, 36. Thanks were formerly extended by the Americans to the captain of the *Cleopatra* for his protection. *Ibid.,* pp. 32, 45.

[68] *Ibid.,* pp. 32-34.   [69] *Ibid.,* pp. 32-33.   [70] *Ibid.,* pp. 32-33, 43.

[71] *Ibid.,* pp. 17-18.   [72] *Ibid.,* p. 26.

ley, the foreign secretary, had assured Bayard, however, that the British government had no desire or intention to establish a protectorate in Central America. Bayard himself believed that the troops had been landed merely for protection to the residents.[73] Some time later Bayard sent further details regarding the incident which went to show that his opinion had been correct.[74]

A telegram from Gresham to Baker, sent on March 14, had brought no further details;[75] but on April 19 Captain Watson, of the American vessel *San Francisco*, which had been sent to Bluefields to protect American interests, telegraphed a statement to the Navy Department. The landing of the British troops, he said, was justifiable, and permission of the Nicaraguan commissioner had been first obtained. The troops had been believed necessary to the protection of life and property. Later, however, the British force had retired and now the Nicaraguans were in full control.[76]

By April 30 a fairly accurate account of the affair had reached Washington, and on that date Gresham wrote to Bayard, objecting to the joint assumption of authority in Mosquito by the British and Nicaraguan agents, as incompatible with the terms of the treaty of Managua. The stipulations of that treaty, Gresham stated, left no room for foreign intervention, or for the administration of affairs in the reserve by aliens. The arrangement for a provisional government would tend to strengthen the assumption that Mosquito was a territorial entity with sovereign rights. Such government could have no support from the United States. While the American government was pleased to learn that the British forces had been landed simply for the

---

[73] *Ibid.*, pp. 26-27.   [74] *Ibid.*, pp. 34-40.   [75] *Ibid.*, p. 26.
[76] *Ibid.*, p. 50.

protection of life and property, the President hoped that the anomalous situation in the Mosquito reserve might speedily cease, and that no foreign agency would be permitted to dictate or participate in the administration of affairs there.[77]

Bayard, on May 22, telegraphed a reply to this. In an interview just concluded with Kimberley, the latter had again assured him that Great Britain had no intention or desire of forming a protectorate over any part of Nicaraguan territory; instead it wished to act thoroughly in concert with the United States, and to continue the treaty of 1850 " in unbroken force and effect ". The British consul, Kimberley had stated, had acted without instructions in helping to form a provisional government, but had done so because he believed the lives and property of the residents to be in danger. It was the wish of the British government to consult with the United States in order to guard against Nicaraguan violence to British and American interests. The British minister at Washington had been instructed to this effect.[78]

Later, a letter from Bayard expressed the belief that the British government had no desire for the abrogation of the Clayton-Bulwer treaty, or to do anything inconsistent with its provisions, or to interfere in any way with the plans or works of the United States in relation to the proposed canal. They desired, he believed, to have only the most friendly and mutually accommodating relations with the American government.[79]

[77] *U. S. Docs.*, ser. no. 3275, doc. 20, pp. 68-69.
[78] *Ibid.*, p. 91.   [79] *Ibid.*, pp. 96-97.

Gresham replied, on July 19, that to accept the implied invitation to join with Great Britain for the purpose of settling the questions originating in the recent incident at Bluefields might indicate a willingness on the part of the existing American administration to depart from the policy of its predecessors in dealing with Central American questions. The government in the reserve was not Mosquito, but alien, especially at Bluefields. No matter how conspicuous the American or other alien interests which had grown up under the fiction of Indian self-government, neither the United States nor Great Britain could fairly sanction or uphold this abuse of Nicaraguan sovereignty. American rights in the reservation must be treated by the United States like similar rights in other parts of Nicaragua, and, should these be invaded, the American residents could look only to the Nicaraguan government for redress.[80]

Meanwhile, the provisional government, supported by the Nicaraguan authorities, had acted in a very arbitrary manner and had become unpopular. Encouraged by the aliens—especially the Americans of poor reputation[81]—the Indians and Jamaica negroes revolted, drove out the Nicaraguans, and restored Clarence, the Mosquito chief, to his office.[82] The two contending parties at first displayed considerable violence, but the presence of marines from the American vessel *Marblehead* helped restore order.[83]

The Nicaraguan authorities, however, soon regained control of the reserve, and by tactful treatment of the

[80] *Ibid.*, pp. 126-128.
[81] *Ibid.*, pp. 128, 158-161, 163, 164, 168, 169.
[82] *Ibid.*, p. 128.
[83] *Ibid.*, pp. 128, 132, 137-142.

Indians won their confidence.[84] In a short time, at the express desire of the Mosquitos, steps were taken towards their incorporation into the Nicaraguan republic. Delegates from the leading tribes met in convention, voted for incorporation, and formally recognized the constitution of Nicaragua. The Mosquitos were given all of the rights of other Nicaraguan citizens and also some special privileges. The former reserve became the department of Zelaya in the republic.[85]

The fact of Mosquito incorporation, made known to the American government through a telegram from Baker, was received with much satisfaction.[86] The arrangement was equally gratifying to Great Britain. On December 22, 1894, Bayard sent the following announcement:

> Her Majesty's Government are well pleased with the prospect of having "Clarence" and his fortunes eliminated from their political responsibility.

> There was the most open expression of satisfaction at the foreign office upon the reported voluntary incorporation of the

[84] The foreigners who were suspected of having incited the Mosquitos to revolt escaped less fortunately. Two American citizens and twelve British subjects, including Hatch, the British vice-consul at Bluefields, were arrested and after rough treatment were sent to Managua. *Ibid.*, p. 173. Upon protest being made from their government, the Americans were soon released; but the release of the British, and particularly of Hatch, was long delayed, as was also the redress demanded by the British government. *Ibid.*, pp. 190-195. Finally, by seizure of the harbor of Corinto, Great Britain forced Nicaragua to restore Hatch and to pay an indemnity of seventy-five thousand dollars. Travis, *Mosquito History*, 31. This roused some Americans who believed that the British were trying to gain control of the Nicaragua canal route; but the American government itself took a more reasonable view, as did the majority of the population. Colquhoun, *The Nicaragua Canal*, 293-295.

[85] *U. S. Docs.*, ser. no. 3275, doc. 20, pp. 204-206. The firm stand of the American government for the rights of Nicaragua in the reserve was a very important factor in producing this final settlement; and the friendly action of the United States was fully appreciated by Nicaragua. *Ibid.*, p. 205.

[86] *Ibid.*, p. 201.

Indians with the rest of Nicaragua, for it was a consummation devoutly to be wished, and they were glad to be free from the subject.[87]

Thus, in a manner agreeable to all concerned, was at last settled the famous Mosquito question, which had been a source of disagreement between the United States and Great Britain for nearly fifty years, and between the latter and Central America for more than two centuries.

[87] *Ibid.*, pp. 203-204. By a treaty with Nicaragua, ratified in 1906, Great Britain formally recognized the abrogation of the treaty of Managua and the incorporation of the Mosquitos into the Nicaraguan republic. *Parl. Papers*, 1906, CXXXVI, " Treaty between the United Kingdom and the Republic of Nicaragua with regard to the Mosquito Territory ", 1-6.

CHAPTER X.

THE NEW CANAL TREATIES, AND NEW CONDITIONS IN CENTRAL AMERICA.

For many years a growing desire had existed in the United States for a transisthmian canal owned and controlled by Americans, but up to the close of the last century there seemed little prospect of its prompt realization. Though the less responsible element in Congress frequently urged abrogation, the members with a clearer sense of international honor felt with Olney that the Clayton-Bulwer treaty could not be set aside except by joint action with England. Such action seemed but a remote possibility, for the British government had expressed its satisfaction with the treaty and its firm determination to stand by it.

The last few years of the century, however, brought a change in British and American affairs which profoundly affected the relations of the two governments. The Boer War and the events immediately preceding it had given rise to a coldness between England and other European powers. England felt herself isolated, and therefore sought support beyond Europe.[1] This new policy undoubtedly influenced the British attitude towards the United States during the Spanish-American War. English sympathy probably would have been

[1] Coolidge, *The United States as a World Power*, 275; Barral-Montferrat, *De Monroë à Roosevelt*, 239.

on the American side in any case, but, as it was, an unusual cordiality accompanied the sympathy.[2]

The friendliness of Great Britain was reciprocated by the Americans, but the British government fully realized that such unusual cordiality would not long survive if the Clayton-Bulwer treaty were maintained as an obstacle to an American transisthmian canal. The long cruise of the *Oregon* around Cape Horn in 1898, for the purpose of joining the Atlantic squadron, had called attention to the need for a canal, while the acquisition of the Philippines and Hawaii, in the Pacific, and of Porto Rico, which strengthened the American position in the Caribbean Sea, further increased the arguments in favor of it.[3] The time was fully ripe for the undertaking, and, in order to place on a secure basis the new Anglo-American relations, Great Britain was inclined to humor the United States in her long-cherished desire.

Accordingly, after the presidential message of December, 1898, had again called attention to the need of the nation and urged action, Pauncefote, the British ambassador at Washington, approached the secretary of state in order to learn the exact attitude of the American government. This was frankly given. The President, Pauncefote was emphatically assured, had no intention of ignoring the Clayton-Bulwer treaty, and would faithfully observe its stipulations; but, in view of the demand for a canal, the United States wished,

---

[2] Coolidge, *The United States as a World Power*, 275; Latané, *America as a World Power*, 63-64.

[3] Coolidge, *The United States as a World Power*, 274; *Parl. Papers*, 1901, [Cd. 438], "Correspondence respecting the Convention Signed at Washington relative to the Establishment of a Communication by Ship-Canal", 4; Keasbey, "Terms and Tenor of the Clayton-Bulwer Treaty", in *Annals of the American Academy*, Nov. 1899, pp. 1-26.

by friendly negotiation with England, to secure such modification of the treaty as would, without affecting the " general principle " therein declared, enable the enterprise to be undertaken by the American government.[4]

The British government expressed a willingness to consider the matter, and, in consequence, a draft convention was drawn up by Secretary of State Hay, and handed to Pauncefote in January, 1899. However, just at this time the Joint High Commission, to which had been assigned the settlement of the Alaskan boundary and other questions between the two governments, had come seriously to question whether an adjustment of these difficulties could be effected, because of the unwillingness of the American government to yield regarding the contested boundary. In consequence, Great Britain hesitated to make concessions on the question of the Clayton-Bulwer treaty, and for some months nothing was accomplished with regard to it. But early in 1900 the British government was again stirred to activity. A bill was before Congress empowering the President to acquire from Nicaragua and Costa Rica the control of territory for a canal route, and directing the secretary of war to construct the canal and make provision for its protection. It seemed likely that the bill would pass, and thus cause embarrassment between the two governments. To obviate such a possibility the British government decided to accept the convention as presented by Hay.[5]

This convention, signed February 5, 1900, gave the American government full power to direct the construc-

<hr />

[4] *Parl. Papers,* 1901, [Cd. 438], " Correspondence respecting the Convention signed at Washington . . . ", etc., 4.
[5] *Ibid.,* 4-5.

tion of the canal and to provide for its regulation and management. In order to preserve the " general principle " of neutralization established by the Clayton-Bulwer treaty, the following rules for the free navigation of the canal, substantially those agreed upon in 1888 for the Suez route, were adopted:

(1) The canal was to be open in time of war as in time of peace to vessels of commerce and war on terms of entire equality.

(2) The canal was never to be blockaded, or any right of war exercised, or any act of hostility committed within it.

(3) War vessels of a belligerent should not revictual or take any stores in the canal, except so far as was strictly necessary; and the transit of such vessels should be effected with the least possible delay. Prizes were to come under the same rule as war vessels.

(4) No belligerent should embark or disembark troops, munitions of war, or warlike materials in the canal except in case of accidental hindrance of the transit, in which case the transit should be resumed as quickly as possible.

(5) War vessels of a belligerent should not remain in the waters within three marine miles of either end of the canal longer than twenty-four hours, except when in distress, in which case they should depart as soon as possible. But a war vessel of one belligerent should not depart within twenty-four hours from the departure of a war vessel of the other belligerent.

(6) The works, etc., necessary to the construction, maintenance, and operation of the canal were to be considered part of the canal and should enjoy complete immunity from hostile attacks.

(7) No fortifications should be erected to command the canal or the adjoining waters, but the United States was free to maintain such military police as would protect it against lawlessness and disorder.

Immediately after the ratification of the treaty the contracting parties were to bring the arrangement to the notice of other powers and invite them to adhere to it.[6]

The treaty was promptly presented to the Senate, but ratification of it was not accomplished before Congress adjourned, though the bill for the American construction and defense of a canal was passed by a large majority, on May 2. When Congress resumed its session in the autumn, the treaty formed by Hay and Pauncefote was ratified, but only after three amendments, seriously changing its meaning, had been added: the Clayton-Bulwer treaty was declared to be superseded by the new arrangement; a new clause was added to rule five stating that the first five rules should not apply to measures which the United States might find it necessary to take for securing by its own forces the defense of the United States and the maintenance of public order; the provision for inviting the adherence of other powers to the treaty was entirely omitted.[7] These changes were practically an elimination of the neutralization policy, and would place the canal in control of the United States with the protection of the route for the use of other powers left entirely to American discretion.

[6] *Parl. Papers,* 1900, [Cd. -30], " Convention between Her Majesty and the United States Supplementary to the Convention of April 19, 1850 ", 1-2.
[7] *Ibid.,* 1901, [Cd. 438], " Correspondence respecting the Convention signed at Washington . . . ", etc., 2-5.

From the first it seemed hardly possible that the British government would favor the amended treaty. Though the British press fully admitted that fifty years of change justified the American demand for modification of the Clayton-Bulwer treaty, it declared that the draft signed by Hay and Pauncefote accomplished this, and denounced the amended treaty.[8] The President also was criticised for permitting its ratification, after being so amended.[9]

A letter written on February 22, 1901, by Lansdowne, the British foreign secretary, to Pauncefote, after calling attention to the conciliatory spirit which had led the British government to resume negotiations, presented the British view of the Senate amendments. The Clayton-Bulwer treaty, Lansdowne wrote, was an international contract of unquestionable validity, and, according to well-established usage, should not be abrogated or modified except with the consent of both parties to the contract. In spite of this, the British government had been confronted by a proposal from the American Senate—without any previous attempt to ascertain British views—for the abrogation of the treaty. But the second and third amendments were even more objectionable. The second, giving the United States control of the canal in time of war, was a distinct departure from the principle hitherto acceptable to both governments. The change proposed by the United States would presumably permit warlike acts, on the part of that government, in or near the canal— acts clearly inconsistent with the neutral character which it had always been sought to give the canal, and

[8] London *Morning Post*, Dec. 5, 14, 1900; London *Daily News*, Jan. 17, 1901; London *Times*, Jan. 16, 18, 1901.

[9] London *Times*, Dec. 24, 1900.

which would deny its free use to the commerce and navies of the world. Such an arrangement would strike at the very root of the general principle of neutralization upon which the Clayton-Bulwer treaty was based. But the import of the second amendment was peculiarly emphasized when considered in connection with the third. If the adherence of the powers were given, the neutrality of the canal would be secured; without that adherence, it would depend only upon the guarantee of the two contracting parties. The last amendment, however, not only removed all prospect of the wider guarantee, but also placed the British government in a position of marked disadvantage, compared with the other powers, which would not be subject to the self-denying ordinance which Great Britain was desired to accept.[10]

In view of these facts, the British government could not accept the amended convention, and, under existing circumstances, preferred to retain the Clayton-Bulwer treaty. The British government, Lansdowne concluded, had shown an earnest desire to meet the views of the United States, and would have been ready to consider in a friendly spirit any amendments—not inconsistent with the principles accepted by both governments—which the United States might have desired to propose; and it would sincerely regret a failure to come to a friendly understanding in regard to this important subject.[11]

The British refusal to accept the amended treaty immediately produced a Senate resolution for the abro-

---

[10] *Parl. Papers,* 1901, [Cd. 438], "Correspondence respecting the Convention signed at Washington . . . ", etc., 5-7.
[11] *Ibid.,* 7.

gation of the Clayton-Bulwer convention.[12] Hay, however, promptly proceeded to form a new draft, which, on April 25, 1901, Pauncefote transmitted to Lansdowne.[13] This draft was similar to the former treaty as amended by the Senate in that by separate article it declared the Clayton-Bulwer treaty to be superseded and made no provision for inviting other powers to adhere to the stipulations agreed upon; but the rules for the regulation of the canal were modified with the aim of meeting British objections and yet preserving the principle contended for by the United States. From the first rule were omitted the words, " in time of war as in time of peace "; rule seven prohibiting the fortification of the canal by the United States was omitted, but to rule two was added the reservation: " The United States, however, shall be at liberty to maintain such military police along the canal as may be necessary to protect it against lawlessness and disorder "; finally, the clause added to rule five in the former draft was entirely omitted.[14]

The changes made by Hay rendered the arrangement more acceptable to the British government, but certain further modifications were proposed by Lansdowne. In order to preserve the " general principle " stipulated for in the Clayton-Bulwer treaty, a new article was added reaffirming this general principle and asserting that the rules governing the use of the canal should as far as applicable control all interoceanic communications across the isthmus connecting North and South

[12] *Cong. Record*, XXXV, 8, 13-22, 23-28.
[13] *Parl. Papers*, 1902, [Cd. 905], " Correspondence respecting the Treaty signed at Washington relative to the Establishment of a Communication by Ship-Canal ", 1.
[14] *Ibid.*, 1-2.

America; and that no change of territorial sovereignty or other change of circumstances should affect such general principle or the obligations of the contracting parties under the treaty. The first rule for regulating the use of the canal was so modified as to admit to it only the vessels of those nations which should agree to observe the rules above described; and to the same rule was appended the stipulation that the conditions and charges in connection with the use of the canal should be just and equitable.[15]

The American government objected to the first change mentioned. This, it claimed, repeated what was already stated in the preamble, and seemed to give a wider application to article eight of the Clayton-Bulwer treaty than was originally intended. Instead of the article added by the British government, Hay suggested a simple statement providing that no change of territorial sovereignty or of the international relations of the country or countries traversed by the canal should affect the general principle of neutralization, or the obligation of the contracting parties. The second change was also objected to, because of the strong American aversion to inviting other powers to become contracting parties to the canal treaty; in its place were proposed the words, "the canal shall be free and open to the vessels of commerce and of war of all nations observing these Rules ".[16]

These modifications were accepted by the British government, which suggested a slight further alteration in the wording of the preamble and of the first article,

[15] *Parl. Papers*, 1902 [Cd. 905], " Correspondence respecting the Treaty signed at Washington relative to the Establishment of a Communication by Ship-Canal ", 2-7.
[16] *Ibid.*, 7-8.

in order to make it perfectly clear that the treaty was meant to apply to all other canals across the American isthmus as well as that through Nicaragua.[17] These changes were in turn accepted by the American government, and the treaty was signed on November 18, 1901,[18] by Hay and Pauncefote. The next month it passed the Senate by a vote of seventy-two to six,[19] and ratifications were exchanged between the two governments in the following February.[20]

In view of the modifications which Great Britain had permitted in the rules providing for the neutralization of the canal, it is difficult to see how neutralization was guaranteed in the case of war between the United States and any other power.[21] The new treaty, however, met the approval of both nations. As Great Britain seemed to think her interests secured by this treaty, she had no objection to giving up some of the earlier measures for which she had contended, or to setting aside the Clayton-Bulwer treaty, which both countries acknowledged to be outgrown.[22] Moreover, the British felt that the right to protect and control the canal was only a reasonable demand, considering that the whole cost of construction was to be borne by the American nation.[23] In fact, the satisfactory completion of the treaty was regarded as the conclusion of a long period

[17] *Ibid.,* 8-9.   [18] *Ibid.,* 10-11.   [19] *Ibid.,* 11.

[20] *Ibid.,* [Cd. 1007], "Treaty between the United Kingdom and the United States of America for the Establishment of a Ship-Canal ", 1.

[21] For a discussion of the neutralization provisions of the treaty, see Latané, "Neutralization Features of the Hay-Pauncefote Treaty ", in Am. Hist. Assn., *Annual Report, 1902,* I, 289-303; also Woolsey, " Suez and Panama—a Parallel ", pp. 305-312 of the same volume.

[22] London *Daily News,* Nov. 18, Dec. 17, 1901; London *Times,* Nov. 19, 1901.

[23] *Parl. Papers,* 1902, [Cd. 905], " Correspondence respecting the Treaty signed at Washington . . . ", etc., 4.

of controversy and misunderstanding, and the opening of a new era of more friendly feeling between the two governments.[24]

Even before the ratification of the Hay-Pauncefote treaty the American government had taken steps towards the construction of a canal. In 1899 it appointed a commission which was instructed to examine into all practicable routes. The following year the commission reported in favor of the Nicaragua route, as the French company which had the franchise for the Panama route seemed unwilling to sell all of its rights to the American government.[25] This report, however, led the French company to change its attitude, and in 1902 it offered to sell out to the United States for forty million dollars. In consequence of the offer, the canal commission altered its decision and advised the adoption of the Panama route.[26] On June 28, 1902, the President was authorized to purchase the French company's property, and to obtain from Colombia the control of the territory traversed by the canal route. If reasonable terms could not be obtained from the company or from Colombia, the President was empowered to form a canal treaty with Nicaragua and Costa Rica.[27]

Negotiations with Colombia followed, and the Hay-Herran treaty of January, 1903, was the result; but the Colombian Senate refused to ratify the agreement,[28] and for a time it seemed as though the United States

[24] London *Times,* Dec. 18, 1901.
[25] Lindsay, *Panama and the Canal Today,* 88; Johnson, *Four Centuries of the Panama Canal,* 116, 120-121; Edwards, *Panama,* 464.
[26] Johnson, *op. cit.,* 121-126; Edwards, *Panama,* 464-465.
[27] Lindsay, *Panama and the Canal Today,* 89-90; Johnson, *op. cit.,* 126-128.
[28] Lindsay, *Panama and the Canal Today,* 90-91; Johnson, *op. cit.,* 130-149; Edwards, *Panama,* 465-467.

would again turn to the Nicaraguan route. However, a revolution which the United States was accused of fomenting,[29] soon took place in Panama, and that province declared its independence of Colombia, in November, 1903, and established itself as a separate republic.[30] A speedy recognition of the new government by the United States followed, and within a month a new canal treaty, which was promptly ratified, was formed between the United States and Panama.[31] Further investigation led to a decision in favor of a lock canal,[32] and in 1907 the American government itself determined to undertake the construction. The commission, with Major G. W. Goethals at its head, was put in control of the enterprise, and work was promptly begun.[33]

By 1912 it was evident that the canal would soon be ready for use; therefore it was necessary that Congress pass measures for its regulation. The Panama Canal bill, originating in the House, was framed for this purpose. Among other provisions it fixed the tolls to be paid by vessels passing through the canal, but exempted all American vessels from such payment.[34] The bill went to the Senate and while it was before that body,

[29] Lindsay, *Panama and the Canal Today*, 92-93. For the part played by the United States in this connection, see the source collections, *The Panama Canal Question*, and " *I Took the Isthmus* ", also *U. S. Docs.*, ser. no. 4587, doc. 51; ser. no. 4588, doc. 95.

[30] Edwards, *Panama*, 467-476; Arias, *Panama Canal*, 64-68.

[31] *Sen. Doc.* no. 456, 63 Cong., 2 sess., pp. 74-84. In consequence of the attitude of the United States, much bitterness has been displayed by Colombia towards that country. This seems likely to be wiped out by a treaty, now ready for the ratification of the American Senate, by which the American government agrees to pay Colombia twenty-five million dollars for the loss of Panama and the transfer of the canal zone to the United States. *Cong. Record*, LI, 12676, *passim*; LII, 403-405.

[32] Edwards, *Panama*, 488-490; Johnson, *Four Centuries of the Panama Canal*, 316-325.

[33] Edwards, *Panama*, 505-510.

[34] *New International Year Book*, 1912, p. 495.

a protest was presented by the British government against such exemption in favor of the United States, on the ground that it was a violation of the Hay-Pauncefote treaty.[35]

The canal bill was the subject of a long, sharp debate in the Senate,[36] and finally the exemption clause was so modified as to include only American vessels engaged in coastwise trade. In this form the bill was passed by the Senate on August 9 and was promptly signed by President Taft.[37] On November 13 the President issued a proclamation fixing the rates of tolls to be paid by vessels using the Panama Canal.[38] On the following day the British foreign secretary instructed Bryce, the British ambassador at Washington, to present to the American government a protest against the canal legislation. This protest, which was presented December 9, was an amplification of that of the preceding July. "The intention of the Hay-Pauncefote treaty", the protest stated, "was that the United States was to recover the right to construct the transisthmian canal upon the terms that when constructed the canal was to be open to British and United States ships on equal terms." If any American vessel were permitted to pass through the canal toll free, British vessels would be forced to bear more than an equal share of the cost and current expenses of the canal. The British government, the communication intimated, expected the United States either to repeal the objectionable part

[35] *Sen. Doc.* no. 11, 63 Cong., 1 sess., pp. 10-11.

[36] *Cong. Record,* XLVIII, 1818-1825, 9168-9189, 9221-9227, 9231-9239, 9278-9284, 9359-9365.

[37] *New International Year Book,* 1912, p. 495.

[38] *Sen. Doc.* no. 11, 63 Cong., 1 sess., pp. 10-11.

of the canal act or to submit the matter to arbitration.[39]

The reply of the American government was evasive and its arguments unsound. The protest of the British government, it implied, was premature, as the canal was not yet complete and no unfair tolls had yet been paid by Great Britain; consequently, there was nothing to arbitrate. After all, the remission of tolls to American ships was only a subsidy for which America had to pay, and not Great Britain. The protest of the British, the reply intimated, was really an attempt to read into the Hay-Pauncefote treaty a surrender by the American government of its right to regulate its own commerce. The letter concluded, however, with an expression of willingness to submit the matter to arbitration.[40]

But it early became evident that the American government by no means had the undivided support of the nation. Expressions of disapproval came from all over the country, on the ground that such discrimination in favor of the United States was inexpedient as well as a violation of treaty obligations.[41] In the face

[39] *Ibid.,* pp. 11-19. The protest also called attention to the fact that vessels of Panama had been exempted from the payment of tolls by the canal treaty with Panama in 1903, and intimated that discretion seemed to be given the President to discriminate, in fixing the tolls, in favor of American vessels in general as against foreign vessels. *Ibid.,* pp. 16, 18.

[40] *Ibid.,* pp. 3-10. The toll controversy was probably influential in rousing a fear in the United States that Great Britain or some other foreign power, dissatisfied with American regulation of the Panama Canal, might determine to construct a rival route. In an effort to guard against this, a treaty, now ready for ratification by the Senate, was formed with Nicaragua. This treaty secures to the United States a perpetual and exclusive right of way across Nicaragua for an interoceanic canal, and also establishes a virtual American protectorate over the Nicaraguan republic. *Nation,* XCVII, 92-93; *Outlook,* CVI, 20-21.

[41] *The " Coastwise Exemption "*: *the Nation Against It*; *Cong. Record,* XLIX, 1818-1825; Root, " Panama Canal Tolls ", in *World Peace Foundation Pamphlet Series,* III, no. 3; *Nation,* XCVI, 26; *Outlook,* CIII, 249-253; *Independent,* LXXIV, 224-226; *Century Magazine,* LXXXV, 630-631; *Literary Digest,* XLV, 1165-1166; LXVI, 220.

of opposition from home and protest and criticism from abroad it seemed unlikely that the toll legislation could long stand. A definite attitude of disapprobation on the part of President Wilson shortly after his accession to office hinted at an early reversal of government policy regarding the question; and on March 5, 1914, in an address delivered at a joint session of the houses of Congress the President asked for the repeal of the Panama Canal Act, on the ground that exemption of American vessels from the payment of tolls constituted a mistaken economic policy and was a " plain contravention of the treaty with Great Britain ".[42] On the day following, a bill for repealing the exemption clause of the canal act was introduced into the House, and it was passed by the House a few weeks later. In the Senate the measure was hotly debated, but it was finally passed on June 11, with an amendment attached. The amendment provided that the repeal of the exemption clause should not be regarded as a relinquishment of any right which the United States might have under the Hay-Pauncefote treaty or the treaty with Panama, or otherwise, to discriminate in favor of American vessels by exempting them from the payment of tolls; or as impairing any right of the United States under those treaties, or otherwise, with respect to the sovereignty over or the control of the canal.[43] The House promptly concurred in the Senate amendment, and President Wilson signed the repeal bill on June 15.[44] Thus was removed the latest cause for friction between England and the United States with relation to the Central American isthmus.

[42] *House Doc.*, no. 813, 63 Cong., 2 sess.
[43] *Cong. Record*, LI, 5895-11214, *passim*.
[44] *Nation*, XCVIII, 711, 712.

The abrogation of the Clayton-Bulwer treaty by the Hay-Pauncefote agreement removed the former restraint upon British and American relations in connection with Central America. Upon Great Britain this change had merely a negative influence; she reduced her garrisons in the West Indies and withdrew her war vessels, thus practically recognizing American supremacy in the Gulf region.[45] But with the United States the case was quite different. The large investment of American capital in Central America and the proximity of the region to the Panama Canal Zone was bound greatly to increase American interest in the Central American states, and to cause the United States government to assume a decided policy towards them.

In consequence, a system of interference in Central American matters, resembling tutelage, developed. Repeatedly the United States stepped forward to prevent the states from meddling in one another's affairs, and to prevent or end war between them.[46] Nicaragua, because of her disorganized condition, has received the largest share of attention. In December, 1907, under the auspices of the United States and Mexico, a convention of Central American delegates met at Washington and formed a treaty providing for the arbitration of all international differences.[47] However, Zelaya, the Nicaraguan dictator, refused to abide by the arrangement, and while the convention was still sitting he planned an invasion of Salvador.[48] The American government prevented the execution of the plan,[49] but

[45] Coolidge, *The United States as a World Power*, 276.
[46] Palmer, *Central America and its Problems*, 291-292, 294-295; Calderon, *Latin America: its Rise and Progress*, 292.
[47] Palmer, *Central America and its Problems*, 292-293, 307-330.
[48] *Ibid.*, 294-295.   [49] *Ibid.*, 295.

shortly afterwards a revolt, aided by American citizens, was started against Zelaya's rule. Two American captives from the revolutionary army were shot at the order of the dictator. This act, and Nicaragua's failure to observe the arbitration convention, caused the suspension of diplomatic relations between her and the United States. In consequence, Zelaya, realizing that his position was hopeless, fled from the country.[50] Anarchy in Nicaragua followed, and the United States again interfered, for the purpose of promoting a free general presidential election and the establishment of a stable government.[51]

The Nicaraguans, however, failed to follow the plans of the American government, and confusion and disorder increased to such an extent that Nicaragua finally appealed to the United States for aid. In response, the American government appointed Thomas C. Dawson, who had had much diplomatic experience with the Latin-American republics, for the purpose of aiding the disorganized state to establish itself politically and economically on a sounder basis. Under Dawson's influence the political leaders pledged themselves to agree upon a presidential candidate in 1913.[52] Dawson's financial plans were similar to those which he had recently put into execution in San Domingo;[53] Nicaragua's debt was to be taken over by New York bankers and her customs houses were to be put under American protection.[54] This arrangement was approved by the

---

[50] Palmer, *Central America and its Problems*, 296, 330-335.

[51] Hale, " With the Knox Mission to Central America ", in *World's Work*, XXIV, 184; Hale, " Our Danger in Central America ", *ibid.*, 446.

[52] *American Review of Reviews*, XLVI, 572.

[53] *Ibid.*; Hale, " With the Knox Mission to Central America ", in *World's Work*, XXIV, 183-185.

[54] *Ibid.*, 184.

Nicaraguan government, but the American Senate refused to ratify the treaty.[55]

The actions of the United States in San Domingo and Panama, however, had roused general suspicion in Latin America against American designs. In Central America this suspicion was aggravated by constant interference by the Washington authorities, and by the Dawson mission. Annexation to the United States was feared and a strong faction opposing all American interference had developed.[56] In order to allay these fears, Secretary of State Knox went to Central America in 1912, while the Dawson treaty was still before the American Senate. The aim of the visit was to explain that the United States wished merely to establish such conditions of peace and security as would remove all necessity for direct intervention.[57] However, aside from revealing the full extent of dislike and suspicion felt by the Central Americans for their northern neighbor, the Knox mission appears to have accomplished but little.[58]

Following the Senate's refusal to ratify the Dawson treaty,[59] war broke out in Nicaragua between the partisans of the United States and the foes of American intervention. American naval forces took part in the struggle and defended the capital against the anti-

[55] *Ibid.*; *Outlook*, CI, 845-846.

[56] Hale, " With the Knox Mission to Central America ", in *World's Work*, XXIV, 184, 190; *Current Literature*, LIII, 377.

[57] Conant, " Our Mission in Nicaragua ", in *N. Am. Rev.*, CXCVI, 63; Hale, " With the Knox Mission to Central America ", in *World's Work*, XXIV, 179-180.

[58] *Ibid.*, 182, 186, 190-193; *Literary Digest*, XLV, 286.

[59] Though the treaty failed, Nicaragua voluntarily placed the administration of her customs in the hands of an American, to decided advantage, and obtained a loan of New York bankers, so she was soon on a better basis financially. *Outlook*, CVI, 21-22.

American party, which was led by Mena, the former secretary of war.[60] During this disturbance, in September, 1912, a note of warning was issued from Washington, setting forth the policy of the Taft administration towards Central America. Under the Washington convention of 1907, the note declared, the United States had a " moral mandate " to exert its influence for preserving peace in Central America. Its aim was to foster true constitutional government and free elections, and to this end it would support established governments against revolutions based upon the selfish designs of would-be despots. Force would be used, if necessary, to maintain free communication with American legations, and to protect them.[61] The announcement of the moral mandate was an exposition of what was denounced as " dollar diplomacy " by opponents of the Taft administration. These claimed that it was the policy of the administration to support Central American leaders favorable to the United States government or friendly to American business interests in Central America.[62] The situation formed an interesting contrast to that existing in Central America in 1848 and 1849. At that time Great Britain was practicing " dollar diplomacy ".[63]

As the Panama Canal approached completion the constant confusion in Central America gave rise to serious questions regarding future relations between the United States and the Central American Republics, and in this connection the Monroe doctrine became the

[60] *Current Literature*, LIII, 376; *Literary Digest*, XLV, 286.
[61] *Outlook*, CII, 150-151; *Literary Digest*, XLV, 505.
[62] Palmer, *Central America and its Problems*, 304-305; *N. Am. Rev.*, CXCVII, 58-61; *Current Literature*, LIII, 376; *Literary Digest*, XLV, 505-506.
[63] See above, pp. 55 ff. Also see above, p. 313, note 40.

subject of considerable discussion and criticism, in the United States as well as in Europe and Latin America.[64] Many Americans felt that the doctrine had outlived its usefulness, for while it no longer aided Latin America, it caused the United States to be hated and feared by her neighbors to the south.

Within the preceding few months, however, a decided reaction has developed in favor of a " new Monroe doctrine ". President Wilson is a strong exponent of this doctrine, which carries with it a less selfish and more helpful Latin-American policy than that which has existed during the past decade.[65] Coincident with this change of attitude has developed the idea that the rapid progress of Argentina, Brazil, and Chile, and the degree of stability and culture displayed by these states, entitle them to a voice in the management of the affairs of the Western World. Consequently, the conviction is growing that the United States should invite these republics to become partners with her in supporting the Monroe doctrine and in promoting peace and progress in the weaker parts of Latin America. The American acceptance of mediation offered by representatives of the " A. B. C. republics " in the difficulty with Mexico in the spring of 1914 was in conformity with the new attitude of the United States towards her southern neighbors. And this mediation not only relieved the

[64] Calderón, *Latin America: its Rise and Progress,* 298-312; Palmer, *Central America and its Problems,* 284-287; Crichfield, *Rise and Progress of the South-American Republics,* II, 632-644; Winter, *Guatemala and her People of Today,* 226-227; Bingham, *The Monroe Doctrine: an Obsolete Shibboleth;* Hale, " Our Danger in Central America ", in *World's Work,* XXIV, 443-452; *Literary Digest,* XLIV, 583, 978-979, 1151-1152; XLV, 412, 1117-1118.

[65] Brown, " A New Era of Good Feeling ", in *Atlantic,* CXV, 99-111; *Current Opinion,* LIV, 3-5.

strained situation between the United States and Mexico, but it also established a new precedent by recognizing these powers as equals of the United States; and it virtually admitted that " differences which gravely menace the relations of individual American states are matters of concern to all the American nations ".[66] The recent appointment, by the Pan-American Union, of a commisssion to consider the problems of international law which have risen in consequence of the great war in Europe is another noteworthy step in the same direction.[67] If this policy is continued, genuine Pan-American friendship and understanding are bound to result, and solidarity upon questions of Western international interest. The Central American states, with the remainder of Latin America, will participate in the benefits resulting from the change.

[66] Moore, " Is there a Latin America? ", in *Independent,* LXXXI, 91-93.
[67] *Nation,* XCIX, 702.

CHAPTER XI.

GENERAL RÉSUMÉ.

In the preceding chapters has been traced a century of British-American diplomatic relations regarding the Central American isthmus, with the purpose of showing the changes in attitude which have taken place between the two governments and also of determining the causes producing these changes. This has necessitated —in addition to a consideration of the main question— a study of the relations of the Central American states to each other, as well as notice of the attitude of the British and American governments regarding other matters whenever an influence upon the question under consideration was evident or probable.

For more than a century and a half previous to the formation of the American Union, Great Britain encroached upon Central America; and for more than four decades after the establishment of the United States, the aggressions continued in a fluctuating manner without rousing any feeling between the two countries. But British suspicions of American opposition were roused by the publication of the Monroe doctrine. Consequently, for the following twenty years, through a desire to avoid trouble with the United States, as well as because of a temporary waning of governmental interest in Central America, Canning's anti-American policy was neglected; British encroachments were slow and were initiated largely by British agents in the region. With the rapid movement of the

United States to the southwest, however—insuring the acquisition of California as well as other Mexican territory—the British government became fearful that the Americans meant to seize the isthmus, and, by monopolizing the transisthmian routes, to strike a blow at British commerce. As a result, under governmental direction, British interest in Central America now greatly increased. The weakness and subsequent dissolution of the Central American republic, produced partly by the intrigues of the British agents, particularly favored foreign interference.

When California became an American possession, the interest of the United States in Central America was for the first time thoroughly roused. This was largely because the Nicaraguan isthmus was then believed to supply the most feasible route to the Pacific coast. Attention thus being directed to Central America, the nation came to realize the predominance of British influence there, and promptly showed resentment at finding the eastern terminus of the San Juan route across Nicaragua controlled by the British in the name of the Mosquitos. Determination to eliminate British control from Central America was influential in producing a more aggressive version of the Monroe doctrine by President Polk; but plans to assert America's leading position on the isthmus, delayed by the Mexican War, were as yet unrealized at the close of the Polk administration. The discovery of gold in California greatly increased American demand for a transisthmian highway, as well as added to the resentment at apparent British intention to monopolize the best route.

This situation faced the new Whig administration and led it to take definite steps, primarily for securing a neutral transit route, but also with the aim of forcing the British to withdraw from Central America. With this in view, negotiations were begun early in 1849, but under unusual difficulties. Though at the time neither nation desired to monopolize the Nicaragua route, each suspected the other of such a purpose. After such suspicions were partially removed, there remained the serious difference of opinion concerning the British protectorate over the Mosquitos; but since feeling in America was so strong as to threaten a hostile outbreak between the two nations, it was decided to negotiate for the guarantee of neutrality of the interoceanic transit and to avoid discussion of the Mosquito question, on which an agreement was little likely to be reached. The Clayton-Bulwer treaty, which violated the spirit of the Monroe doctrine, was the result. This agreement contained self-denying clauses with reference to Central American territory, and stipulations intended to secure the entire neutrality of the prospective Nicaragua canal, as well as articles for extending the guarantee to all other practicable routes across the American isthmus. But as Clayton had labored to secure such word-, ing as would force British withdrawal from Central America and as Bulwer had endeavored to preserve the Mosquito protectorate, the language of the treaty was vague, and augured future trouble.

Promptly after the ratification of the Clayton-Bulwer treaty, the British government began negotiations for adjusting its Central American relations in conformity with the new treaty; but the disorganized condition of affairs in Central America, the unwillingness of the British to make sufficient concessions, and the lack of interest of the Fillmore administration in securing a just and final settlement, all tended toward delay, and no result was reached after two years of effort.

When Pierce became president a more aggressive American policy was asserted, since the Democrats were more favorable than the Whigs to a stiff tone in foreign relations—especially as regarded England. British action served to increase this attitude; shortly before the accession of Pierce, the Bay Islands, contrary to treaty engagements, had been formed into a British colony. A dispute over the interpretation of the Clayton-Bulwer treaty followed. The American government declared that the treaty required British withdrawal from the Mosquito protectorate, the Bay Islands, and the Belize territory between the Sibun and the Sarstoon rivers. The British government in reply assumed the untenable stand that the treaty was merely prospective in its operation and did not affect existing British possessions in Central America.

The emphatic presentation of these conflicting points of view produced a deadlock in Central American relations lasting for more than a year. During this time the American government displayed an active determination to stand upon its own view of the treaty, and to force Great Britain to recede from her extreme interpretation.

In the autumn of 1855 the question became complicated with the recruiting dispute; suspicion increased on both sides, and the situation grew more serious. The British government, however, somewhat relieved the tension early in 1856 by a formal offer to submit the Central American controversy to arbitration. But the evident determination of the American government to dismiss Crampton, and the growth of suspicion in both countries that each nation was interested to some degree in the filibustering movements in their relation to the Central American dispute gave a bad turn to affairs, so that by the last of May, 1856, the possibility of war was freely discussed by both nations.

But the British government had no intention of provoking war with the United States. It had come fully to realize how unjustifiable was its position upon the Central American question and was convinced by the determined attitude of the United States that an attempt to maintain this position would be likely to end in open hostilities between the two nations. The British government knew, moreover, that it would lack the support of the British people in a war over such a question. Finally, Great Britain, government and people alike, was anxious to avoid a conflict with the United States, under any circumstances, because of the resulting damage to commerce between the two countries—especially commerce in raw cotton and cotton products. Consequently, the British foreign secretary quickly responded to the firm but conciliatory tone assumed by the American government during the height of the crisis, and the relations of the two countries took on a more friendly appearance.

In a spirit of good understanding negotiations were resumed, and produced the Dallas-Clarendon treaty. This was a compromise arrangement, providing for British withdrawal from Mosquito Shore and the Bay Islands; but by it the United States acquiesced in the Sarstoon as the southern boundary of Belize. The treaty failed of ratification, however, largely because an earlier treaty made between Great Britain and Honduras for the transfer of the Bay Islands was rejected by the Honduran Senate.

After the failure of the Dallas-Clarendon treaty, a strong movement towards the abrogation of the Clayton-Bulwer treaty by congressional action was manifested in the United States. In order to avert this, and consequent hostile relations between the two governments, Great Britain determined to settle the question by direct negotiation with the Central American states. The American government was notified of this plan, and in order further to allay unfriendly feeling in the United States, the offer of arbitration was renewed. The aim of the mission to be sent to Central America, the British government explained, was to carry out the general tenor of the American interpretation of the Clayton-Bulwer treaty as reflected in the Dallas-Clarendon arrangement. President Buchanan, however, was not satisfied with such an adjustment; he showed little cordiality towards the plan, and in his message of 1857 evinced a strong inclination towards abrogation.

This attitude on the part of the American government and the British determination not to take any action until an answer had been received to the offer of arbitration produced a deadlock which lasted for several weeks.

Meanwhile, the American government was officially notified by Napier, the British minister, that Great Britain would consent to an unconditional abrogation of the Clayton-Bulwer treaty, which would mean a return to the *status quo,* Great Britain retaining her former possessions, including the Bay Islands. This communication was influential in bringing the American government to a decision, and it replied by rejecting arbitration and expressing a preference for direct settlement by a special British commissioner. Therefore, the British government determined that Ouseley, the British commissioner, who had lingered at Washington pending a decision on the part of the American government, should proceed immediately to Central America. But Ouseley's original instructions were modified, because of the attitude of the United States, and he was authorized only to arrange for the disposal of the Mosquito protectorate, of which Great Britain had for some time been anxious to free herself.

The American government, when it realized that Great Britain would not consent to abrogation of the Clayton-Bulwer treaty, in addition to abandonment of her Central American claims and possessions, soon assumed a more cordial manner and displayed a friendly interest in the British plan of settlement. The inclination of Congress, however, was still strongly towards the abrogation of the treaty, and there was danger that if the dispute was not settled before December, 1859, Congress, which would then meet, would attempt to set aside the arrangement. Consequently, the British government, in order to expedite matters, appointed Wyke, who had already formed a treaty with Guatemala, defining the Belize boundaries, to take the place of Ouseley. The latter, indeed, had conducted his mission in an unsatisfactory manner and had accomplished nothing towards the settlement of the Central American question. Wyke, accordingly, made a treaty with Honduras for the transfer of the Bay Islands and the sovereignty over the Mosquitos within the limits of Honduras to that republic; and by treaty with Nicaragua he transferred to her Greytown as well as the remainder of the Nicaraguan part of the Mosquito Shore. The arrangements made by Wyke were declared by President Buchanan, in his message of December, 1860, to be entirely satisfactory.

During the years 1856 to 1860 a shifting of interests had taken place in Great Britain and the United States; the former lost her territorial interest in Central America and, with it, her jealousy of the United States; the latter, on the other hand, had become convinced that Central America must eventually be hers—a conviction which probably would have become a fact had not the Civil War swept aside slavery.

Shortly after the close of the war the United States began to show a tendency—hinted at by her actions in 1856 and 1857—to regard the terms of the Clayton-Bulwer treaty as not applying to the Panama route. This tendency became an open declaration with the granting of the Panama concession to de Lesseps, and with it came the demand for an American canal controlled by Americans. In order to obtain this, a strong effort was made, from 1881 to 1883, by the United States to secure the modification or abrogation of the Clayton-Bulwer treaty. This attempt was resisted by the British government, which showed that the American arguments were unsound, that the Clayton-Bulwer treaty by its eighth article had established a general principle of neutralization for all routes on the American isthmus, and that this principle had been recognized by the American government in subsequent treaties.

Following the vain attempt against the Clayton-Bulwer treaty, the United States still manifested a determination to secure an American canal; but with the failure of de Lesseps's undertaking interest was shifted from the Panama to the Nicaragua route. This called attention to the fact that Great Britain, in spite of the treaty of Managua, was still interfering with the Mosquito Indians. American jealousy was roused because of the proximity of the Mosquito reserve to the canal route; and the opposition of the American government to the British policy was influential in producing the incorporation of the Indians with Nicaragua in 1894, which removed all further cause of dispute over the Mosquitos.

In the closing years of the nineteenth century an unusual feeling of friendliness developed between the United States and Great Britain. The British government, in particular, was anxious to preserve this cordiality. Therefore, in 1901 it consented to the Hay-Pauncefote treaty, which superseded the Clayton-Bulwer arrangement and made possible an American transisthmian canal, controlled and protected by Americans. When the canal was nearing completion the American government passed an act for regulating its use which discriminated in favor of American coastwise vessels. The act was protested against by the British government as a violation of treaty engagements and was disapproved by a large proportion of Americans. In consequence of this, the objectionable clause was repealed, June, 1914.

The Hay-Pauncefote treaty produced a marked change in British and American relations towards Central America; British interest lessened, while that of the United States increased; and there developed a system of American interference in Central American affairs which has become objectionable to the Central American states and has seemed little productive of good. The unsatisfactory nature of the situation, however, has come to be realized in the United States, where a distinct revolution in Latin-American policy has begun, which seems likely to terminate in more satisfactory relations between the United States and her southern neighbors, including Central America.

BIBLIOGRAPHY.

The critical comments following the titles listed below are based wholly upon an estimation of the value of the writings to this present study.

GUIDES AND BIBLIOGRAPHIES.

Cannon, Henry Lewin, *Reading References for English History*, Boston, [c. 1910].

Channing, Edward, Albert Bushnell Hart, and Frederick Jackson Turner, *Guide to the Study and Reading of American History*, revised and augmented edition, Boston, 1912.

Paullin, Charles O., and Frederic L. Paxson, *Guide to the Materials in London Archives for the History of the United States since 1783*, Carnegie Institution of Washington, Publication No. 90-B, Washington, 1914. A valuable guide for the subject, but it appeared too late to be of aid in the preparation of this work.

Phillips, P. Lee, *A List of Books, Magazine Articles, and Maps Relating to Central America, Including the Republics of Costa Rica, Guatemala, Honduras, Nicaragua and Salvador, 1800-1900*, Washington, 1902. Valuable; includes many obscure works as well as those better known.

Van Tyne, Claude Halstead, and Waldo Gifford Leland, *Guide to the Archives of the Government of the United States in Washington*, second edition, Carnegie Institution of Washington, Publication No. 92, Washington, 1907. Especially useful, as the arrangement of the Central American correspondence in the State Department is unusually complicated.

MANUSCRIPT SOURCES.

Department of State, Washington, Bureau of Indexes and Archives. Offers much material not printed in the *American State Papers*, the *United States Documents,* or the writings of Buchanan and Webster. Especially valuable for instructions to and despatches from American diplomatic agents in Central America and England. The manuscripts in the Department of State for the period 1815-1860, inclusive, were examined. For a classification of the American diplomatic correspondence bearing on the present study, see Van Tyne and Leland's *Guide to the Archives* listed above.

Public Record Office, London. By far the most valuable source was found in the British manuscript archives, which contain a vast amount of material not printed in the *British and Foreign State Papers* or in the *Parliamentary Papers*. The following is a complete list of the records consulted for the years 1815 to 1860, inclusive:

Admiralty Office.—Admiralty Secretary's In-Letters, Admiralty Secretary's Out-Letters. (Cited as " Ad. Sec. In-Letters ", etc.)

Colonial Office.—Honduras. (Cited as " C. O., Hond.")

Foreign Office.—America, Central America, Costa Rica, France, Guatemala, Honduras, Mexico, Nicaragua, Salvador, Spain. (Cited as " F. O., Am. ", etc.)

Foreign Office, America was the most important series, but many valuable letters were found in Foreign Office, Central America, Foreign Office, Guatemala, and Colonial Office, Honduras. The material in the other records was meagre or of less importance. In every case throughout the present work citations to Foreign Office material have reference to the Foreign Office Records, which consist of the papers, or in-letters, received by the office, with their inclosures, and copies or drafts of letters originating there. All Public Record Office citations in the foot-notes are to the old classification, as the reclassification was not complete when the records were examined.

PRINTED SOURCES.

Adams, John Quincy, *Memoirs of John Quincy Adams, Comprising Portions of his Diary from 1795 to 1848,* edited by Charles Francis Adams, 12 vols., Philadelphia, 1874-1877. A little material.

American State Papers, Foreign Relations, 6 vols., Washington, 1833-1859. Useful for Panama Congress.

Annual Register, London, 1758. Contains texts of treaties.

British and Foreign State Papers, London, 1841. Valuable.

Buchanan, James, *The Works of James Buchanan, Comprising his Speeches, State Papers, and Private Correspondence,* collected and edited by John Bassett Moore, 12 vols., Philadelphia, 1908-1911. Extremely important. Besides the Buchanan correspondence found in the Department of State, it includes copies of that in the collection of the Historical Society of Pennsylvania, as well as in some private collections.

Calendar of State Papers, Colonial Series, America and West Indies, 1675-1700, London, 1893-1910. Slightly useful.

" Canning and Cuba ", in *Publications of the Southern History Association,* vol. ii, no. i. Two illuminating letters from George Canning.

" Canning to Vaughan," in Massachusetts Historical Society, *Proceedings,* XLVI, 233-235. A pertinent letter from George Canning, not found elsewhere in print.

The " Coastwise Exemption": the Nation against it, New York, 1913. A compilation of expressions of opinion.

Congressional Globe, Washington, 1834-1873.

Congressional Record, Washington, 1873-.

Fox, Charles James, *Memoirs and Correspondence of Charles James Fox,* edited by John Russell, 2 vols., Philadelphia, 1853. Contains a few letters of worth.

Hertslet, Lewis, [and others], *A Complete Collection of the Treaties between Great Britain and Foreign Powers,* 22 vols., London, 1840-1901. Valuable for texts of treaties difficult to find elsewhere.

Historical Manuscripts Commission, *Report on the Manuscripts of Mrs. Stopford-Sackville,* vol. 2, London, 1910. A few letters regarding the British expedition to Nicaragua, 1780-1781.

'I Took the Isthmus": Ex-President Roosevelt's Confession, Colombia's Protest, and Editorial Comment by American Newspapers on " How the United States Acquired the Right to Build the Panama Canal", New York, 1911.

" Letters of Bancroft and Buchanan, on the Clayton-Bulwer Treaty, 1849, 1850", in *American Historical Review*, V, 95-102. Important; not found elsewhere in print.

MacDonald, William, *Select Charters and Other Documents Illustrative of American History, 1606-1775*, New York, 1906.

Moore, John Bassett, *A Digest of International Law*, 8 vols., Washington, 1906.

New York Historical Society, *Collections, 1884, Kemble Papers*, II, New York, 1885. Material on the British expedition to Nicaragua, 1780-1781.

Panama Canal Question: a Plea for Colombia, New York, 1904. Diplomatic correspondence.

Parliamentary Debates, edited by T. C. Hansard [and others], London, 1812-

Parliamentary Papers, London, 1801–. These papers, with the *United States Documents,* are essential to any study of the subject from printed sources alone.

Polk, James K., *The Diary of James K. Polk, 1845-1849*, edited by Milo Milton Quaife, 4 vols., Chicago, 1910. Slightly useful.

Richardson, James D., *A Compilation of the Messages and Papers of the Presidents, 1789-1897*, 8 vols., Washington, 1896-1898.

Rush, Richard, *A Residence at the Court of London,* London, 1833. A small contribution.

—— *Memoranda of a Residence at the Court of London,* Philadelphia, 1845. A continuation of the preceding.

—— *The Court of London from 1819 to 1825, with Subsequent Occasional Productions, now First Published in Europe,* edited by Benjamin Rush, London, 1873. Subject matter largely similar to that of two preceding works.

United States Documents, Washington, 1817-. Under this title are included all public documents of the American government. They are an indispensable complement to the *Parliamentary Papers.* The new classification by serial numbers has been used in the foot-notes.

Webster, Daniel, *The Writings and Speeches of Daniel Webster*, National Edition, 18 vols., Boston, 1903. Very valuable; contains copies of private correspondence as well as of that existing in the Department of State.

Wells, William V., *Walker's Expedition to Nicaragua; a History of the Central American War*, New York, 1856. Contains copies of useful letters, speeches, etc. See same title below under "Contemporary Special Works and Articles."

Wharton, Francis, *A Digest of International Law of the United States*, second edition, 3 vols., Washington, 1887. Includes a few extracts from American diplomatic correspondence, subsequent to 1860, not printed in the *United States Documents* or Moore's *Digest*.

CONTEMPORARY SPECIAL WORKS AND ARTICLES.
(Written before 1861.)

Alcedo, Antonio de, *The Geographical and Historical Dictionary of America and the West Indies*, translated and enlarged by G. A. Thompson, 5 vols., London, 1812-1815. Useful.

Allen, Bird, "Sketch of the Eastern Coast of Central America", in *Journal of the Royal Geographical Society*, XI, 76-89.

Appleton, Nathan, "Memoir of Hon. Abbott Lawrence", in Massachusetts Historical Society, *Proceedings*, III, 68-82.

Baily, John, *Central America; Describing each of the States of Guatemala, Honduras, Salvador, Nicaragua, and Costa Rica*, London, 1850. Almost valueless.

Bard, Samuel A. [Ephraim George Squier], *Waikna; or Adventures on the Mosquito Shore*, London, 1855. Important. Squier was bitterly opposed to British encroachments in Central America, but this does not appear to have made his writings any the less authoritative.

Bonnycastle, R. H., *Spanish America; or a Descriptive, Historical and Geographical Account of the Dominion of Spain in the Western Hemisphere*, 2 vols., London, 1818. Largely descriptive, but contains a little material.

Burney, James, *History of the Buccaneers of America,* reprinted from the edition of 1816, London, 1891. Valuable, though prejudiced in favor of the British.

Byam, George, *Wild Life in the Interior of Central America,* London, 1849. Useless.

Churchill, Awnsham, and John, *A Collection of Voyages and Travels, Some Now First Printed from Original Manuscripts, Others Now First Published in English,* 8 vols., London, 1752. Volume six contains an account of " The Mosqueto Indian and his Golden River; Being a familiar Description of the Mosqueto Kingdom in America . . . Written [in or about the Year 1699.] by M. W. ". An important source, written by one who had spent some time on the Mosquito Shore.

Crowe, Frederick, *The Gospel in Central America, Containing a Sketch of the Country,* London, 1850. Crowe was a British missionary at Belize. Authorities generally cited. Reliable and very important.

Dampier, William, *Voyages,* 3 vols., London, 1703-1705. A valuable source.

Dunlop, Robert Glasgow, *Travels in Central America,* London, 1847. Contains a clear and fairly accurate account of Central American history from 1821 to 1846.

Edwards, Bryan, *The History, Civil and Commercial, of the British West Indies, with a Continuation to the Present Time,* fifth edition, 5 vols., London, 1818-1819. Important.

Esquemeling, John, *The Buccaneers of America,* a reprint from an early translation, London, 1911. Esquemeling was a buccaneer. Of slight value.

Fancourt, Charles St. John, *The History of Yucatan from its Discovery to the Close of the Seventeenth Century,* London, 1854. This volume was meant by the author, who was superintendent of Belize, as an introduction to a history of Belize, which seems never to have been written. The introductory volume covers a too early period to be of much use.

Froebel, Julius, *Seven Years' Travel in Central America, Northern Mexico, and the Far West of the United States,* London, 1859. Somewhat helpful.

Galindo, Juan, "Notice of the Caribs in Central America", in *Journal of the Royal Geographical Society*, III, 290-91.

—— "On Central America", in *Journal of the Royal Geographical Society*, VI, 119-136.

Henderson, George, *An Account of the British Settlement of Honduras*, London, 1811. Good. Henderson was superintendent of Belize.

Johnson, Charles, *A General History of the Pyrates*, 2 vols., fourth edition, London, 1726. An account by a pirate.

Juarros, Domingo, *A Statistical and Commercial History of the Kingdom of Guatemala*, translated by J. Baily, London, 1825. Some material; used by later writers.

L. L., "Note sur la colonie anglaise de Balise, et ses rapports sur le Yucatan mexicain", in *Nouvelles Annales des Voyages et des Sciences Géographiques*, C. 51-67.

Long, Edward, *The History of Jamaica; or General Survey of the Antient and Modern State of that Island*, 3 vols., London, 1774. Valuable.

Michell, R. C., "A Statistical Account and Description of the Island of Ruatan", in *United Service Magazine and Naval and Military Journal*, 1850, pt. 2, pp. 541-546.

Scherzer, Carl, *Travels in the Free States of Central America; Nicaragua, Honduras, and San Salvador*, 2 vols., London, 1857. Of slight use.

Sloane, Hans, *A Voyage to the Islands Madera, Barbados, Nieves, S. Christophers and Jamaica, with the Natural History of the Herbs and Trees, Four-footed Beasts, Fishes, Birds, Insects, Reptiles, etc., of the Last of those Islands*, etc., 2 vols., London, 1707-1725. Useful.

Squier, E. G., *Nicaragua, its People, Scenery, Monuments, and the Proposed Interoceanic Canal*, 2 vols., New York, 1852. Good account of British encroachments.

—— *Notes on Central America; Particularly the States of Honduras and San Salvador*, New York, 1855. Good; supplements the author's *Nicaragua*.

—— *Travels in Central America*, 2 vols., New York, 1853. Valuable; subject matter similar to that in two preceding works.

Stephens, John L., *Incidents of Travel in Central America, Chiapas, and Yucatan,* 2 vols., New York, 1841. Slightly useful.

Stout, Peter F., *Nicaragua; Past, Present and Future,* Philadelphia, 1859. Contains considerable material, fairly accurate, but shows bias against England. Stout was American vice-consul in Central America.

Strangeways, Thomas, *Sketch of the Mosquito Shore,* Edinburgh, 1822. Good.

Roberts, Orlando W., *Narrative of Voyages and Excursions on the East Coast and in the Interior of Central America,* Edinburgh, 1827. Much useful material; written by a resident British trader.

Wafer, Lionel, *A New Voyage and Description of the Isthmus of America,* reprinted from the original edition of 1699, edited by George Parker Winship, Cleveland, 1903. Of little worth.

Walker, William, *The War in Nicaragua,* Mobile, 1860. An account from Walker's point of view of his career in Nicaragua previous to May, 1857.

Wells, William V., *Explorations and Adventures in Honduras,* New York, 1857. Helpful.

—— *Walker's Expedition to Nicaragua; a History of the Central American War,* New York, 1856. Considerable material, but poorly organized. Wells was a strong supporter of Walker. See same title above under "Printed Documentary Sources."

CONTEMPORARY REVIEWS AND NEWSPAPERS.

Blackwood's Magazine, vols. 79, 80, 81.

Boston *Post,* July 31, 1854.

Boston *Transcript,* July 28, 29, Aug. 3, 1854.

Daily Alta California, Dec. 5, 16, 1855, Jan. 22, 1859.

De Bow's Review, vol. 27.

Dublin Review, vol. 40.

Harper's Magazine, vols. 10, 12.

Littell's Living Age, vol. 14.

London *Daily News,* Jan. 31, 1853, April 2, 1854.

London *Daily Times,* Nov. 1, 1849, June 13, 1850, Jan. 19, 1856. Dec. 20, 1858.

London *Economist,* vol. 14.

London *Globe,* Mar. 3, 1853.

London *Morning Post,* Dec. 5, 1854, Dec. 23, 1857.

New York *Times,* July 26, 31, Aug. 1, 2, 1854, Jan. 3, 19, Feb. 1, 23, Mar. 6, July 15, 1856.

New York *Tribune,* Aug. 2, 3, 5, 16, 1854.

Niles' Register, vol. 61.

San Francisco *Evening Bulletin,* July 18, Aug. 1, 1856.

United States Magazine and Democratic Review, vols. 17, 21, 25.

GENERAL HISTORIES AND BIOGRAPHIES.

Babcock, Kendric Charles, *The Rise of American Nationality, 1811-1819,* New York, 1906.

Bancroft, Hubert Howe, *History of Central America,* 3 vols, San Francisco, 1886-1887. Useful for study of early period.

Bourne, Edward Gaylord, *Spain in America, 1450-1580,* New York, 1904.

Crichfield, George W., *The Rise and Progress of the South American Republics,* 2 vols., London, 1909. Of little use.

Curtis, George Ticknor, *Life of Daniel Webster,* 2 vols., New York, 1889.

—— *Life of James Buchanan,* 2 vols., New York, 1883.

Dewey, Davis Rich, *National Problems, 1885-1897,* New York, 1907. Some material.

Fortier, Alcée, and John Rose Ficklen, *Central America and Mexico,* Philadelphia, [c. 1907]. Good brief account of Central American history.

Foster, John W., *A Century of American Diplomacy,* Boston, 1900.

García Calderón, F., *Latin America: its Rise and Progress,* translated by Bernard Maill, New York, 1913. Latin-American viewpoint.

Garrison, George Pierce, *Westward Extension, 1841-1850,* New York, 1906. Helpful for background.

Hart, Albert Bushnell, *The Foundations of American Foreign Policy,* New York, 1901.

Helps, Arthur, *The Spanish Conquest in America and its Relation to the History of Slavery and to the Government of Colonies,* 3 vols., London, 1855-1857. Some material.

Henderson, John B., *American Diplomatic Questions,* New York, 1901. General account.

Holst, Hermann Edouard von, *The Constitutional and Political History of the United States,* 8 vols., Chicago, 1881-1892.

Keane, A. H., *Central and South America,* 2 vols., edited by Clements Markham, London, vol. 1, revised 1909; vol. 2, first edition, 1901.

Latané, John Halladay, *America as a World Power,* New York, 1907. Useful.

Lucas, C. P., *A Historical Geography of the British Colonies,* 6 vols., Oxford, 1888-1907. Helpful for early period.

McMaster, John Bach, *A History of the People of the United States from the Revolution to the Civil War,* 8 vols., New York, 1907-1913.

Rhodes, James Ford, *History of the United States from the Compromise of 1850,* 7 vols., New York, 1900-1906.

Schouler, James, *History of the United States of America under the Constitution,* 7 vols., New York, [c. 1894-1913].

Smith, Edward, *England and America after Independence: a Short Examination of their International Intercourse, 1783-1872,* Westminster, 1900. Strongly prejudiced against America.

Smith, Theodore Clark, *Parties and Slavery, 1850-1859,* New York, 1906. Good.

Snow, Freeman, *Treaties and Topics in American Diplomacy,* Boston, 1894. Good perspective.

Sparks, Edwin Earle, *National Development, 1877-1885,* New York, 1907.

Trendell, A. H. R., *Her Majesty's Colonies,* London, 1886. Of little use.

Turner, Frederick Jackson, *Rise of the New West, 1819-1829,* New York, 1906. Contribution to the background of the study.

Winsor, Justin, editor, *Narrative and Critical History of America,* 8 vols., Boston, 1884-1889.

Woodward, William Harrison, *A Short History of the Expansion of the British Empire,* 1500-1902, Cambridge, 1907. Slightly useful.

Woolsey, Theodore Salisbury, *American Foreign Policy,* New York, 1898.

RECENT SPECIAL WORKS.

(Written since 1860.)

Adams, Ephraim Douglass, *British Interests and Activities in Texas, 1838-1846,* Baltimore, 1910. Valuable for background. Based principally on documents in the Public Record Office.

Anderson, C. L. G., *Old Panama and Castilla del Oro,* Washington, 1911. Contains brief general account of the filibusters.

Arias, Harmodio, *The Panama Canal: a Study in International Law and Diplomacy,* London, 1911. Good general account of the American canal policy.

Barral-Montferrat, H. D. de, *De Monroë à Roosevelt,* 1823-1905, Paris, 1905. Unreliable.

Beaumarchais, Maurice D. de, *La doctrine de Monroë; l'évolution de la politique des États-Unis au XIX° siècle,* deuxième édition, Paris, 1898. Of slight value.

Bingham, Hiram, *The Monroe Doctrine: an Obsolete Shibboleth,* New Haven, 1913.

Bryce, James, *South America: Observations and Impressions,* New York, 1912. Good for general background of study.

Butte, George G., *Great Britain and the Panama Canal: a Study of the Tolls Question,* 1913. A defense of exemption in favor of American vessels.

Colquhoun, Archibald Ross, *The Key of the Pacific, the Nicaragua Canal,* New York, 1898. An uncritical but fair treatment.

Coolidge, Archibald Cary, *The United States as a World Power,* New York, 1908. General view; good prospective.

Dunning, John C., *Die Neuesten Anwendungen der Monroe Doktrin,* Borna-Leipzig, 1908.

Edgington, T. B., *The Monroe Doctrine,* Boston, 1905. A mediocre work.

Edwards, Albert, *Panama: the Canal, the Country, and the People,* New York, 1912. A popular account.

Egerton, Hugh Edward, *A Short History of the British Colonial Policy,* London, 1897.

Fiske, Amos Kidder, *The West Indies,* New York, 1906.

Froude, James Anthony, *The English in the West Indies,* London, 1888. Slightly useful.

Gibbs, Archibald Robertson, *British Honduras: an Historical and Descriptive Account of the Colony from its Settlement, 1670,* London, 1883. The best history of British Honduras.

Haring, C. H., *The Buccaneers in the West Indies in the XVIIth Century,* London, [1910]. A careful, critical work.

Johnson, Willis Fletcher, *Four Centuries of the Panama Canal,* New York, 1906. Contains considerable information on the Panama question, but is biased in favor of the American government.

Keasbey, Lindley Miller, *The Nicaragua Canal and the Monroe Doctrine,* New York, 1896. Sound as to simple facts; but conclusions colored by an anti-British feeling, and a prejudice in favor of a Nicaragua as against a Panama canal.

Latané, John Halladay, *The Diplomatic Relations of the United States and Spanish America,* Baltimore, 1899. Good general account.

Lawrence, T. J., *Essays on Some Disputed Questions in Modern International Law,* second edition, Cambridge, 1885. Good general discussion by an Englishman, with emphasis upon the American attack on the Clayton-Bulwer treaty, 1880-1883.

Lindsay, Forbes, *Panama and the Canal Today,* new revised edition, Boston, 1912. Fair general account.

Lucas, Daniel B., *Nicaragua: War of the Filibusters,* Richmond, 1896. A popular account based largely upon Walker's *War in Nicaragua.*

Mahan, A. T., *The Interest of America in Sea Power, Present and Future,* Boston, 1898.

Martin, Percy F., *Salvador of the Twentieth Century,* New York, 1911.

Moses, Bernard, *The Establishment of Spanish Rule in America*, New York, 1898. Slightly useful.

Nicaise, Auguste, *Les flibustiers américains: Walker et l'Amérique Centrale*, Paris, 1861. Fair brief account.

Oppenheim, L., *The Panama Canal Conflict between Great Britain and the United States of America: a Study*, Cambridge, 1913. A British view.

Palmer, Frederick, *Central America and its Problems*, New York, 1910. A clear, unbiased view of the present situation in Central America.

Paxson, Frederic L., *The Independence of the South American Republics: a Study in Recognition and Foreign Policy*, Philadelphia, 1903.

Reddaway, W. F., *The Monroe Doctrine*, second edition, New York, 1905. Good.

Reeves, Jesse S., *American Diplomacy under Tyler and Polk*, Baltimore, 1907.

Roche, James Jeffrey, *By-ways of War; the Story of the Filibusters*, Boston, 1901. A popular account.

Rodway, James, *The West Indies and the Spanish Main*, London, 1896. A popular history of the buccaneer period.

Siegfried, A., [and others], *Les questions actuelles de politique étrangère dans l'Amérique du Nord*, Paris, 1911. Of little use.

Smith, Justin Harvey, *The Annexation of Texas*, New York, 1911. Useful for background. Based chiefly upon manuscript records.

Squier, E. G., *Honduras; Descriptive, Historical and Statistical*, London, 1870. Ground covered very similar to the author's *Notes on Central America*.

Travis, Ira D., *British Rule in Central America: or a Sketch of Mosquito History*, Publication No. 5, Michigan Political Science Association, July, 1895. Good.

—— *The History of the Clayton-Bulwer Treaty*, Publication No. 8, vol. 3, Michigan Political Science Association, Jan., 1900. Carefully prepared and reliable as to facts, but conclusions at times unsound. The best work on the subject.

Tucker, George F., *The Monroe Doctrine: a Concise History of its Origin and Growth*, Boston, 1885.

Walker, J. W. G., *Ocean to Ocean: an Account, Personal and Historical, of Nicaragua and its People,* Chicago, 1902. General account of the Central American question. Perspective good, but some inaccuracies.

Winter, Nevin O., *Guatemala and her People of Today,* Boston, 1909.

RECENT ARTICLES IN PERIODICALS AND NEWSPAPERS.

(Signed Articles.)

Bell, Charles N., " Remarks on the Mosquito Territory, its Climate, People, Productions, etc.", in *Journal of the Royal Geographical Society,* XXXII, 242-268.

Bingham, Hiram, " The Monroe Doctrine: an Obsolete Shibboleth ", in *Atlantic Monthly,* CII, 721-734.

Brown, L. Ames, " A New Era of Good Feeling ", in *Atlantic Monthly,* CXV, 99-111.

Conant, Charles A., " Our Mission in Nicaragua ", in *North American Review,* CXCVI, 63-72. Useful for recent period.

Grahame, Leopold, " The Canal Diplomacy: a British View ", in *North American Review,* CXCVII, 30-40.

Hale, William Bayard, " Our Danger in Central America ", in *World's Work,* XXIV, 443-452. Valuable.

―――― " With the Knox Mission to Central America ", in *World's Work,* XXIV, 179-194, 323-337. Valuable.

Keasbey, Lindley M., " The National Canal Policy ", in American Historical Association, *Annual Report, 1902,* I, 275-288.

―――― " Terms and Tenor of the Clayton-Bulwer Treaty ", in *Annals of the American Academy,* Nov., 1899.

Keely, Robert N., Jr., " Nicaragua and the Mosquito Coast ", in *Popular Science Monthly,* XLV, 160-175. A good description.

Latané, John H., " Neutralization Features of the Hay-Pauncefote Treaty ", in American Historical Association, *Annual Report, 1902,* I, 289-303. A valuable discussion.

Moore, John Bassett, " Is there a Latin America? " in *Independent,* LXXXI, 91-93. Good.

Paxson, Frederic Logan, "England and Mexico, 1824-1825", in *Colorado University Studies,* III, 115-119. Contribution towards the background of the study.

Rives, George L., "Mexican Diplomacy on the Eve of War with the United States", in *American Historical Review,* XVIII, 275-295. Useful.

Root, Elihu, "The Obligations of the United States as to Panama Canal Tolls", in *World Peace Foundation Pamphlet Series,* III, no. 3. Speech delivered in the Senate against exemption of American vessels, January 13, 1913.

Scroggs, William Oscar, "William Walker and the Steamship Corporation in Nicaragua", in *American Historical Review,* X, 792-812. Valuable.

Showalter, William Joseph, "The Countries of the Caribbean", in *National Geographic Magazine,* XXIV, 227-249. Describes present conditions.

Temperley, H. W. V., "The Later American Policy of George Canning", in *American Historical Review,* XI, 779-798. Valuable for understanding of early period.

Woolsey, Theodore S., "Suez and Panama—a Parallel", in American Historical Association, *Annual Report, 1902,* I, 307-312. A helpful comparison.

(Unsigned Articles.)

American Review of Reviews, vols. 46, 47.
Century Magazine, vol. 85.
Current Literature, vol. 53.
Current Opinion, vols. 54, 56.
Harper's Weekly, vol. 60.
Independent, vols. 74, 77.
Literary Digest, vols. 44, 45, 46.
London *Daily News,* Nov. 18, Dec. 17, 1901.
London *Daily Times,* Nov. 19, Dec. 18, 1901.
Nation, vols. 96, 97, 98, 99.
North American Review, vol. 97.
Outlook, vols. 91, 92, 93, 96.

INDEX.

347